Sprawling PLACES

Sprawling
PLACES

David Kolb

THE UNIVERSITY OF GEORGIA PRESS
Athens & London

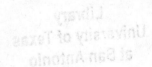

© 2008 by the University of Georgia Press

Athens, Georgia 30602

All rights reserved

Designed by Walton Harris

Set in 10/13 New Baskerville

Printed and bound by Thomson-Shore

The paper in this book meets the guidelines for
permanence and durability of the Committee on
Production Guidelines for Book Longevity of the
Council on Library Resources.

Printed in the United States of America

08 09 10 11 12 C 5 4 3 2 1

08 09 10 11 12 P 5 4 3 2 1

Library of Congress Cataloging-in-Publication Data

Kolb, David.

Sprawling places / David Kolb.

p.   cm.

Includes bibliographical references and index.

ISBN-13: 978-0-8203-2988-8 (hardcover : alk. paper)

ISBN-10: 0-8203-2988-6 (hardcover : alk. paper)

ISBN-13: 978-0-8203-2989-5 (pbk. : alk. paper)

ISBN-10: 0-8203-2989-4 (pbk. : alk. paper)

1. Sociology, Urban. 2. Cities and towns. I. Title.

HT151.K594 2008

307.76—dc22   2007039038

British Library Cataloging-in-Publication Data available

Contents

Preface

This book argues that, contrary to what many detractors believe, today's society is still creating real human places. Theme parks and suburban sprawl and anonymous functional places such as airports and parking lots are more than nonplaces. To see them aright, we have to measure them in terms of their own new forms of connection rather than against classic hierarchical unities.

The book first describes the changes that have set new places apart and altered the context of older places. It offers a general theory about what turns a given area into a social human place, and argues that places today should be evaluated according to criteria of linkage and complexity rather than classical authenticity and centered unity. Complexity brings greater self-awareness of the ways places are multiple and linked, and of how we inhabit them and keep them alive. I disagree with those urban theorists and social analysts who claim that places have become commodities and pale simulacra of what places should be. I defend theme parks and themed places while arguing that they have to be experienced more complexly than they officially want to be. The final two chapters take up suburban sprawl, defending it against many criticisms while agreeing with others. Suburbia is more internally multiple and it is interconnected in more ways than by spatial proximity. So despite the seeming thinness of many suburban places, they are more complex than they appear to be. The book closes by suggesting interventions and changes in policy that could make suburbia more complex, just, and humane.

THE BOOK AND THE WEB SITE

The book is part of a larger project that also includes a Sprawling Places Web hypertext presentation of the ideas. The Web site offers hundreds of images of places discussed in the book and of many others. It presents the main argument in a complexly linked way and in a variety of styles.

Each version treats some topics in more detail than the other. The site overlaps about a third of the book but also incorporates many narratives, background materials, and self-reflective turns. The book treats its topics in a more linear fashion with many references and footnotes.

The Web site is at http://www.dkolb.org/sprawlingplaces. On its pages the list in the left-hand column includes a link to Outlines of Some of the Discussion. Clicking on this reveals links to outlines, and also Links from the Book Version. Clicking on this takes you to a page with links to the topics where this book suggests that the Web site provides useful images or treats something more fully. For instance, the Web site discusses in more detail the creation of real places in virtual spaces.

The hypertext Web version and the book exist together as part of a project to compare the experience of writing and reading in the two diverse media. That project is discussed in the essay "Twin Media," which is linked from http://www.dkolb.org.

ACKNOWLEDGMENTS

This project received generous support from the Phillips Endowment at Bates College and made great strides during a welcome sojourn at the School of Architecture at Lund University, Sweden. I thank those who heard and reacted to presentations at the University of Kentucky, Aarhus University (Denmark), the Accademia Danica, the Open University, Lund University, the Sandbjerg Conference (Sønderborg, Denmark), the University of Texas, Texas A&M University, and Bryn Mawr and Bowdoin Colleges. Thanks to Edward Casey for an attentive reading of an early version, to anonymous readers for comments on later versions, to Nancy Gerth for the book's index, and to Derek Krissoff at the University of Georgia Press for insight and enthusiasm. For helpful discussions, long or short, I thank Mona Ålend, Gregers Algreen-Ussing, Shunjuku Arakawa, Michael Benedikt, Mark Bernstein, David Brent, Joan Claffey, Jane Douglas, Andres Duany, Will Dudley, Joseph Flay, Luis Francisco-Revilla, Rick Furuta, Judy Gammelgård, Madeline Gins, Trish Glazebrook, Diane Greco, Cecilia Häggström, Andrew Hargadon, Martin Jay, Matthias Kärrholm, Stephen Kemper, Ruth Kisch, Harry Kolb, Mary Kolb, Patricia Kolb, Tony Koltz, John Leggett, Marjorie Luesebrink, Ben Macri, Clara Mancini, David McBride, John McCumber, Anthony Meyer,

Lee Miller, Stephen Moore, Dee Mortensen, Stuart Moulthrop, Anne Niemiec, Angelica Nuzzo, Ib Omland, Jonathan Powers, Geoff Pynn, William Richardson, Paul Ricoeur, John Sallis, Gunnar Sandin, Frank Shipman, Simon Buckingham Shum, Lars-Henrik Ståhl, Thomas Tracy, Cheryl Troxel, Gregory Ulmer, Finn Werne, and Tomas Wikström.

Sprawling PLACES

CHAPTER ONE

Places Today

*Our sense of place keeps getting vaguer . . . We find ourselves
uprooted, adrift in an uncharted, alien terrain. . . . We've
failed to accept that the old definitions of place no longer
apply; place is now as much virtual as it is physical. . . . Our
notion of place, then, must be reinvented. . . . If we are at
last to create a contemporary sense of place . . . We need to
acknowledge the ugly as well as the beautiful, the disturbing
as well as the cozy, the virtual as well as the real. It is this
totality that today constitutes the "here."*
(Bartolucci 1997, 60–61)

CRITICS OF TODAY'S CITIES AND SUBURBS often appeal to idealized older places. Earlier, people enjoyed Paris and the hill towns of Italy, or Charleston and small-town America. Now, we are stuck with banal suburban sprawl and vapid city entertainment centers. We have tourist attractions and Disneyfied places that are created only for consuming. When our places grow, we get Houston. Looming virtual reality will divorce stranger places even more from natural locales.

Is it as bad as they say? Is there no hope? My goal in studying contemporary places is to get beyond criticisms that concentrate on the problems of place today, and instead discover and examine the new spatial and social possibilities they offer. Can our new kinds of places make room for new kinds of community?

We have all lived in or visited locales that seemed just right, perhaps in Greenwich Village, a clearing in the woods, a Japanese house, or a white town in Vermont set in a valley with the embracing hills just so. We know places that make us feel centered and more alive. Often these satisfying places are older, perhaps because they have more layers of history and detail, perhaps because they resonate from childhood.

Other places, though, are not likely to be favorites: shopping malls, tract housing developments, suburban commercial strips. There are also places we are ambivalent about, such as Disney-like theme parks and other touristy locales that we may feel embarrassed to have enjoyed. Such places feel brittle, and they are remembered more for quick thrills than for opening our minds and settling our lives.

Many criticisms of places today take their orientation from classic examples: small communities (the primitive village, the medieval manor, the old New England town), or centralized cities (Renaissance piazzas, Roman processional streets, Parisian squares, Savannah's street plan), or places of ritual (the Greek temple precinct, the medieval cathedral square), or pastoral places (the English countryside, the Nordic farm). But these are no longer adequate for understanding the new kinds of places being created since the middle of the twentieth century. Today's economy is not the same; our images of past places are too idealized; today's society is less restricted. Places today are different because our lives are different. We are more mobile, perhaps more self-conscious, certainly more fragmented yet abruptly linked together.

New kinds of places, such as those that are themed and those within suburban sprawl, certainly deserve criticism for their many problems. Their architecture is usually clichéd, but even when it is of higher quality, the lives offered may be overly simplified. Shiny surfaces may conceal injustices and inequities. Nonetheless, these places have within them the makings of their own betterment. Urban theorists should understand their new modes of unity and connection, and not hasten to measure them by old examples. Planners should seek inspiration from places that are sprawling, fractured, multiple, paratactic, intersecting—from the suburban commercial strip, from the Net, from speeded-up, fragmented, virtual, discontinuous, mobile inhabitations rather than classic piazzas and small towns.[1] By looking at today's places theorists and architects can locate key features of new kinds of places as well as neglected features in older places, then turn and use these features to fight the current thinning and dumbing down of all our places.

"Mediterranean hill towns, in all their wide variety but equally undeniable kinship, are mandatory places of pilgrimage. . . . [yet] equally fascinating are the North American suburbs, at all levels of income" (Habraken 1998, xix). But many social critics think they know all about suburbs; they think they are bad. But perhaps that is so because they do not see suburbs in their full form and processes. By considering the complete linkages and interrelations in Manhattan, crowded and growing Asian cities, virtual worlds, and new kinds of places with complex and novel structures, our sense of what is possible is broadened. But how do we apply that wider view to suburbia, which seems to be the antithesis of such dense places? How can both new and old places be lived with a more-than-traditional awareness?[2]

This book develops a theory of complexity and connection that is general enough to apply to both cities and suburbs; it also offers ways to see suburbia's complexities and increase them. Granting the validity of many critical concerns, I argue that returning to traditional unities is an unhelpful and ultimately wrongheaded response. I offer new definitions and criteria, evaluate alternative concepts, cite empirical studies, and show the effects of applying the proposed concepts.

SOME EMBLEMATIC CONTEMPORARY PLACES

Many contemporary places have the feel of flimsy surfaces left over from once-solid localities. It is true that places do not hold as tightly as they once did. Even those places created according to today's best insights into how to make a shelter or a community no longer seem so firm. Some people respond to the sense of loss by seeking a return to closed and hierarchical places. That attempt can only succeed through bad faith and averted vision. Some try to isolate themselves, but there is no closure—only places linked to and overlapping one another, new contexts, and mixtures. Some respond by celebrating total rootlessness, often with a forced joviality that ignores or treats ironically the ways in which places still help define and locate us. Some seek a deeper universal home ground beneath the flow of empirical places. I sympathize with that attempt, but I see us not so much rooted in a universal or natural place as at home in the continual embodied process of making and remaking social meanings and places.

There are some places that have become emblematic of the problems with places today.

Themed Places

Theme parks, festival markets, and the like can seem the epitome of unreal places. The sign over the entrance to California Disneyland tells patrons that they are about to leave the ordinary world. Inside all is bright and slick, planned in detail for intended effects. Everything is clean and efficient, with the infrastructure hidden under the vast podium that holds the park. In terms of its architecture and its functioning, Disneyland is thoroughly real, but its functions are fantasy and money, selling the experience. The embodiment of the fantasy has been branded "hyperreal" as not just an escape but also a revelatory sample of what our world is becoming (see Eco 1990).

Fantasy architecture is not new—kings and nobles have often indulged—but now you don't need a palace or even a theme park. You can live a fantasy in a themed apartment complex, at a decorated mall, or in a themed restaurant. These fantasies multiply as market segmentation accelerates. In place of the monuments modernist planners hoped to erect celebrating universal values, we see commercial temples for market niches, including commodified versions of whatever resistance against commodification is currently popular.

No matter whether they are aesthetically pleasing or not, many contemporary places are condemned as commodities, spectacles, or machines for a standardized consumerist routine that pales in comparison to older and thicker, more rooted, modes of living. This superficial life is attributed to a mix of global capitalism, technological changes such as the automobile and the media, and modernization as an inevitable loss of roots.

I evaluate such complaints in detail in chapter 5. Theme parks do call attention to both the dominance of commerce and the way gritty economic and political realities can be covered with a sheen of fantasy. Still, if they are taken as the key to understanding places today, theme parks will confuse the issues. Just as the parks tend to reduce the complexity of life, so critiques that take them as central examples tend to oversimplify in making facile contrasts with "real places." Seeing theme parks with more complex vision leads to seeing the complexities of other kinds of places amid the processes that support them.

Suburban Sprawl

A second emblematic contemporary place is suburban sprawl full of random agglomerations of housing developments, shopping strips, office campuses, and highways. Following are examples of different kinds of sprawl in the United States.

An early suburb: I grew up in Garden City, a town on Long Island a few miles outside New York. The town was planned in the late nineteenth century and mostly built before World War II. Typical of that era's railroad suburbs, it has its own downtown shopping area, broad avenues, tree-filled streets laid out with blocks in varying patterns, green spaces, parks and schools, and a railroad station that links it to the metropolis. Garden City's leafy streets resemble television sitcoms about suburban life, but the town does not resemble the actual suburbs built after World War II, which are single-use residential areas that lack downtowns and public transport. When I lived there, Garden City was near the outer edge of development; now it is a node in an expanded net of suburbs that reaches far beyond. Suburban malls and commercial strips came later to Garden City, but they are not essential to the town the way they are to the further developments.

Austin: When I first began visiting Austin in the early 1970s, the outlying town of two thousand inhabitants where my parents had retired was twenty-some miles northwest from the center of the city, and was reached on two-lane roads that wound through close-in wealthy developments, then through hilly ranch country. Now Austin has sprawled. The retirement town on Lake Travis has become a bedroom suburb of ten thousand surrounded by other residential developments. The two-lane road past the Lakeway town entrance is now a five-lane commercial strip with thirteen banks and miles of small shopping centers. The chamber of commerce has moved its office from the small shopping area inside the town out to the busy strip on the edge.

The town had only two entrance roads off this new commercial strip; now more are being built. The roads into Austin are now six lanes speeding past walled developments with golf courses, amenity packages, and predictable names. Houses have gotten larger; traffic can be intense. The nearby town of Bee Cave, once scattered ranches around a few wooden stores and restaurants at a highway intersection, is now a big-box power center.

Austin was destined to sprawl as it attracted people who wanted suburban living. The metropolitan area's population has gone from half a million to over a million in the twenty-five years between 1975 and 2000, and may double again in the coming decades. The boom in and around Lakeway accelerated when the residents seceded from a rural school district and set up their own. With the prospect of better schools, the tax base developed rapidly as developers bought up ranch land and found ways to deal with the restrictions environmental groups were trying to impose for the sake of water and local habitat. The school district now has five thousand students and predicts it will have thirteen thousand by 2015.

The result is hills carpeted with houses, charming and not-so-charming in all the styles of the past three decades. Long, open views have been restricted by decades of tree growth. Cul-de-sacs are plentiful and sidewalks few. Garden-apartment complexes crowd the hills closer to the city. Little municipalities have arisen to defend their property values and push costs off onto others. Speed limits and zoning requirements vary abruptly over short segments of road. Public transportation is nonexistent; the private vehicle rules. Roads grow wider, new highways are planned, built, and elevated on stilts, but still congestion increases.

Older residents bemoan the loss of country living. Newer residents keep arriving for an attractive bedroom suburb by the lake. No one is happy with local stores closing and the landscape disappearing, but they enjoy the conveniences. Mexican maids and garden workers commute from Austin's southern suburbs. Downtown Austin, with its rich urban life, is a destination for special events; there are few shopping needs that cannot be met in the local strip or in the large malls half-way to the city.

Washington, D.C.: Driving north from Washington, D.C., you meet tall buildings in Silver Spring, Maryland, then row houses, then single-family houses in developments with countrified names but no country: Heath Field, Fir Glen, Aspen Hill, Milestone, Hunting Hill Estates. Then you come to the old town of Wheaton, then Brooke Manor Estates without trees. Near Gaithersburg you can visit a Flower Valley with attractive houses but no visible cars or people.

All of these connect to the strips, not to the old town centers. Then you come into the New Urbanism at Kentlands. Farther out you pass a community that describes itself as "The Preserve, an Estate Development in a Wooded Enclave," and you reach horse country with large houses on treeless lots, and finally emerge into farms with signs offering more house lots. The Virginia suburbs to the west are similar, though with more thin strips of trees along the roads masking many developments.

Portland, Maine: The state of Maine, with its 41 people per square mile, would not seem a likely candidate for sprawl problems, but it has them. Sprawl in most of the state looks different from that found around a city such as Washington, D.C., because Maine subdivisions are small and hidden by hills, or the housing is strung out along country roads rather than batched in neighborhoods with their own entrances. There are only two interstate highways, so the hierarchy of roads is not as layered as in metropolitan areas. But the effects are the same as in denser subdivisions elsewhere. Infrastructure is overstressed, rural land uses are diminished, animal habitats are cut up, and outlying school systems are forced to expand. Towns struggle to cope with unplanned growth and traffic, while older city neighborhoods see their tax base diminish even as they provide services for the larger area. The largest city in the state, Portland, shows the most sprawl, but sprawl also surrounds smaller cities such as Lewiston or Augusta, and even smaller market towns such as Bridgton.

Portland, Oregon: Across the country in Oregon, Portland has a deserved reputation for fighting sprawl successfully. The city is surrounded by an urban growth boundary that has retained nearby open space and agriculture, deflecting development in toward the center, where there has been a significant amount of new housing, rehabilitation of older areas of the city, and infill rather than greenfield building. The average density of the city is higher than in most U.S. cities, and there is good civic spirit. Public transit links some parts of the area and has been slated for expansion.[3]

Nonetheless, the outer regions inside the urban growth boundary have acquired many of the characteristics of standard sprawl. They are denser, with small house lots and big apartment complexes, but the suburban pattern holds: large single-use tracts of land are zipped together by commercial strips and dotted with the occasional large mall at a highway interchange.

The preceding paragraphs have offered some examples of sprawl, uncontrolled overall but planned in detail with an eye for profit. Suburban sprawl houses the life of millions, but those lives and these places are criticized by partisans of city life as thinned out, homogenized, unjust and unequal, and lacking richness and challenge. In chapters 6 and 7 I discuss causes and patterns, pros and cons, and make some suggestions how suburbia might be made to increase its actual and symbolic density.

Suburban sprawl and themed places stand out as examples of what many urban and social theorists see as the ongoing collapse of older,

denser, centered and *real* places. On the other hand, these examples
are scarcely the whole story. Nor do they reveal a single deep essence
of today's places. Other qualities of places can be mobilized to question
overly general critiques while developing a new value perspective. In the
remainder of this chapter I look at some of those qualities, and close
with an example that shows them in operation.

I seek a way of talking about places that is not biased against information explosions, social divisions and connections, multiplicity and discontinuity, and themed and self-conscious living in place. The next chapter presents a theory about the nature of places that stresses the role of
shared norms and expectations in turning an area of space into a social
place. What I will call *places* are those locations that are places-where-we-
do-something, rather than just places-where-something-is. Places in this
sense involve patterns of activity that prescribe divisions within the space
and govern what is expected or appropriate to do and not to do in these
locations. Such norms and expectations may be explicit in a highly ritualized locale such as a church or a courthouse. Less explicit and looser
norms apply to a dining room or a corridor. The norms of a place can
be clear where patterns of appropriate action have long-standing accep-
tance, but there are also norms involved in temporary places, as might
happen when a group lays down a picnic blanket or rearranges chairs in
a cocktail lounge. Here is where you sit, and if you move that chair too
far you are violating a (temporary) expectation and thereby making a
statement about your role in the conversation.

There's no doubt that many newer places have little to recommend
them aesthetically. But they remain places shaped by social norms and
expectations. Their oversimplified lives are what need to be investigated,
not just their aesthetics. What I suggest aims at improving the concreteness and social thickness of places; improvements to their aesthetic character should follow upon that. Beautiful but oversimplified places can be
worse for us than complex junkiness.

My general idea is that complexly linked, more self-aware places can
provide antidotes to the consumption of one flattened social role and
place after another. There are ways, even in suburbia, to increase the
awareness of links and connections, context, and of the interplay of economic, political, and cultural processes and pressures. These can work
to make more visible multiple norms and forces and flows even in seemingly monotone regions. With these rhythms more evident, there is a

better chance to fight attempts to damp places down to a single beat, keeping open the possibility of new possibilities and of active participation in defining places for our lives.

In talking about places I employ several general distinctions, such as between causal and normative connections, and between structures and processes. A handful of basic philosophical moves recur throughout this book. The first move is to insist on mediation, complexity, and linkage; there are no one-dimensional, isolated identities for places, communities, or individuals. The second is to be alert for illicit transformations of empirical generalities into universal laws, which happens in many totalizing critiques of today's places. The third is to show how the conditions that transform an area into a place—social norms for actions unified across space and time—also make it impossible to have either perfectly closed places or perfectly open homelessness. The fourth move is to show how contemporary places embody new kinds of unity and connection. The fifth is to argue that though normative distinctions are needed, they should discriminate among different kinds of place unity rather than between authentic and counterfeit places. The sixth is to insist that neither social process nor social structure can be taken as primary, since each exists through the other.

It is tempting to envision traditional places as solid unities eroded by destructive flows (of capital, media, commodities, information, immigrants, and so on). But in social life, structures exist within processes that continually renew them. What seems firm is in fact always changing, perhaps slowly, but by the twenty-first century the speed of change has increased. So have the speed and reach of those flows. To fight the bad effects of this acceleration we cannot appeal to some naturally solid resistance outside those flows. Instead we should become aware of and use the overlooked complexities, linkages, eddies, and twists within the flows. By doing so, we discover that more is going on than the usual definitions indicate. In dealing with contemporary places we need to learn how to see them in their complexities and to take advantage of their new modes of unity and connection to fight their dumbing down.

NONCONCENTRIC AND NONHIERARCHICAL PLACES

Traditional places that refer to a hierarchical center create a reassuring sense of being settled and located convincingly (see Harries 1997).

Activities feel unified when they are referred to clearly demarcated central points within an ordered hierarchy of actions and identities. Communities usually anchor and define themselves with reference to monuments and ceremonial centers.

Such concentric identities can be graphed onto tree structures, where each smaller branch connects neatly to one larger branch. Legitimacy flows along the tree. Depending on which political or epistemological theory is applied, it flows from the universal to the particular or vice versa, but in either case it flows along the neatly ordered branches of the tree.[4]

Contemporary places break hierarchies, ignore centers, and replace tree structures by networks that are multiply connected. Nodes in the network of identities and places are accessible from one another by many routes without going through fixed higher-level norms or central places. There may be self-declared summaries or groupings, but these can be routed around, since they have little structural dominance. Linkages can bypass them or create rival overviews.

Urban areas no longer dominate their regions. The urban areas themselves become multifocal as different functions locate their "centers" here and there: a stadium, a department store, a civic building. There is no single central palace or market square, and the urban core is surrounded by suburbia that may separate residential from commercial but spreads them out into a spotty mix.

Travel, too, used to be more concentric. To go from one place to another was to experience a series of intervening borders belonging to ever more inclusive places that were nicely nested one within the other: the city, the state, the region, then back down to another center. Now airplanes and satellite links allow people and information to flow above borders and bypass concentric nesting. We step out of Boston into an intermediate zone with its own flowing rhythm of similar terminals and planes, then from that flow step into Paris. Or we pick up the phone and contact a Parisian friend without experiencing any traversal at all, not even the former sequence of clicks, delayed response, and international operators in different countries.[5]

Today's identities are less tied to concentric places. Once groups nested in territorial boundaries such as those for towns, church parishes, school and voting districts, and so on. Now identity is spread among many groups that are often not associated with any fixed territory.

Beneath hierarchical trees and outside the control of centers there have always been discontinuities: cases that didn't quite fit, illegalities, and multiple connections that ignored neat structure. Now more places and identities have become aggressively connected in nonconcentric and nonhierarchical ways. The hierarchical structures that remain have become shallower, so that there are fewer levels and one never has to go very far up in order to transit to a distant node. These shallow hierarchies, moreover, have lost most of their substantive power to define. When social universals enable a flow with few if any substantive intermediate levels—that is, when there are modern identities—then there is little to support hierarchy.[6]

As early as 1961, Jesse Reichek claimed that "the elements used in the design of the physical city such as the square, the closed vista, and the greenbelt may have matched prior social orders and fitted prior conceptions of order; but they are compatible neither with contemporary social processes nor with modern conceptions of order. Within older systems of thought, afocality was a sign of disorder. But today, many of the signs that are so frequently mistaken for 'urban chaos' are, instead, the marks of emerging new forms, new kinds of order that reflect the increasingly pluralistic and afocal structure of changing social relationships" (Reichek, 1961, 141).[7]

Reichek may confuse multifocal structures with afocal structures, but he is right that older forms cannot sum up our new places and processes. Neither can any single new form. This does not imply, however, that traditional forms cannot be used to enrich individual nodes and local foci when these are recognized for what they are, local nodes in wider networks.

It is liberating to have more than hierarchical and concentrically related places and topologies of connection. On the other hand, there is no need to shun or flee hierarchical and concentric places. There is no need to live in nomadic tents in order to be free from hierarchy and centers, as long as those are open to a wider network of possibilities. That proviso is important because many hierarchical and concentric places still embody substantial inequities that try to close off connections and mobility. In this sense, the more complex inhabitation that I suggest has political implications against such closures. Yet while the new kinds of unities in newer places can increase freedom, they too can be used in the service of domination. Michel Foucault has shown how nonhierarchical arrangements can embody detailed oppression (see Foucault 1979). Even a spacious openness to wider possibilities, though generally liberating, can lead to a "surfing" mode of being-in-places that avoids confronting the inequities and harms of any particular place.

LINKING TO OTHER PLACES

With the development of communication and transportation, a place today has far more active links to distant locations. These links are not external add-ons; they are essential to the place. Near and far are both present. "The very tissue of spatial experience alters, conjoining proximity and distance in ways that have few close parallels in prior ages" (Giddens 1990, 140). Local places are not closed off and complete by themselves; "the local community is not a saturated environment of familiar, taken-for-granted meanings, but in some large part a locally-situated expression of distanciated relations" (Giddens 1990, 109).

This linkage and connection contrasts with the way premodern societies are typically thought of as closed and focused only on the local set of places. "In pre-modern societies, space and place largely coincide, since the spatial dimensions of social life are, for most of the population, and in most respects, dominated by 'presence' — by localized activities. The advent of modernity increasingly tears space away from place by fostering relations between 'absent' others, locationally distant from any given situation of face-to-face interaction. In conditions of modernity, place becomes increasingly *phantasmagoric*: that is to say, locales are thoroughly penetrated by and shaped in terms of social influences quite distant from them" (Giddens 1990, 18–19).

Considering ancient trade even among tribal societies, and conquests, pilgrimages, and relations to distant sacred sites, premodern places may not have been as closed off as is claimed. But modern places not only have many more links; those links are more central to the reality and life of the places.

In the mid-1960s the British architect Cedric Price developed a plan to turn a region of old ceramic factory towns into a dispersed educational facility formed by a set of linkages. According to art historian Stanley Mathews, Price's Potteries Thinkbelt proposal "was not a 'building' and perhaps not even 'architecture' as it was understood at the time.

Price proposed utilizing the derelict railway network of the vast Potteries district as the basic infrastructure for a new technical 'school.' Mobile classroom, laboratory and residential modules would be placed on the disused railway lines and shunted around the region, to be grouped and assembled as required by current needs, and then moved and re-grouped as those needs changed. Modular housing and administrative units would be assembled at various fixed points along the rail lines" (Mathews 2000).[8]

Price's plan acknowledged both linkage and change. The Thinkbelt resembles proposals for dispersed virtual educational institutions on the Internet. However the Thinkbelt was not merely dispersed, it was also rooted in a particular area's needs and its physical links. It would have led to greater understanding of how a particular region's history connected to and could be reinvigorated by wider flows in science and the economy. That kind of mixed local-global focus is needed today, when the media and the Internet tend to turn attention away from local connections.[9]

Some linkages today are not to other places but to activities and organizations that do not need to be in any appropriate place of their own. They may have buildings and headquarters and other facilities, but these can be abandoned and the organization or group moves elsewhere when economic or other circumstances change. Their activities take up space, though not an assigned place. Joshua Meyerowitz studied the way in which new media break down the isolation of formerly separated social situations, and argues that social separations depending on restricted information flow cannot be maintained. One effect is a growth of social settings and actions divorced from any geographical place. In this the modern begins to resemble very early modes of life. "Many of the features of our 'information age' make us resemble the most primitive of social and political forms: the hunting and gathering society. As nomadic peoples, hunters and gatherers . . . have little 'sense of place'; specific activities and behaviors are not tightly fixed to specific physical settings." He then notes that "electronic media create new types of social situations that transcend physically defined social settings and have their own rules and role expectations" (Meyerowitz 1985, 315–17, 333).[10]

Both the increase in linkage and the increase in actions that can be carried on anywhere change the meaning of what is present in a place.

"What structures the locale is not simply that which is present on the scene; the 'visible form' of the locale conceals the distanciated relations which determine its nature" (Giddens 1990, 19). The ways the structure and life of a place can exceed its architectural form will be important for the discussion of suburban sprawl.

MULTIPLE AND CONTESTED PLACES

Today's places are multiple in new ways. Links, new means of communication, media penetration, commercial ventures, migration—all these blend in new ingredients. Sometimes these mixtures are enriching. Japanese culture is famous for taking foreign influences and products into a mix that juxtaposes them with native elements without conflict. Discussing his experiences in Japan, Charles Moore remarked that "[in the Japanese writing system] four concurrent alphabets [exist in] a cheerful simultaneity. . . . Neon and tatami mat can coexist, to the detriment of neither. This, damn it, is the conceptual triumph that may save the world, if there's any air left in it to breathe" (Moore 2001, 281).

The contemporary weakening of hierarchies of centered places frees up "a simultaneous multiplicity" of places that are "cross-cutting, intersecting, aligning with one another, or existing in relations of paradox or antagonism" (Massey 1994, 3). Doreen Massey has pointed out how much changes when places are no longer neatly nested and bounded. Places cease to be the site of "an authenticity as singular, fixed and unproblematic in its identity" (1994, 3). Contested places can become violent, but often the tensions result in less dramatic but continuous rival attempts to stabilize meanings.

Such conflicts continually occur, whether loudly or quietly. They may focus on laws and legislatures, or planning boards and referenda, or just on daily activities and alternations. They may be peaceful yet still express underlying social tensions. For instance, next to Norman Foster's Hong Kong and Shanghai Bank building in Hong Kong is a park filled with customers, busy executives, messengers, and trucks delivering supplies or money or data, tourists off the ferry, and other players in Hong Kong's business life. But on weekends the area fills with migrant laborers, mostly from the Philippines. They redivide and redefine the park. The plaza's physical features function in new ways: linear plantings along which business lunch-goers had set up many small temporary conversation places now define a few larger areas where groups listen to preachers or dance to recorded music. What goes on is neither culturally Chinese nor English. The division and the definition of the place changes.

Parks have multiple uses, and it is not surprising that in a multicultural society space might get used in different ways. But the users are not just alternating. The separation of place uses would only be complete if Martians came down secretly at night and used the place for their sacred rituals. The executives and the migrant laborers are not just diverse, they are aligned as owners and servants, and they are quietly contesting the definition of the city and of appropriate behavior in its public places. No single definition prevails, and the borders of the place or places change as the uses change.

Different populations can show themselves in their norms for movement. In a town center that offers tourist attractions as well as daily facilities, tourists seldom acknowledge one another unless they get in each other's way, so the everyday people and the tourists have different gestural and body languages for dealing with oncoming groups on the street. The ordinary inhabitants more easily set up temporary places for conversations and interactions, and those interactions take longer because there are ongoing relations to be reaffirmed. The place looks different to the two groups; locals notice clues that are set by custom or habit; tourists notice clues set by guidebooks or by comparisons with their experiences of places far away.

City residents are familiar with the idea that different groups within a city may lead disparate lives that move on spatial trajectories among institutions and commercial establishments unique to each group, coming together only occasionally in special places or for special events. The city space supports many parallel, overlapping, and intersecting networks of places with their own layers of social norms. The same is true of suburbs. Multiple but interpenetrating enclaves composed of archipelagos of residences, roads, and institutions allow multiple ways of life within the seemingly homogeneous sprawl. In neither city nor sprawl do these multiple places stand in any clear hierarchical relation to one another.

REPEATED PLACES

On the commercial strip and elsewhere in today's world, the "same place" can be multiplied many times in separate locations. Franchise repetition goes beyond similarity. It is not accidental that one McDonald's restaurant looks like another. Their similarity provides the reassurance that encourages sales. Different location, different context, "same" place—but what kind of sameness? Franchised places are not all parts of one big place. We don't expect the movements or rituals of a single action to involve multiple McDonald's restaurants. Yet those restaurants are more than buildings that happen to resemble one another. They are controlled by a normative relation to a rule.[11]

The original hamburger stands built by the McDonald brothers in California no longer exist. The corporation tore them down despite the protests of preservationists. Nostalgia lost, and it doesn't matter whether or not current restaurants look like the originals or serve the same menu. If historians discovered that the McDonald brothers had never really been associated with the original restaurants, or that the restaurants had really been latte bars, that would not affect the legitimacy of the current restaurants. Franchises get their authenticity not from a relation to a privileged original but from faithfulness to a rule. (Faithfulness is necessary but it is not enough; you might build a faithful replica of a McDonald's, but without the proper corporate approvals you'd be in deep legal trouble.)

Repetition can become more complex than a franchise. While commercial franchises do not depend on any relation to a privileged original, some repeated places do have such special relations. One example would be a U.S. embassy with extraterritorial rights. It is "the same place" as the United States, for certain juridical purposes. An embassy's relation to its mother country is stronger than the relation of one franchise to another.

Even stronger relations exist. Although there is no original McDonald's left, there is an original Vatican, a single Big Ben, a single Grand Shrine at Ise. Each has a unique history tied to its location. You could Disney-reproduce Ise Shrine, or the Vatican, but that would not be like a franchise—it would be more like a souvenir. The replica would not be *a* Vatican in the way a restaurant can be *a* McDonald's. You can't have *a* Vatican, you can only have *the* Vatican. This is not just because there is a unique physical location in Rome but also because of the claims of special historical events and recurring rituals. Communal events make the tie to place.

VIRTUAL PLACES

To the degree that technology allows us to experience expanses of virtual space in which movements and gestures can take on different social meanings, we can speak of "real places" in virtual space. This depends on the development of social conventions for virtual topographies, which may closely imitate physical space or may diverge in strange ways of their own. In the Sprawling Places Web site I discuss many questions surrounding the notion of real yet virtual places.[12] But the influence of virtual reality is not confined to massive multiplayer online games and Star Trek holodecks. Web sites can provide adjunct spaces and meeting places for people whose daily routines now include a virtual component. Financial traders can work in a "place" composed of widely scattered but electronically linked locations supplemented by virtual presentations and visualized data spaces. Teens and students can change the spatiality of their environment by making the distant close and keeping group cohesion through computer e-mail and instant messaging, as well as cell phones and text messages.

CHANGING PLACES

Change has now become expected. People are eager to sell you guidance on how to manage change, but no one can sell you an absence of change. Part of the challenge of urban and suburban planning is to create physical and institutional structures that allow and accept change gracefully. Some changes are consciously directed, some occur unnoticed. Architects are sensitive to the different ways a place can change, because they are often asked to reuse older structures or to build new structures that alter a place. Some changes happen without self-awareness, at least in the beginning. "Parlors" in American homes became "living rooms," which became "family rooms" and are now "great rooms." Marketers pick up such trends and amplify them, but the trends have no single origin. Acceptable attire for university professors has become informal, but there was no particular moment when this happened nor any central source decreeing it. Or, suppose there have been many ways to walk across a plaza, all the same as far as the norms of the place were concerned, but these ways cease to be equal when a controversial political party opens an office that layers a gradient of approach and avoidance onto the plaza. After a time people realize that new expectations have developed and that the place's norms have altered without conscious decision, so that their paths across the plaza have a new differential political significance.

It would be satisfying to tell a unified story of change as a decline from a past golden age or as an ascent toward a coming golden age, but the sources of change are not so unified. Change in the textures of action happens for contingent reasons and from all directions. Ordinary changes tend to have ordinary explanations. New functions may demand a conscious search to establish new kinds of places. Railroad stations developed a standard arrangement quite early, whereas airports still struggle toward a suitable form. Because of new shopping habits linked perhaps to the spread of two-career families, strip malls have experienced a resurgence. Other changes are quite conscious. A legislature passes new rules for behavior in its chambers. When the U.S. Air Force Academy opened in Colorado in 1954, a committee on traditions examined the way things were done at the other military academies and posted notices stating that on a certain date it would become a tradition that such and such things were to be done.

Today those changes in places that happen through deliberate intervention have become more common. These bring the explicit generation of new social norms for possible actions, new kinds of transition and gestures, new rituals and expectations. Themed places show this process, and it also happens as people weave the separated units of suburban sprawl into linked patterns of living.[13]

Some places have gone further to offer gestures more familiar from experimental writing and artworks. In such works a peaceful-looking linear sequence of text may contain complex nonlinear movements of thought or twisted and frustrated narrative temporality. Meanings may be being created by harsh juxtapositions or ironic meta-moves repeated on themselves. Places too can be ordinary looking but still offer norms and textures of action that break previous kinds of unity. "On the horizon, then, at the furthest edge of the possible, it is a matter of producing the space of the human species—the collective (generic) work of the species—on the model of what used to be called 'art'" (Lefebvre 1991, 422). Derrida speaks about the ideal of a work of literature that produces its own new readers. "The work then becomes an institution forming its own readers, giving them a competence which they did not possess before" (Derrida 1992, 75). This is happening in today's places as well. Museums redefine themselves. Malls try to become agoras. Civic institutions mix previously separated functions. Computer games and themed places change expectations about connection and reference. When suburbs are compared to theme parks, the comparison may have more positive connotations than the critics intend.[14]

Avant-garde architects and artists sometimes dream of a condition of permanent novelty, an artwork or place that can never be caught in a general classification. But deviant uses eventually are recouped by extended norms. Places become routinized despite efforts to keep their novelty fresh. While new modes of action may concretize the general conditions for place making in new ways, the novelty will become routinized. Then the technologies and social changes that have made unusual places today may create wilder and more strangely textured places tomorrow.

A FURTHER EXAMPLE: THE STRIP AND THE LIST

Travel any distance, and there is a suburban commercial strip. The strip combines land-gobbling sprawl with the artificiality of themed stores and malls. The strip's disorder asserts itself over the commercial structures it contains, much to the frustration of architects trying to make individual buildings stand out as complete in themselves. "Architects of exclusion have for generations perfected their art, and built their buildings on plots assigned to them. But somehow the special strip which they abhor has arrogated to itself more vitality, more power of growth . . . than the whole of their tidy output" (Moore 2001, 156). With its endless garish seductions and banal repetitions the strip seems a terrible decline from an ordered cityscape. Back in 1955, Victor Gruen complained about the antecedents of today's commercial strips, which he called subcityscapes. "The degrading facade of suburbia, the shameful introduction to our cities, the scourge of the metropolis. *Subcityscape* consists of elements which cling like leeches to all our roads, accompanying them far out to where there was, once upon a time, something called landscape; *subcityscape*—consisting of gas stations, shacks, shanties, car lots, posters,

billboards, dump heaps, roadside stands, rubbish, dirt, and trash. . . .
Subcityscapes spread their tentacles in all directions, overgrow regions,
states, and country" (Gruen 1955, 194–95).

Gruen proposed a remedy. He designed America's first centralized
shopping centers, the precursors of today's malls. He wanted to avoid
"long rows of one-story structures along the arterials." Now we have
the malls he begat, but they stand amid the long rows of the strip he
hated.

Robert Venturi once wrote that "Main Street is almost all right" and
praised an earlier version of Las Vegas (Venturi 1966).[15] The strip is not
Main Street; it is too dispersed and hostile to the pedestrian. Nor is the
strip the old Las Vegas; its signs point to familiar franchises rather than
to unique mini-worlds. In fact, could anyone affirm that the strip is "almost all right"?

In this book I affirm that what seems terrible fragmentation and ba-
nalization holds new forms of unity that have not been well understood
or well treated architecturally. Despite its general ugliness, the commercial strip shows a new kind of order that appears more and more often: the list with links. You cannot understand the strip—or any other
place in suburban sprawl—just by looking at the local architectural
form, because the sprawl's form involves connections other than spatial
proximity.

Suburban strips seem all too familiar, so we might see them afresh
by considering the way the strip can remake a downtown. Foremost in
importance is discontinuity combined with linkage. In an elegy for van-
ishing urban form, Paul Goldberger lamented the discontinuity along
Chicago's Michigan Avenue:

> It is a great boulevard, one of the finest in any American city,
> its noblest stretch—the Magnificent Mile—running from the
> Chicago River to Lake Shore Drive. This part of North Michigan
> once was the province of Chicago's most elegant shops, most of
> which were set in handsome, medium-size commercial buildings
> of limestone and brick. A few apartment buildings, some hotels
> and a couple of office buildings joined to create one of those truly
> civilized boulevards whose buildings are individually distinctive
> yet have enough in common to make a coherent whole. The ar-

chitecture was neo-everything: classical, Renaissance, Art Deco, Georgian. The styles worked together because the building scale was similar and the architects' intention was to play not a solo but a part in the larger symphony of the street. . . . North Michigan is now a street of malls, and if you think that is an oxymoron, come see this parade of suburban architecture metastasizing into a new kind of urban form. For that is what North Michigan is now, a series of suburban shopping malls turned on end to become vertical urban malls, with high-rise towers plopped on top. They march, one after the other, down the avenue, now less a true urban street than a funnel to carry cars and taxis past the line of monoliths. (Goldberger 1996)

According to Goldberger Michigan Avenue used to be a unified cityscape with an architectural rhythm supporting a form of life appropriate to that unity, but now it has become a characterless pipe for flows of shoppers heading into malls that except for their height might as well be along a suburban strip. Yet Goldberger's lament does not pay enough attention to the character of the strip.

Construction of enclosed malls peaked some years ago in the United States, but commercial strips continue to expand.[16] Indoor malls, once the pride of their areas and the first to lure shoppers from downtown, have been supplanted by smaller strip malls and big-box stores. Older enclosed malls may be retrofitted as strip malls where all the shops face a parking lot and there is no common space inside the building, thus increasing rentable space and allowing customers to move directly from their cars to the store of their choice, which fits the habits of people with little time and a particular product in mind. Newer "lifestyle" malls that cluster shops around squares, and other combinations of separate buildings, may resemble older downtowns but are merely the strip of franchises in a new geometry.[17] Trendy downtown neighborhoods can also become strips of franchises. The enclosed mall must now become itself an attraction by offering special ways of spending time and minding the children. The Mall of America in Minnesota and its parent in Canada transform themselves into tourist destinations. Malls host quasi-civic events; the enclosed mall tries to become a (privatized) agora.[18]

Enclosed malls tried to maintain a unified atmosphere, but the strip glories in discontinuity. Along the strip, shops are viewed and chosen from one's car, then one parks and walks quickly. There is an abrupt transition among the discontinuous worlds inside the various shops. These worlds are no longer mediated by any shared interior decor in an enclosed mall's public space. This is the discontinuity that Goldberger lamented on Michigan Avenue. The flow of traffic slides you along as you choose your next destination, then dart in and out. There are no mediating spaces except the almost characterless street itself.[19] Although it is continuous, the street has little quality of its own except its convenience or inconvenience. Its blandness highlights the seductive presences and the abrupt transitions among the various enterprises. The major continuities are the spatial size and rhythms of the enterprises, the level of signage and visual noise, and the music on your car radio.

One branded island abuts another, McDonald's next to Wal-Mart next to Kinko's. There is no continuity to the spatial transitions except for parking and whatever commonalities result from the marketing imperative of instant recognizability. Amid the glitz, some older establishments—car repair shops, dry cleaners, and the like—may survive, but they look cheap and shabby even though they may offer more effective services than businesses in the tarted-up buildings around them. They are historical survivals from a different spatiality of shopping, but they may outlive their flashier kin.

Strip transitions are abrupt and follow no order: supermarket, motel, Chinese restaurant, tire store, travel agency, burger barn, bookstore, animal hospital. Nor is there continuity in time; substantial-looking enterprises suddenly disappear and are abruptly replaced. In Venturi's terms, most of them are decorated sheds pretending to be ducks, an architecture that allows for rapid remodeling.

The strip needs no hierarchy; all is available and adjacent, and all transitions are sudden. The discontinuous yet linked structure of a list prevails. The road offers only a corridor for flow, not a principle of content. Stores, texts, places, and identities can be related one to another without any significant connection through more general unities or meanings.[20]

Looked at abstractly, what has happened is that clamorous discontinuity has replaced cooperative unity. Driving the strip is like scanning a list. You travel facing transitions and seductions, just as when reading the ads in the newspaper, or the Yellow Pages, or surfing Web lists. Whether one scans for a purpose or on impulse, the list remains. The unified character of the street recedes as each item on the list vies for your attention. Some items on the list are malls, which are themselves more lists offering more seductions.

Because it is expensive to be well positioned on the strip's list, larger chains will be favored, whereas being on the lists on the Web or in the Yellow Pages requires less investment, so those can offer more differentiations. But these differentiations make those lists longer and unsurveyable, so the meta-lists appear, the category guide in the Yellow Pages, the informal compilations of Web links, the Web search engines that provide still more lists.

If the strip is a list with seductions, it is in danger of being replaced by online lists. Another set of discontinuous seductions arrives at the door every day, as each catalog tries to entice readers into its carefully crafted atmospheric world. The structure of catalog shopping resembles the strip or the on-line search. A straightforward extension will create virtual strips, such as the Street described in Neal Stephenson's novel *Snow Crash* (Stephenson 1993).

The commercial strip differs from the urban ideal forcefully espoused by Jane Jacobs, which encourages multiple use and interaction.[21] The strip is oriented to isolated shoppers in the insulated environment of the car, rather than to crowd interaction in a street market or pedestrian urban retail. City walkers on Fifth Avenue or in Greenwich Village are pulled out of themselves into multiple rhythms and complex continuities and meetings on a city street, but the strip has no continuities except within each themed island, and once inside we remain alone, as Marc Augé points out in his discussion of shopping emporia as places where each shopper relates to the corporation within a shared solitude structured by restricted social roles (Augé 1995).

Not only is the street-list discontinuous, but also many items on the list are discontinuous in another way. This is *a* McDonald's, not *the* Jones family store. You step out of the flow into a place that is the same as others of its sort, as I've already described. You know the script and the expectations to follow; you recognize the symbols and the atmosphere.

Amid these lists and discontinuous little worlds there are few truly public spaces. Enclosed malls are an intermediate case; they hope for crowds but their private owners control the environment. City merchants in Soho or on Fifth Avenue want to maximize exposure and flow just as do mall owners, but city merchants cannot easily control the space around their stores, so more happens there, both for good and bad. Yet a divided agora does persist dematerialized on the airwaves as talk shows, and on the Internet as chat rooms, blogs, and bulletin boards. These, however, threaten to become private clubs, on yet other lists.

Lists as next-to's and inside-of's, on their own and inserted into other lists; Web links to lists of links, lists of products, mailing lists, MTV as a discontinuous list of little worlds, phone books, dictionaries and encyclopedias, to-do lists, multithemed places, course lists, guidebooks, advertising maps of localities, magazine racks listing links to discontinuous communities, bits of one world showing up inside another. To make a list you need separated items, which may however be from many conflicting levels.

On a list items seem peacefully exterior to each other, even if in fact they include or oppose each other. A local car repair shop can be next to a global franchise. A specialty store can be next to the Wal-Mart that is out to destroy it. On a Web page or in the telephone directory, items of very diverse kinds stand on the same list. A list needs criteria for what counts as a single item, and some way of marking that distinction. In the book and on the Web there are visual clues in the layout. The suburban strip separates by parking lots and storefronts. A list needs some relatively neutral backdrop for the list to appear against, whether this be the yellow page, a Web graphic background, or the space along the street or in the mall. There has to be a dimension within which the list items appear together, no matter how disparate or conflicted they may be.

That list background is not really neutral, though, for within that space items on lists are interacting with each other. Besides conflict and inclusion, some items interact just by being adjacent on the list. My store's business is affected by what you sell next door, or by the location of the entrance to your parking lot, or by the fact that my store is listed on a page that also includes a popular destination. You and I might become friends because a waiting line uses designated letters of the alphabet ("A through K stand here"). These interactions are not easily controlled, and they are fought over by the people and institutions involved.

For lists are linear manifestations of more complex linked structures and processes. Not all the structure found on a list is contained within the individual items and their proximities on the list. There are links among the items, and to items on other lists. The links may or may not be visible. Throughout this book I argue that contemporary places need to find architectural ways of emphasizing their links.

Lists both offer and paralyze choice. Unlike a centered hierarchy, a list disseminates in many directions. People today are self-conscious of having to face lists, of being themselves items on lists, and of confronting lists within their own identities. A city—or a self—with too many isolated monuments needs to find or create more links.

To lament the lack of older continuities and centers is to miss the new kinds of unity. Paul Goldberger did not see that the strip might be offering a new kind of unity. He said of the new shape of Michigan Avenue: "Even the most sophisticated urban mall has a way of seeming suburban, a place too much like other places. Enter any one of these North Michigan Avenue malls and you could be almost anywhere. The stores are the same as the ones you see everywhere. . . . The special identity of this once-unique urban street is lost" (Goldberger 1996).

The avenue is now a list, and its "almost anywhere" comes from the need for seductive recognizability. Yet there is still form-giving, though it is discontinuous. The form comes not just in the spatial locality of Michigan Avenue but also in the scattered connections of McDonald's or Nieman-Marcus, and in the economic and commuting patterns involved. That these may not be interesting localities is due more to their purposes and the technology available than to the kind of unity being created. When Goldberger calls this unity "suburban," we should reply by asking: Just what kind of unity do the suburbs possess? They too have a complex linked and list structure that extends beyond what is immediately visible. To think of suburbs as collections of ersatz mini Mount Vernons alternating with meaningless strips doesn't deal with what they have already become, and the new transport and telecommunication nets will make them even more complex.

Is such linked discontinuity new? Consider the historical jumble in the Roman Forum, consider not the harmonious Greek temple but the mix of activities in its temple precinct, think of traditional markets and fairs. Linked discontinuity is not new, but something has changed. It is not the introduction of mixture where none was before, but rather the thinning of older concentric and hierarchical identities that had imposed control

on intermediate zones. Freed, more transitions can become discontinuous; more kinds of links can develop, because places and worlds can be
"next to" one another without spatial continuity.

Even the lost urban form Goldberger mourns was laid on something
like a list. Cities have always presented a density of links that did not
coincide with their spatial structures. Linked discontinuity has always
been at war with hierarchy. Now the hierarchy is weaker. The old concentric centers had more content to impose. Michigan Avenue's older
community was not so inclusive, and the new urban form is more democratic, attracting more people than those who could afford old Michigan
Avenue's stores and clubs.

I have been using the commercial strip's flowing street and attractions
as an example of a new kind of unity within suburban sprawl. What you
see from the road or from the air are nodes sitting next to one another.
The links that connect the nodes are not so visible, however; they are
carried by the trucks on the roads, the packets on the cables and fibers,
and in the habits and movements of people. What may appear as a dull
one-thing-after-another involves complicated rhythms and intersecting
linkages. These intersecting and mingling activities can resemble urban
density, though they are not so spatially compressed. In chapter 7 I argue for improving suburban sprawl through further increasing its density by self-conscious linkage and awareness of process.[22] Once we see
how spatial relations are not the only connections that unify a place, we
begin to notice many more kinds of place unity.

Should I then be talking about "postmodern places"? Nowadays I don't
find that term useful, although I once wrote a book about it (Kolb 1990).
As a term, *postmodern* seems to have become debased far more quickly
than *modern*, which has had a run of centuries compared to decades. In
architecture *postmodern* started by naming a liberating reaction against
the strictures of orthodox modernism, then it acquired more positive
content as the assertion of locality and particular history, and then it
became attached to historicist styles of surface decoration for modern
boxes. Now it often functions as a term of disparagement. More recently,
places have been claimed to be postmodern if they make room for decentered fluid identities for selves and bodies and encounters—as in online self-presentations, raves, and festival spaces. Most recently, whether
from older traditions or from resurgent modernists, there has come a

reaction against such claims; the postmodern is seen as a nihilistic de-generation of identity and community. I disagree with all these analyses. Universal claims, radical or conservative, are all over-generalized. I seek less radical but still emphatic assertions of a new condition, arguing that there are indeed new games in town, while the older continue, changed by their new context. Some of the characteristics of new places can be used to counter their other less desirable traits. There is liberation to be sought, though it is neither total nor assured.

CHAPTER TWO

What Is a Place?

Lived-in space is in our view best conceived as the
social construction of shared frameworks in which
people orient themselves and act.
(from the brochure for the Space and Virtuality Studio,
University of Malmö, Sweden)

JUST WHAT ARE PLACES, and how do they come about? Places are sometimes opposed to mere expanses of space, and that is one contrast I will be making. Often today places are also opposed to what are called *nonplaces* in another sense, all those malls and subdivisions and theme parks and parking lots that differ from classic dense and centered places in the ways described in the previous chapter. In this chapter I honor the concerns about such places but demonstrate that that way of describing the problem is unsound. Parking lots on the perimeter of a mall are real places inscribed with communal activities.[1] They have their usages and modes of life. To say that the parking lot and the mall are nonplaces questions their simplicity and their thin social roles, yet even so they remain human places. Identifying real places with centered, hierarchical locales for unified communities applies overly rigid concepts to our world, even as the realities of global markets and communication remake old centered places into multiconnected nodes. Those who declare that we live in nonplaces distort past lives and fail to see contemporary possibilities. They do point to real problems with contemporary places, but I argue that many (though not all) of what are taken as negative qualities can also enable positive achievements. There are new possibilities already inherent in the very features of contemporary places that their detractors despise.

THE CONCEPT OF PLACE

In daily American English *place* and its related terms (such as *area, position, location, locale, site*) are used in overlapping ways. The White House is a place, a field of flowers is a place, the broom has its place in the closet, the children's place is upstairs, the first line on the form is the place to fill in this year's income. Although there may be some differences among saying that this is the place for the fair, the site of the fair, or the position of the fair, in daily usage the terms tend to run together. But not completely.

If I exclaim "What a wonderful place!" when I see Venice's Piazza San Marco, I am saying something more than if I say "What a wonderful site!" The word *site* suggests that I have in mind some function, or that I like the contours of the general location. The word *place*, on the other hand, can suggest a more general praise of the piazza as a place for human life to flourish. Charles Moore, borrowing from Suzanne Langer, describes place making as the creation of an "ethical domain" that expresses a culture's sense of itself and its world. "I have employed the perhaps vaguer notion of place, the ordering of the whole environment that members of a civilization stand in the middle of, the making of sense, the projection of the image of the civilization onto the environment. This projection can be manipulated by the architect in ways spatial and formal, but it has as its purpose not simply the making of shapes or of spaces but the making of a sensible image of a culture, to give people a sense of where they are in it and to make the framework for whatever happens in the civilization" (Moore 2001, 292). If that is lacking, Sim Van der Ryn argues, "If our image or perception of a specific environmental order is confused or unclear then there is no place. We don't know when we are there; we don't know where we are. Organic synthesis, human possession have not occurred. Our lives are increasingly spent in just such meaningless environments" (Moore 2001, 99).

This notion of place is based on hierarchical public places such as church squares and public monuments. Moore says that places should provide "a controlled inside surrounded by layers" (Moore 2001, 77). Places should single out locations for special public importance where life is enacted in public (Moore 2001, 119). "One can hope, too, for the day when the gradual loss of differentiated place, the gradual emerging of the gray no-places and the inundation of the places of special significance will cause the slumbering citizenry to awaken, to demand to spend its money to have a public life" (Moore 2001, 138). In his outline of topics concerning place making, Moore lists "accommodating or celebrating human activity," "taking possession of space," "establishing a hierarchy of importance," "distinguishing inside from outside," "conditioning the inside," "manipulating scale . . . space and shape . . . sequence in time" (Moore 2001, 78–79). Moore says that he wants architects to create a "sense of a hierarchical system (I've been calling it a sense of place)" (295).[2]

One obvious worry about this notion of place is that the "we" of "our lives" is now more multiple. A single symbolic center might not gather the diversity of cultures around us. A deeper problem is that even if our culture were homogeneous, our places do not make hierarchy in the way Moore wants it done. As we saw in chapter 1, today's places are increasingly interlinked, multiple, and changing. There are still hierarchically organized places and domains with central symbolic precincts, but they lose their primacy as they are enfolded within a network of connections and relations that is not centered nor organized hierarchically.

Moore admits that his notion no longer fits our reality. Americans move about every five years, so we lack the firm commitment to a piece of territory that gave strength to central hierarchical places and monuments (Moore 2001, 296). Nor do our activities fit in classical spaces. "The most powerful and effective places which our forebears made for themselves, and left for us, exist in contiguous space. They work on an organized hierarchy of importances, first dividing what is inside from what is outside, then in some way arranging things in order of their importance. . . . Our own places, however, like our lives, are not bound up in one contiguous space. Our order is not made in one discrete inside neatly separated from a hostile outside. . . . Our new places, that is, are given form with electronic not visual glue" (Moore 2001, 151–52).

When a civilization is changing rapidly, the demand for centered hierarchical places becomes questionable.[3] A notion of place based on classic models misses what is unique and novel about today's "ethical domain." We need more flexible notions about place making. Moore acknowledges this when he remarks that the fact that places today all seem the same may be due to the lack of sufficiently precise tools for talking about them (Moore 2001, 136). Although he is implying that better mathematical tools are needed, I suggest that the problem lies in his basic concept of place itself, which is flawed and needs to be rethought.

There are many kinds of places today and many different dimensions along which places might be evaluated. A blunt contrast between places and nonplaces is not helpful. Instead of using *place* as an honorific term for all that ought to be good about places, I suggest a more neutral notion of place that will apply to parking lots and theme parks and suburban sprawl as well as to the Acropolis and Central Park and Monticello. Further distinctions and evaluations can then be made within the notion of place. In subsequent chapters I argue that notions about linkage and connection, and evaluative contrasts such as complex/simple and thick/thin can provide a vocabulary for talking about the possibilities and problems of contemporary places without biasing the discussion in favor of hierarchical centers.

AREAS, PLACES, AND LOCALES

My strategy for developing a more useful concept of place is to separate from the hierarchical notion of place the core idea that a place is where social norms spread out possibilities for action across a spatial landscape.

There are beautiful areas in a forest that are obviously "somewhere" locatable on a map, and present a striking unified character, but are "nowhere in particular" in the sense that there are no expectations or rituals or actions associated with their areas. Many things are happening in those areas as the plants grow and the birds fly, but nothing human or social happens there. Such areas are places in one sense of the word but not in another. I want to distinguish those senses.

In this book I assign distinctions to words that in ordinary use are not so distinct. The distinctions do not fall into a neat hierarchy; in some cases the same area can be described by more than one of the terms. To develop the new notion of place I distinguish *areas*, *locations*, *locales*, and *places*. There is nothing wrong with the ordinary flexible usages of these terms. However, theorists and writers such as Moore and Norberg-Schulz use *place* with a bias toward centers and hierarchies. The definitions suggested below avoid that bias and allow important distinctions to be shown more clearly.

An *area* is an expanse of space. Areas can be designated very precisely by measurements, or by reference to landmarks, or indicated loosely as "over there." There can be many purposes in designating areas, but doing so does not automatically make them places in the sense relevant here.[4] Since areas can be designated arbitrarily, an area may or may not coincide with distinct regions that have unified textures, so an area could include half of this qualitative array (a cornfield) plus a third of that one (a nearby factory).

Most areas of space are also *locations*. A location is an area where a thing or an event is found. Strictly speaking, events occur everywhere. Over there the flowers bloom, the wind blows, and even that boulder's sitting unmoved for millennia is a long event, as is its slow erosion, whether or not people are here to notice it. There is the location the fish migrate by, the location where the wind makes that odd sound. The location of the tree. The location of the battle. This last example comes perhaps closest to one common use of *place*.

Some locations have a character that makes us perceive the area as unified and complete. I call such satisfying and unified locations *locales*. The clearing in the woods and the Piazza San Marco are locales. They might also be places in a social sense, but they do not have to be. (Locales can be similar to what Christian Norberg-Schulz calls *places*. Anthony Giddens, however, uses *locale* to designate more or less what I call *places*.) I argue below that places do not have to be locales with a unified character. (In the Sprawling Places Web site I also argue that places in a social sense do not have to be continuous single areas of space, and that real places can be in virtual space, as well as in combinations of physical and virtual spaces.)

Out of areas and locations we make *places*. For instance, there is the place where we worship, or vote, or sell melons. That area over there is just an arbitrarily defined expanse, but this one here is where we dance on Thursday evenings, or is a picnic spot, or an examination hall, or a bedroom. The parts of an area stand in spatial relations of adjacency, position, and distance. The parts of a place stand in more complex relations. At a political speech the speaker's area and the press area might be adjacent, but the contrast between them is more than geometrical.

A *place* in the sense I propose is an extended location consisting of one or more expanses of space where social norms of action define significant areas and transitions for activities. Places are permeated by social norms offering possibilities for action. In philosophical jargon, places have an intentional unity and a modal or normative character.[5]

Places in this sense do not have to be organized in hierarchies. They may overlap: the dancing place may also be where the town meeting occurs. A place's borders may be as vague as the borders of the activities involved. Places can also be analyzed in other ways than as places. The building that is the legislative hall is an object composed of such and such materials in this or that style, costing a particular amount to maintain, and so on. The dancing field can be analyzed for its soil content. A virtual meeting room can be discussed as a software object.

This notion of place has relatives in the social sciences. For example in a discussion of systems for cooperative work, Harrison and Dourish remark that

> Physically, a place is a space which is invested with understandings of behavioural appropriateness, cultural expectations, and so forth. We are located in "space," but we act in "place". . . . A conference hall and a theatre share many similar spatial features (such as lighting and orientation); yet we rarely sing or dance when presenting conference papers, and to do so would be regarded as at least slightly odd (or would need to be explained). We wouldn't describe this behavior as "out of space"; but it would most certainly be "out of place"; and this feeling is so strong that we might try quite hard to interpret a song or a dance as part of a presentation, if faced with it suddenly. It is a sense of place, not space, which makes it appropriate to dance at a Grateful Dead concert, but not at a Cambridge high table; to be naked in the bedroom, but not in the street; and to sit at our windows peering out, rather than at other people's windows peering in. Place, not space, frames appropriate behavior. (Harrison and Dourish 1996, 69)

I would add to this social scientific notion a phenomenological claim. We experience a place in time as we move through it in space, but that experience is more than a simple temporal sequence of "now here this color and shape, now there that color and shape."[6] To experience a place is to encounter an expanse of space *as* manifesting a web of social *possibilities* and norms. Indeed, a sequence cannot be experienced *as* a sequence unless there are ongoing memories and anticipations that knit the experience together according to conceptual norms.[7]

Places open possibilities for action, but possibilities are not positively sensed contents like red or green; they exist as a halo or horizon of expected futures and current absences-to-be-filled that give meaning to what is present. Any present perception gets its meaning from its relations within a net of other connected but absent perceptions and socially defined actions for the past and future. For instance, perceiving this visual outline as a house involves the expectation that walking around the object will reveal its back side, that it can be entered, that it has certain typical uses, and so on. Action possibilities give practical meaning, as to a doorknob or a ballpoint pen. We know what to do with those objects. Their meanings are captured in the norms for their use, norms that can vary from explicit rules to habitual understandings.

Usually we sort items and actions under already-existing concepts and norms. We enter a place and classify it as a shopping mall, and we know what behavior is expected or discouraged. At other times, though, we must construct a new concept or norm. Faced with a new kind of animal, or a new kind of artwork, a new social movement, or a new kind of place, we create a concept to define and relate it to other items. This creative kind of judgment creates a new concept, or more likely a new set of concepts—a set of norms and criteria that recognize and reveal a new field of possibilities. A concept classifying a new kind of artwork creates new criteria for making distinctions among artworks. It also changes the relations among previous kinds of artworks as they are seen in new contrasts and relations. It suggests still newer kinds of artworks by variation on the new rules. This act of creating new concepts looks very much like the process of setting up social norms. In such judgments neither the universal rule nor the particular item is fully given in advance. The process reveals and determines them, as the norms and the things normed emerge together. The things revealed by the new concepts are most often already available under other descriptions; for instance, before we can see a new artwork as art, we might see it as an object made of wood including a fish tank and TV screen. There are questions about whether objects and places can be present in perception prior to any distinction of universal meanings from particular instances. I do not engage those issues here, though they were debated in the nineteenth century and are still active in the discussions about place in writers such as Casey and Harries.

Larger actions such as founding an institution or passing a law also acquire meaning through the ranges of possibilities they open and define. Those possibilities in turn get their significance from connections to still others in a net that has no definite boundaries. No present moment or area stands isolated on its own. No spatial or temporal experience is meaningful unless it is immersed within a wider network of absent possibilities governed by practical and conceptual norms. In chapter 4

I discuss the ways in which that field of possibilities exceeds those shaped by a place's explicit social norms, but my point now is that being in a place is not just a simple positive presence but a complex melding of presence and absence, actual and possible movements and perceptions.

Place norms specify types of things and movements and locations, along with their appropriate borders and transitions and performances. This happens with varying degrees of detail. The most elaborate place norms are at thickly ritualized sites such as a legislative hall, a church, or a courthouse. In such places there are zones of general movement (you enter here, not through the door for the judge) and zones that are forbidden to most people (only the jury sits over there). There is a directionality to movement in these places (members walk to the rostrum before speaking); there are crossings where one moves into a new zone (the audience sits here, the press there); there are norms about what parts are in the same zone; there are some actions to do here, others there, and some done by movements from here to there (the bride walks down the aisle). Some items should or should not be present (a flag is mandatory in the courtroom, optional in your dining room); some changes make or don't make sense in the place (redecorating is much restricted in a church or courtroom). Such highly ritualized places are more exacting than less formal locations, but "less formal" is itself a normative category, not an absence of normative categories. A house, a street, a family room: each has its own map and choreography.

A place opens a landscape of action possibilities set in a spatial landscape. Place norms create salience (the decoration on the jury box is less salient than the symbols on the wall behind the judge; the style of the table has little importance in a committee meeting room, whereas the same table's style becomes prominent in a dining room). In making (or remaking or continuing) a place, different regions are distinguished, as are different actions and stages of actions. These two sets of distinctions generate a large number of combinations of zones with actions. Some of those combinations are established as normative, so that the stages and connections and intersections of the actions are related to the regions and connections and intersections of the surrounding expanse. Describing the process of place making this way makes it seem that it happens in stages: making spatial and action distinctions, combining them, making norms. But these occur in a mutual emergence, each taking cues from the other.

A group might make a temporary place by establishing limits and dimensions for conversation in a bar or by a tree in a park. By a few gestures they establish zones of action, borders, and some dimensions of approach and avoidance. Items of furniture and spatial relations could become salient; the act of moving the chair can take on a meaning it did not have in other settings. Standing up or sitting on the ground might no longer be an accidental accompaniment but might take on significance as a move in the conversation. This temporary place remains defined if someone steps away briefly, but it soon dissolves. Not every conversation creates such a place; our talking might be an event that has a location but few if any special expectations for its surroundings, as in a chat among friends walking together on a sidewalk.

In most temporary places people easily map standard roles onto the local environment. But temporary places can encourage new spatial and social roles. Socially liberating novelty can emerge from the carnival, the street demonstration, the performance art happening, but also from the unexpected "new self" that I find when a conversation conducted somewhere else than in its accustomed place opens new possibilities.

Not every action performed in a place makes a move in the ritual of the place. Some acts belong to normatively assigned courses of movement and action in the place. Walking up the aisle to the front of the church at a wedding is a significant action that not everyone is supposed to perform, but shifting three feet to the left in the church pew is an action available to all and does not change your normative location as would shifting three feet to the right into the middle of the aisle. The appropriate range for how you can express yourself changes as you move from the courthouse steps into a courtroom. In a city park, taking off your shirt would not make much normative difference, while in a courtroom it would make an enormous difference to your "position" in the place if the court were in session. Even if your physical location was no different, by taking off your shirt you would have moved along a dimension of significance, which would change your "distance" from other people and the possible actions available to you.[8]

If places involve action patterns, and if most actions are temporal and spatial performances, and if for most actions to happen there have to be transitions between stages specified by goals and meanings, then places will involve divisions, distinctions, and borders. The continuity of a place will be articulated into divisions and transitions united by spatialized

norms for actions. This internal differentiation can involve clearly defined border zones (this rope sharply separates the audience from the
press section) or it can involve landmarks (over toward the rostrum is
where the legislators meet for discussion, but there is no exact border
for that region). The borders could be temporal (a city park might have
different uses at lunchtime than in the late afternoon, so that someone
might rightly complain at four in the afternoon about your picnicking in
the middle of the ball field, but at noon you might reject that complaint
because the customary usage was different then).

There can be no place without some divisions, for in such a place
no form of human life could be enacted. At least there will be a border, however vague, between this place and others, and usually there
will be internal divisions corresponding to different actions or stages of
actions.[9] The greater discontinuity typical of contemporary places thus
emphasizes a condition that has always been true of places. Any place
will have internal divisions, but contemporary places have new kinds of
discontinuities held together by new kinds of unities.

SYSTEMS AND PLACES

In addition to the social norms that link areas into places, there is a
different kind of connection among areas of space. Actions here have
causal effects there. Certain chemicals dumped into the river will cause
fish downstream to die, no matter what the local social norms may be.
Building a highway here will mean more traffic there. Causal links are
independent of social norms. I will call them *systemic* connections or
linkages, arrayed in *systems.* Systemic connections carry environmental
effects, the impact of spatial infrastructure, and many economic constraints. In chapter 4 I examine this distinction in more detail, since critiques of today's places often confuse systemic and normative issues. The
relevant point now, though, is that systemic connections constrain the
creation of social norms. Once that highway is built, the flow of goods
and people will change in ways that may make some social patterns of action impossible to continue, or it may help create new patterns. Building
highways and pipelines and ports, cutting down forests, locating housing
here and not there, these have systemic effects that alter the possibilities
for social places.

Social norms and place making can work around some systemic ef-

fects, but place making has to begin with the available array of spaces
and areas. For the systemic effects we can control, deciding where they
will fall and how they will be distributed is partly a matter of engineering and partly a matter for political conflicts. Where will we locate the
landfill or the airport or the highway? Where will the wind take this pollution? The spatial arrangement of costs and benefits raises issues of dis-
tributive justice and becomes a central stake in place-related disputes.

Henri Lefebvre studied the creation of geographical and social spaces
that cement productive relations and social differences. Discussing hierarchical and other assemblages of places, Lefebvre uses the term *space*
(*l'espace*) in a way somewhat analogous to my use of *place*. He speaks of
social spaces that are produced by, and themselves reproduce, modes of
acting and ways of living. His *spaces* usually encompass a multitude of the
locations that I would call *places*, as well as their geographical distribution and system interactions. He describes, for instance, "a remarkable
instance of the production of space . . . supplied by the current transformation of the perimeter of the Mediterranean into a leisure-oriented
space for industrialized Europe" (Lefebvre 1991, 58). Lefebvre distin-
guishes places as nodes within the larger space of a given civilization or
mode of production (see, for instance, Lefebvre 1991, 288).

Lefebvre's social spaces are areas that have been defined by and in
turn shape social actions. They are sustained by habitual patterns of
movement and gesture. His *spaces* are wider and more generic: the space
of modern transport, urban space, the space of medieval town production or Roman rule, and the space of work, which he describes as consisting of "production units: businesses, farms, offices. The various networks
which link these units are also part of the space of work" (Lefebvre 1991,
191).

In my terms, Lefebvre's spaces are a mix of normative places and
systemic arrangements. Lefebvre stresses that they are complexes with
many historical layers.

> Social space . . . is neither a substantial reality nor a mental real-
> ity, it cannot be resolved into abstractions, and it consists neither
> in a collection of things in space nor in an aggregate of occupied
> places. Being neither space-as-sign nor an ensemble of signs re-
> lated to space, it has an actuality other than that of the abstract

signs and real things which it includes. The initial basis or foundation of social space is nature—natural or physical space. Upon this
basis are superimposed—in ways that transform, supplant or even
threaten to destroy it—successive stratified and tangled networks
which, though always material in form, nevertheless have an existence beyond their materiality: paths, roads, railways, telephone
links, and so on. (Lefebvre 1991, 402–3)

Lefebvre's discussion emphasizes how places, in the sense I propose,
come linked to one another and intertwined with causal systems that
influence social norms. So places can be directly ideological, defining
action possibilities, locating people into roles and tracks, and mandating
attitudes.

It is the way they spread out norms and expectations across space that
makes places sites of both oppression and liberation. Systemic effects
constrain possibilities. Place norms define movements and meanings
and connections, and so open roles for individual and social subjects
who inhabit the place. These social roles and values fill the landscape.
Once there are places for everything and everyone is in his or her place,
the normatively defined relationships can seem natural and inevitable.
They influence us without our notice; their oppressions may be taken for
granted. Spatial arrangements and place norms categorize and bias our
behavior patterns and views, make groups invisible, and confine people
to diminished roles. Places can channel actions and make alternatives
unavailable. They can segregate, and they can degrade possibilities even
when there is no oppression of one group by another, since the quality
of actions and roles available in the place may be less than is needed for
human flourishing, even if no one is differentially oppressed. Places are
not the single origin of oppression, but they spread it over space and
people.

Social scientists view norms as a particular kind of expectation of appropriate behavior. In analyzing the way places are lived, they sometimes
find it useful to distinguish normative expectations for what "should" occur from other expectations about what "will" occur. If office employees
have a habit of standing by the window when they talk about their budget, but there is no norm that they do so, it will be unexpected though
not normatively inappropriate if they talk about it elsewhere. If, on the

other hand, there is an official norm that budget talk is to be done in a secure conference room, then, supposing that in practice they hardly ever talk about the budget in the conference room, it will be inappropriate though not unexpected that budget conversations happen by the window. It may be expected that the conversation will take place at a normatively inappropriate location. Such combinations add to the complexity of a place, since actors then have to weigh different directives. The example also implies that norms about what *should* be done can survive even when they are not followed, while expectations about what *will* be done weaken when they are not reinforced by continuing practice.

The point of this distinction is that place norms are not simple controls or programs; they are lived within an interpretive process that demands tactical decisions and adjustments. Place norms may try to normalize behavior, but they exist through ongoing negotiations that can warp or evade their influence. The same is true of system effects. Practical living in places is not formed by complete and formalized systems of rules. Pierre Bourdieu's discussion of the relation of practice and structure is useful in this regard (Bourdieu 1977). Daily elisions and decisions both reproduce the social norms and introduce changes. "The unpredictability that comes with use is never quite contained with cultural preferences for completeness and closure" (Liggett 2003, 27).

Social norms and expectations are maintained in processes that interpret and modify them; neither the process nor the structure can exist without the other. Poets use and abuse grammar; yet if there were no regularities in language, no usage could be experienced as novel. As with language, no social norms can suppress the possibility of new patterns arising in unexpected ways, either deliberately or through an accumulation of small accidents. Subsequent chapters argue that one means of liberation is an increased awareness of interconnection, systemic forces, and of this constant process of place making and remaking.

There are always possible alternative actions and movements that are improper or unacceptable by the current norms, but might become better responses to local realities. Performing new and currently inappropriate actions can cause a rift in the continuity of social places, challenging accepted definitions. Such acts alter the perceived landscape of possibilities. They may or may not help create new norms, but at least they will make the current structures and forces more obvious.

In the next chapter I urge that we try to increase in the structural and lived complexity of places. This does not by itself undo oppression, but it can make connections and absences and processes more evident. Greater awareness of the complexity of places allows greater awareness of the joints and links in processes where new gestures and expectations, or new movements and pressures, might be created. Understanding the complexity and connections of apparently simplified places, and becoming more active in their processes of place making, help people to be more than programmed functionaries for established norms and spatial arrangements.

BODIES IN SPACE

Places stand against a background. At the end of the hike, the cabin appears within the forest. The city rises amid the surrounding desert. Is that expansive background encountered prior to constructing social places? Yes and no. Edward Casey proposes the phrase "surrounding array" to name that which encompasses us in our lived experience (Casey 1993, 205). The surrounding array is not geometrical space; it is textured and apportioned into regions with their own intensities and elasticities (see Grosz 2001, 127). Casey argues that what is first encountered is not a space considered geometrically but a space that is already divided into regions oriented as up/down, right/left, front/back, and near/far with reference to the perceiver's body. These contrasts make experienced places more than a set of purely geometrical relations between points and volumes; the background is always local, oriented, and directional. In contrast, geometrical space is a matrix seen from nowhere in particular, or if it is seen from one location, that point can be exchanged for others.[10]

Lefebvre shows how places "embody 'properties' (dualities, symmetries, etc.) which could not be imputed either to the human mind or to any transcendent spirit, but only to the actual 'occupation' of space" (Lefebvre 1991, 171; see also Flay 1985, 472). Foremost among such forms, for him, is the relation of center and periphery. Like Casey, Lefebvre argues that spatial logics such as center and periphery, or right and left symmetries, come about not as abstract geometric patterns but within an orientation established by the perceiving body. As Casey puts it, place has "placial properties that evade the parameters of distance and position, [or] sheer relation" (Casey 1997, 334). He claims that "place . . . locates things in regions whose most complete expression is neither geometric nor cartographic" (Casey 1997, 201).[11]

But places involve more than individuals centered in bodily phenomenological space. Casey is right that there is an individual bodily inhabitation of oriented space that makes it possible for us to be in places. Yet places are not just dimensions of front and back, near and far, but socially defined action possibilities within areas always already mediated by social norms and influenced by local and remote social processes and events.

The oriented and already-structured quality of places is one reason we cannot simply say that places are differentiated out of some neutral background of "experience." Another reason is that if experience is equated with a sequence of fully positive events (as in classic empiricism and sense-data accounts) then places disappear, since they involve an awareness of possibility and modal qualities, which disappear in a linear series of positive moments with no relations to one another. Guidance for knowing what portions of a temporal and spatial sequence count as experiences of the same place will not emerge from the positive items alone. If a conception of experience is rich enough to include the possible and the normative, then experience is being conceived as more than a straight temporal sequence of separated positive events.

The inhabitation of place cannot be split into natural and social components. We are never in naked space prior to place making; we always find ourselves within an ongoing world of bodily and social meaning. Still, by an abstraction we can say that a bodily oriented array or expanse is a necessary condition for place making.

Lefebvre, too, sees the interaction of individual and social factors in place making. On the one hand, he wants to emphasize the ways in which economic and political arrangements create large-scale spatial structures and norms. Yet he also will say that the social patterns "are not imposed upon material bodies, as many philosophers suppose, by prior thought. Bodies—deployments of energy—produce space and produce themselves, along with their motions, according to the laws of space" (Lefebvre 1991, 171). Lefebvre says that "this is a truly remarkable relationship: the body with the energies at its disposal, the living body, creates or produces its own space; conversely, the laws of space, which is to say the laws of discrimination in space, also govern the living body and the deployment of its energies" (Lefebvre 1991, 170).[12] Energy and work are structuring and structured, social and individual, in a dialectic where there is no simple first cause.

As people move and work within spaces that are always already socially structured, places get established with varying degrees of awareness. Patterns can begin to structure our expectations and actions without our notice. Suppose I always look at a certain tree as I pass by, or always tie my shoes leaning on a certain rock before climbing a hill. Place creation can range from such insensible settling in of expectations, through communal avowal of already accepted norms, up to explicitly debated legislation.[13] At the less aware extreme, such as at the shoe-tying rock, there may be no clear answer to the question of whether or not an area has acquired a social norm. Sheerly habitual actions that generate no expectations make not a place but only a location. At the more aware extreme, places with explicitly codified norms often become the battlegrounds for protests against and defenses of social norms, as the norms are both explicit and resilient there.

Even very explicitly established places do not come about because dominant individual or communal creativity simply imposes norms on a neutral passive space. There is an interaction between the features and rhythms of the area and the details of the social norms.[14] The particular textures of this or that spatial region may invite the assignment of possible actions from a social repertory that is already mostly defined (this area will make a good picnic area, this room has good light for an office, that area is too steep for a park). Given our evolutionary heritage, certain configurations of space and certain kinds of surroundings will seem more appropriate for certain actions. In addition, social norms have their histories. Even if we were pioneers moving into a genuinely uninhabited area, we would be coming from established places that have shaped our expectations and we would be speaking a language with an existing vocabulary for describing actions and parts of places. Making places is not creation from nothing; both the social content and the spatial array suggest connections and possibilities. And that suggestiveness is not exhausted by the creation of any one place. Areas of space always have more texture and more resources than are highlighted by any one social definition. As Elizabeth Grosz points out, "space is the ongoing possibility of a different inhabitation" (Grosz 2001, 9).

PLACES IN PROCESS AND CONTEXT

The first context for the social structure of a place is the existing local architecture. Sometimes the norms for a place can be more enduring (imagine a legislative body that rebuilds its meeting place in a new style). More often the building outlives its original place norms. The Pantheon in Rome has had different identities as a temple, a church, a museum, and a tourist attraction. Place norms are not identical to the programs or the styles of buildings.

Social norms are not in total control. I have already pointed out that the geography of physical and systemic connections affects place creation. Places are also affected by architecture. The Roman Pantheon's authoritative design, with its symmetrical domed interior opening to the sky, obviously has had tremendous influence on whatever social norms it acquired. The Pantheon brings to bear on its current identity powerful spatial and geometric experiences with cosmological and historical associations that transcend any current norms. Architectural effects can occur quite independently of place norms. Buildings are not neutral containers, and their own effects may or may not be consonant with the norms for the place. Sometimes the social norms will ignore or go against the architectural effects in the place, as may happen when a new institution is founded in an older building, for instance a democratic assembly in a former royal palace.

For an area to become a place it is not necessary — though it is nearly inevitable — that people mark, shape, and build to adjust the features of the area and the place norms to accommodate each other.[15] When architects build a place, they usually strive for such adjustments, though today architects such as Peter Eisenman sometimes design buildings that deliberately chafe against the textures of action in the place.

I have been emphasizing how the structure of a place is both physical and normative. It includes the physical layout of landscape and architecture with their structures, effects, divisions, continuities, and affordances. It also includes the social norms that divide and assign actions to areas and subareas. Place structures have their own importance and complexities, and they offer occasions for greater awareness of the context of the place and its processes of place making.

There are two kinds of processes of place making. First, there is the local ongoing activity of interpretation and reinterpretation. Place norms are always being passed on, being reread, having their conflicts resolved, being adapted to alterations in the place or its context. This keeps place norms active while it supports and revises their meanings.

Second, there are the larger intertwined causal and political processes that shape the physical environment and its resources. These both make possible and constrain the creation of social norms. Often these systemic and political processes are distant in time or space, but they do not have to be. A suburb stands where it does, with the landscape and geography it has, because of the local geology, the governmental tax policies, incentives set up by the various levels of government, decisions by developers and financial markets, older decisions locating highways and infrastructure and industries, pressures in distant lands causing migration, laws about the environment, court decisions, and on and on. Such influences come in many kinds and need not work in parallel. They affect different dimensions of local places in different ways. Some of these processes and effects are systemic in the sense I defined earlier in this chapter; they produce causal effects that will happen whether intended or not. Whatever the social norms, pollution let loose there will kill trees here; tax relief there will cause decline here. Some processes are explicitly normative, such as laws and court decisions, but most of these larger processes mix systemic and normative factors.

The structure of a place never exists on its own; it results from larger social processes and decisions received into local processes of interpretation and embodiment. Architectural interventions can be at once the results of larger processes and means for local interpretation, modulation, and perhaps resistance to those larger processes. Local interpretation keeps normative and physical structures flexible, and it keeps larger causal and political processes from forcing every detail in a place. On the other hand, outside processes provide resources and keep local interpretive processes from closing in on themselves.

All aspects of places have their own complexities: spatial and normative structures, embodied interpretative living, and larger causal and political processes. Further complexities can arise from how these are played off against one another in a more active and self-conscious in-habitation of places that are argued for in the next chapter.

PLACES WITH DEEP NARRATIVES

The terms I have been using (*area, location, locale, place*) are not orga-nized into a hierarchical or concentric set. My distinctions are in some ways more flexible and in some ways more restrictive than in other theo-ries, because they offer no simple negative term in opposition to *place*. That is, there can be *nonplaces* that are areas and locations, and there can also be nonplaces that are locales with a striking unified character but that are still not places for social activity. Especially, there is no no-tion of nonplace that applies to the sort of thing that many others call nonplaces: suburban strips, malls, sprawling subdivisions, theme parks, and so on. As I identify them, those are fully places, though their social norms may define oversimplified or oppressive lives. Malls and suburban strips are as real places as are cozy villages or the Piazza San Marco. They may not be as complex or as thick, but to call them nonplaces blunts the critical mind just when it is needed most. We should rather question what kind of places they are and how they can be brought to improve on their own possibilities.

The way I characterize places, though, may still seem too thin. What about the way narratives, dreams, associations, and histories get attached to places that define us (for examples, see Tuan 1977)? What about the unified character of a place, its aesthetic appeal, and the way it fits in with the subtleties of the natural or built landscape? Isn't there much more to places than just social norms?

Yes there is, but it is a mistake to demand that a "real place" have a deep narrative history and a harmonious character. That paralyzes thought by condemning en masse too many contemporary places when what is needed is a concept of *place* flexible enough to describe the kinds of places we find and able to allow us to make critical judgments among different kinds of thin and simplified places.

It is important to be able to talk analytically about social places that lack narrative richness and unified character, because that lack is often what makes them special and "modern." In the next chapter I introduce more tools for discussing contemporary places, using the notions of complex versus simplified, thick versus thin, and dense versus diluted places.

Given this new notion of place I am proposing, social norms are necessary, but narratives and associations are neither necessary nor sufficient for an area to become a social place. In fact it is crucial to some contemporary places that they lack rich associations and narratives (see the references in chapter 3 to Marc Augé). On the other hand, a forest area could be rich in personal or familial associations without having any norms established for what is done there. It could be a *location* that stimulates certain memories, but not a socially defined *place*. (More typically, though, such an area would quickly acquire familial or social norms as the place where family members go to reminisce.) Usually shared narratives involve social norms, but they do not have to. Associations with a place could be peripheral to the social definition of the area: the parking lot is where our farm used to be, or where Cousin Jim hit the light pole, or where I am reminded of a movie chase scene, but these associations are irrelevant to its function and to the social roles and actions there.

Associated narratives and a unified pervasive character do enrich places. However, they are not necessary and they can be dangerous. "Enrichment" can be taken literally when unified character and strong narratives become commodities. A street offering a strikingly resonant experience and echoes of history may be old and revered, or it may have been designed last month to attract tourists and shoppers. Narratives are manufactured for themed places to sell, or are produced to supplant unsavory real histories.

Barry Lopez, describing an attitude that would improve our awareness and respect for the land, speaks of "paying intimate attention; a storied relationship to a place rather than a solely sensory awareness of it; and living in some sort of ethical unity with a place" (Lopez 1997). We need, he says, to become *vulnerable* to a place. This is as true for a Manhattan street as for an Alaskan valley, and includes, in his telling, stories about industrial and economic forces as well as about animals and native cultures. Beyond commodification and beyond personal associations there are important stories about the forces and decisions involved in the current shape of a landscape or a place. Such narratives increase the lived complexity of the place and may stimulate action, but they are not what place theorists usually intend when they talk of narratives attached to places.

UNIFIED PLACE CHARACTER

Associated feelings and narratives are neither necessary nor sufficient to make an area into a social place, and the same is true of a unified place character or overall atmosphere. It follows from the notion of a place as involving social norms that many striking and effective locales, such as a clearing in the woods or a beautiful mountain valley, are not necessarily places in the social sense of the word. The effects of such locales on us may resemble the effect of a fine day with wonderful clear weather. We become centered, energized, and alert; we feel we have escaped a heaviness we may not have been aware of. Still, such locales need not have any social norms established for activity there.

Some effective social places, such as temporary quarters for a legislature, may lack aesthetic and spatial character. So places in my sense do not require the feeling of a unified and centered locale. Whether or not a locale gives us a feeling of unity and at-home-ness is separate from what kind of social possibilities the place offers. Some spaces and locales that make us feel wonderful are not associated with any patterns for action. Others might be social places, but their harmonious feeling might hide serious oppressions. The social landscape of a place is usually more complex than a single unified place character can convey.

It sounds jarring to insist that some wonderfully unified and impressive locales are not places. Nevertheless, I emphasize this distinction because critics often confuse issues of atmosphere and character with issues of complexity and justice. Whether a place produces a feeling of appropriateness and completeness is quite different from whether or not its social norms for action are complex, appropriate, humane, and whether the local system effects are fairly distributed. The problems with many newer places have more to do with their oversimplified social norms and their relation to larger systems than with their aesthetic character, inadequate as that may be.

There is no doubt that a satisfying unified character and complex humane textures of action may go together in wonderful ways, and places feel better when they have an overall character that fits their patterns of action. But also a satisfying character can mask narrow or oppressive social norms. Among writers who worry about the character of today's places, Karsten Harries is the most aware of both possibilities. While he wishes for a felt fusion of centered place design and wholeness of life, he understands how that feeling may reinforce social evils. He is not sure that modern democratic society allows the older deeply felt and historical centered place character to be designed any more, because it may restrict freedom (see Harries 1997).

It may still seem wrong to insist that places do not *need* special harmony between their social norms, their typical actions, and their natural and architectural character. Don't places need to have *some* unified character to match their normative unity? No, they do not.

Perhaps the most vocal proponent of unified place character has been Christian Norberg-Schulz. His writings provide sensitive descriptions of the natural characters of different regions and cities. He asserts that every place must possess a unified character derived from the natural environment.

> [A place is] a totality made up of concrete things having material substance, shape, texture, and colour. Together these things determine *an "environmental character," which is the essence of place.* (Norberg-Schulz 1976, in Nesbitt 1996, 414, my emphasis)

> The character [of a place] is determined by the material and formal constitution of the place. We must therefore ask: how is the ground on which we walk, how is the sky above our heads, or in general how are the boundaries which define the place. How a boundary is depends upon its formal articulation, which is again related to the way it is "built." . . . The existential purpose of building (architecture) is therefore to make a site become a place, that is, to uncover the meanings potentially present in the given environment. (Norberg-Schulz 1976, in Nesbitt 1996, 420–22)

Norberg-Schulz is careful to distinguish his claim that places must have an appropriate and unified character from the stronger claim that places must have a character that elicits an "Ah!" of contentment. Places can have many different characters, some quite humdrum. Still, he attacks contemporary places as lacking the kind of character that would let people dwell properly. He argues that we need places that support more than just our functioning in machines for living. He develops from

Heidegger a general theory about what spatial and natural dimensions constitute place and what character should be built into today's places.[16] Norberg-Schulz attends especially to the features of a region's landscape and climate. He develops a description of what a full human life would be in a full place, and for that too he finds clues in Heidegger's theories of authentic human dwelling. So his doctrine of place character includes an implicit set of social norms for different kinds of places.

Although Norberg-Schulz writes evocative descriptions, his arguments do not prove that unified place character is either necessary or sufficient for an area to be a social place. Unified character is not *necessary* for an area to be a place, because many social places, especially in their early stages, lack unified character, as can be seen from the many informal rooms where institutions reside when they take their start. These rooms tend to look alike although the institutions might be quite different. Nor is unified character by itself *sufficient* to make an area into a place, because character can distinguish a locale and make it feel unified and appropriate, yet the locale not be a place in any social sense. A striking valley that feels like a unified whole might include half of an agribusiness farm and half of a neighboring nature preserve, which have different social norms and different ways of relating to nature. Or a coexisting plurality of rival social norms for the use of a public square might contrast with the unified historical character of a town that contains diverse immigrant communities.[17]

As a critical tool, the concept of unified place character is aimed against areas that possess little or no character and become mere conjunctions of stuff that cannot provide rooted evocative surroundings for human dwelling. It is similar to Moore's idea that places should lay out a unified social domain with hierarchies of importance. Norberg-Schulz's concept has a stronger environmental component than Moore's. The environment plus the activities combine to provide guidance about what kinds of places to create.[18] Different actions demand places with different characters. A dwelling has to be "protective," an office "practical," a ballroom "festive," and a church "solemn" (Norberg-Schulz 1976, in Nesbitt 1996, 419–20).

However, both the critical and the prescriptive aspects of this concept of place character are unstable. The number of defined actions and characters has to be small enough to offer guidance, yet there will always be pressure to expand the list to include more and more types of action and more characters. Critical uses of the concept of character demand a clear sense of what counts as good character—it won't be enough to indicate *whatever* togetherness some conjoined items happen to have. Norberg-Schulz seems to draw his normative theory of character from nature, but he also has an a priori list of what he has identified as the fundamental needs for dwelling. Such lists of approved needs and characters force certain ideals of social unity as the only ones appropriate for real places. For him, a unified character demands architectural and social centering; the lack of such centering condemns contemporary places. Centering is harder now, because places want to be multiple and complex and linked, yet Norberg-Schulz's approach recommends changes that would enforce simpler social patterns and lives. If one tries to avoid such overly simple social prescriptions, one weakens the notion of place character. As the list of acceptable needs and activities lengthens, it includes too many kinds of character. Maybe it will even include the character of disunity, or metacharacters, but long before then the idea will have lost its critical bite.

Because of this instability, the concept of character does not provide adequate diagnostic tools. It remains too strongly within the arena of aesthetic questions about perception, which do not get to the root of the problems today, and which suggest inadequate solutions. The unity of a place occurs more fundamentally in its social norms than in its perceived character, and it is in the kinds of unity enabled by their norms that contemporary places are most different. Since today multiple or loosely linked place norms often coexist or overlap in the same area, it would be wrong to expect each of them to correspond to a distinct unified character. It is also possible to have adjacent places with quite different social norms existing in neighboring areas that are architecturally indistinguishable from one another.

Although place norms and place character do not imply each other, planners and architects should consider both without one being taken as the definitive key to the other. Are there place characters appropriate for complex linked, multiple, nonhierarchical, and nonconcentric places? How could we create through architecture and planning a spacious sense of inhabitation that need not rely on a single fixed identity? My guess is that answering these questions will involve an architectural and visual complexity that we may have to learn to distinguish from clutter. Even traditional-looking harmonious and centered places, and their contemporary equivalents such as New Urbanist developments, will come to show new place characters, not because they look much different than before, but because of their explicit and self-conscious insertion into wider processes and more complex norms.[19]

CHAPTER THREE

Place Complexity

*There is nothing, whether in actuality or in thought, that is
as simple . . . as is commonly imagined. [Claiming that things
are simple and self-sufficient] is a mere opinion based on a
lack of awareness of what is actually present.*
(Hegel 1969, 829)

WE HAVE ALREADY EXAMINED some key characteristics of today's places
and offered a theory about the nature of places; this chapter turns to
criteria for evaluating and improving contemporary places. I suggest a
criterion using the term *complexity*. This offers leverage on contemporary
places without making totalizing claims, and without demanding a distinction of genuine originals from denatured imitations. The more common criterion of place, *authenticity*, is vague and usually tied to centered
and hierarchical places. It condemns too much in today's world and offers too little guidance about how to proceed. It is better to distinguish
complex from simplified places and to make the related distinctions of
thick from thin, and dense from diluted places (see definitions later in
this chapter). The contrast of complexity with simplification captures
many of the negative features criticized in contemporary places, while
offering helpful ideas for their improvement.

Here are three claims about complexity: a frequent problem with
places today is the replacement of complex interwoven identities and
places by series of simpler identities and places; because of their inherent temporality, because of the way social norms involve meanings and
contrasts and linkages that cannot be fully controlled, and because they
exist within multiple processes of place formation, even the most simplified places contain the seeds of a restorative complexity; and more
complex places can support a richer and more self-aware inhabitation
that embodies more fully and explicitly the conditions and processes
that make places possible at all.[1]

Today we often find archipelagos of intense but simplified places and stripped-down brief role identities. Advertisements entice consumers to become simplified versions of parents, workers, bosses, and tourists, one after another. Single-issue politics simplifies political complexities. Modernist urban planning tried to break cities and lives into homogeneous zones for residence, work, recreation, and commerce. Many contemporary places prescribe simple total roles that shift quickly to other equally simple roles. Be a quiet airline passenger, then all eyes for the bus tour, then a jovial diner. Enjoy this spectacle, then be a canny shopper. Play this game, now this other one.

These simplified roles are not necessarily bad in themselves, but complexity cannot be avoided. No amount of immediate intensity can preclude the development of cross-time connections and awareness that bring the series of roles and places to interact with itself. No amount of compulsion can keep webs of possibilities from changing and mixing.

By *complexity* I mean interacting multiplicities. A complex place will have multiple roles, forces, norms, processes, internal spatial divisions, and external links to other kinds of places and to the processes that bring together multiple forces and systems.

Complexity is both static and dynamic; there are interacting multiplicities in a place's structure of social norms and in its processes of formation. There are complex ways of living in a place, involving self-conscious participation in its structure and process. But complexity is not just a matter of personal awareness; a place may have internal and linked complexities without a person being aware of them. Indeed, seemingly oversimplified places, such as suburban sprawl, are more complex than their architecture and plans show, and would be helped by having those complexities made more evident and taken up more self-consciously.

THREE DIMENSIONS OF COMPLEXITY

The discussion in the remainder of this book rests on three dimensions of place complexity: in the physical and normative structures of a place, in its ongoing local process of interpretation, and in its connection to more remote systemic and political processes.

The first dimension is structural complexity in the space of a place and its social norms. Although these aspects can vary independently of one another, each tends to reinforce the others. We might ask: Is the place totally foreground, or does it interweave foreground emphases and more banal, everyday stretches? Are the place's normative routes and paths of action linear or not? Are these routes parallel and loosely connected, or are they interwoven and interacting with one another? Does the place embody a single straightforward social role, or multiple aspects and multiple interacting roles? If the social roles involved in the place are multiple (whether thick or thin), how does the place define them to be together? Do they intersect or do they run in parallel? If there are multiple competing social norms and spatial divisions for different inhabitants of the place, do they coexist in ways that make it more complex or do they make it into several overlapping simpler places? Does the place show explicit spatial or symbolic links or signs of its connection to other places and processes?

The second dimension of complexity is in the processes of local interpretation and reproduction that maintain a place's structure. "Structure only exists insofar as people do things knowledgeably and do them in certain contexts that have particular consequences" (Giddens 1998, 81). Social structure continues to exist through the activities that both conform to and reproduce it. "Social life . . . is continually contingently reproduced by knowledgeable human agents—that's what gives it fixity and that's what also produces change" (90).[2]

While the spatial and normative structures of a place can range from oversimplified to very complex, the processes constituting a place are always complex. So diagnostic questions about complexity in the processes of place formation have to do with the degree of awareness and participation that is present or encouraged: Can the place be lived as an active unification of the multiple factors resulting from its social and spatial divisions and unities? Does the place encourage inhabitants to be aware of their own processes of active interpretation and their resolution of multiple roles and demands? (Increasing the structural complexity of a place can increase the occasions for such awareness. Conversely, finding ways to stimulate such awareness may reveal structural complexities.) Are there opportunities to participate in the reformation or reproduction of the place's spatial structures and social norms?

The processes that sustain and reproduce place norms and social structures are many and various and do not work in parallel. Incentives; imitation; repetition and discipline; the discovery of or the instillation of interests; various kinds of language and behavior learning; laws, rituals, and customs and their means of enforcement and self-monitoring all embody social norms and classifications in a person's habitual behavior according to approved temporal and spatial rhythms. Some of these influences are consciously controlled, some happen without planning. All are open to deliberate alteration and unconscious slippage. A social gesture or a pattern of action or a ritual may be performed the same yet in a new context it could change its meaning because it contrasts with new alternatives. A handwritten letter takes on different meanings depending on whether it is sent in response to an e-mail or to another handwritten letter. A two-week delay answering an e-mail is perceived differently than the same delay in answering a posted letter. An identical bodily or linguistic performance can take on new meanings that are not under the control of those who teach the practice. This happens constantly with styles of dress and slang that age rapidly. Conscious changes are introduced into place norms and social practices (as with laws) when demanded by new needs or new contexts. But even keeping place norms the same presumes that those passing them on "read" them the same from generation to generation. A religious authority may try to keep the interpretation of its symbols identical over generations, but new contexts and new contrasts and applications will raise new questions. Even if the symbols and practices are stabilized, cultural and linguistic change will alter the context and force new interpretations.[3]

Becoming more self-aware of the ways in which place norms and structures depend on active support and interpretation will bring a greater awareness of distant larger processes that impinge on a place. Local interpretation and reproduction can in varying degrees mediate and redefine the effects of larger forces (as when a local culture gives a local inflection to products or images from the global circulation of commodities).

The third dimension of complexity is in that relation with the remote systemic and political processes that shape a place. Both local processes of interpretation and more remote economic, political, and environmental processes are inherently multiple. But while inhabitants are necessarily involved in interpreting and reproducing a place's structure, they may have little or no awareness of or influence on more remote processes. Therefore, diagnostic questions about this third dimension of complexity ask about awareness and participation: Does the place show explicit spatial or symbolic links and signs of its belonging within larger systems, social contexts, and their genetic processes? Does the place enforce the illusion that its social and spatial structures are immediately given and natural? Or do its norms and spatial articulation and architecture make it easier to become aware of the political and economic processes, the systemic pressures and constraints, the varied interest groups within and outside the place, and their procedures of negotiation or imposition? Are there possibilities for intervening in or redirecting those larger processes?

Becoming aware of structural complexity involves living consciously the interacting multiplicity of intersecting roles and the interplay between spatial and social structures. Becoming aware of complexity in the ongoing process of interpretation involves consciously taking up that interpretive task with its internal multiplicities and the different kinds of change and adaptation that it produces. Becoming aware of the larger processes involves being conscious of causal forces and political decisions, of their interactions and intersections, and developing possibilities for intervening in those processes.

When I argue for self-awareness of the processes that generate places I am not suggesting detached critical contemplation. We are always already involved in those processes. Self-reflection and self-reference are already ingredients in our immediate experience of places. Becoming more actively aware of them reveals complexity in what may seem simplified places, and also adds to that complexity by opening up more kinds of explicit possibility and relation.[4]

This chapter deals primarily with structural complexity; the other two dimensions of complexity are present but are discussed more fully in chapter 4.

STRUCTURAL COMPLEXITY AND INTENSITY

A structurally simple place foregrounds itself and its norms all at once, or offers linear routes of action composed of relatively independent serial stages with few second-level connections or references among them, or embodies only one pattern of life composed of roles that don't interact much. A structurally complex place involves more elaborated presences-and-absences of its features and the nonexplicit background of practice and process, or offers nonlinear paths of action and interwoven multiplicities of kinds of life with more potential for conflicting internal tensions.

A structurally complex place can be lived in a relatively simplified and unaware manner, just as a structurally simple place can be lived in a manner more aware of the underlying complexity of its context and its processes of formation. No place can be totally simplified, since even the most structurally simple place will still be inserted into larger contexts and processes, though this may be denied or hidden within the place. Simplification of places is a surface phenomenon that hides the underlying complexity of social processes and the mediations involved in actively inhabiting a place.

A structurally complex place is not present all at once as foreground or focal. A simple place may be more immediately intense. A standard boxy mall may have architectural shapes stuck on its façade so it appears to have gables or be made of bricks. This asserts localness by foregrounding their symbols and archetypes to provide an instantly recognizable experience of locality, but the effect is quite different from day-to-day living in a complex place. Disneyland's Main Street seems more intensely local than the streets it is meant to recall. Disney's version condenses and crowds together typical forms and references that in a real town would be separated by stretches of banal everydayness. By that condensation Disney gains intensity but loses the complexity of what it means to live those forms. Disney so pushes the archetypes forward that forms and symbols cannot recede and shape lives continually and indirectly. Forms and symbols instead demand to be focal objects of perception, each for itself, so they cannot interact subtly with each other or with a quieter background. The place is simplified while it is being made more straightforward and simply intense.

There are different kinds of intensity. Disney's Epcot theme park crowds together mini replicas of famous national monuments from around the world. These tempt the tourist to experience travel to the actual nations as a collection of simplified but intense monuments, each captured in a photograph the tourist takes to commemorate the visit.[5] A properly complex travel experience would encounter the monuments amid everyday life's contested nets of norms and histories and social patterns, and across stretches of less monumental time and space. Such complexity can hold more surprises, though there is another kind of surprise found in a series of simplified places, where one place exercises no influence upon the next. One Epcot reproduction gives few clues about what the next will contain; this is so precisely because they are not linked in a complex whole.

Spatial and social complexities bring references and connections that impose multiple and mutually qualifying norms on the paths of action within a place. The next thing you do there might be affected by the intersection of several norms and thereby require judgment and balance. Not just any arbitrarily chosen stage of action can follow any other, and interpretation or arbitration might be needed. Complex places restrict what should follow upon what, while increasing the number of connections and normative possibilities within the place. This increases the intensity of the place in a different way than would a linear sequence of simpler self-contained intensities that did not impose much on each next step.

Simplified places can provide intense moments whose order is indifferent one to another. Someone might move from one machine to another in a video arcade, where each game world is self-contained. Playing one game imposes no restrictions on which game is played next. Even within a single game world the sequence of experiences may be arbitrary; obstacles and opponents and puzzles could be relocated without much affecting the overall experience. The arcade will become a more complex place if its customers develop rituals involving the games, draw comparisons among them, and impose meanings based on larger patterns of action outside. For instance the arcade could become an element in adolescent rituals that set norms for their behavior in widely separated places yoked together in their lives, so that actions in the game arcade would have consequences for how one speaks or acts in some quite different location.

Without complex actions and norms that link their spatial discontinuities, disconnected areas could be adjoined in ways that emphasize the serial self-sufficiency of each successive locale, as in many tourist bus itineraries. In a different medium, compare the interchangeable adventures inserted to delay the climax of an adventure film with the complex echoes and placement of the comedy scenes in Shakespearean tragedies.

Commodification pushes to increase the seriality of experience and the independence of modules of place one from another. Then more combinations can be consumed, since simple intensities pass quickly and need to be renewed. Yet any series, no matter how simple, still opens a door to complexity, because for moments to be unified at all across time—for them to be experienced as a series—there must be some second-level connections beyond serial sequence. Both the continuity and the discontinuity of the series can then provide lures for complexity.

So a complex intensity is not just a series of simple intensities, although both are experienced in a sequence of temporal episodes. The moments of a complex temporal sequence relate to one another in other ways than sequence. Such nonlinear or nonserial orderings are present within all experiences, but they can be more or less interwoven, more or less self-reflexive, more or less explicit in the ongoing experience of a place.

Complex places demand sensitivity to cultural languages and codes, catching the drift of forms of life, sensing the narrative surrounding an action and realizing that a significant move has happened or is now being called for, knowing what to do and how to go on from here. This kind of complexity does not necessarily lead to singular sudden moments of intensity. The shock at the climax of a Shakespearean tragedy is different from the thrill at the climax of an adventure film.

Nonlinearity is one key to complexity. Nonlinear references and echoes from one part of a story to another make a novel complex. Complex music contains more elaborated and unexpected internal self-reference than easy-listening standard sequences. A place can become complex when there are references and comments from one part to another in its spatial construction, in its normative routes of action, or in its references to its own process of formation. Architects create references and harmonies between one part of a building and another; there are social equivalents when actions here echo and repeat actions there, or what is to be done or avoided here echoes in unexpected ways the norms for actions there. In a mall the normative references between one area and another are flat and repetitious; in a house of worship there may be intricate ways in which actions here echo the statuary there, or the norms for this area contrast while fitting in with those for another area.

Such nonlinear connections need not be spatial, and they could qualify a quite straightforward space. *Complex* means more than *complicated.* Things that are complicated have many parts intricately organized.[6] A place that is complex in its norms and in the possibilities it offers for action might not be spatially intricate or architecturally complicated.

Building a tortuous or intricate spatial arrangement would seem an obvious way to add complexity to a place, but it will not render the place complex unless the spatial intricacies are correlated with differentiated social norms and expectations. This may happen, for instance, with the circulation patterns in a courthouse designed to separate the public from court officials and both groups from people on trial. Spatial qualities can amplify complexity if the local patterns of life are appropriate, but spatial effects are not sufficient by themselves, since spatial complexity could be encompassed by a fairly straightforward form of life, as in a recreational maze or fun house. A simple rectangular room could be a very complex place if intersecting forms of life were interwoven there, as with the factions and undercurrents in a royal court.

Spatial and social arrangements mutually condition each other, but not with strict necessity. A shopping mall's network of subplaces can easily be rearranged when the mall is rebuilt. In a cathedral such as Chartres the arrangement of the elaborate subplaces is constrained by the spatial and symbolic conventions of medieval church building. The Capitol building in Washington holds functional spaces that could be spatially rearranged but would maintain their complex exclusions and intersections.

A structurally complex place offers a density of roles and relations. It may or may not be dense in the usual sense of containing a large population in many buildings per unit area. A place that is dense in that urban sense is likely to be complex in my sense, though there could be cases where it was not, for instance if the large population followed only a few thin and nonintersecting social roles. Dystopias such as *Brave New World* picture dense but simplified cities. Later in this chapter I introduce the notion of historical density, which again is not the usual urban density, though a dense city in the usual sense will usually be historically dense as well.

Complex identities and places (and activities and roles) take time to develop and require time for us to encounter and experience them. Complex gestures and skills have intermediate stages that must be repeated and learned. Spatially complex places need to be explored from different angles and along different spatial routes; normatively complex places invite explorations by different roles and along different routes of action. The place's norms and expectations are interwoven, including multiple actions that may be associated with the building's geometry in unexpected ways, and may intersect and interact in ways that require sensitive judgment. The intensities that develop from this kind of complexity are not immediate bursts of experience; they build up slowly and enrich the horizon of alternatives and possibilities within which actions are performed.[7]

Place complexity does not vary directly with architectural form (this will be important in considering ways to increase the lived complexity of suburban sprawl). The spatial energy and complexity of Frank Gehry's Guggenheim museum in Bilbao does not guarantee that as a place it is more complex than Mies van der Rohe's serene museum in Berlin. A Baroque building may be as differentiated visually as a Gehry building, but if the Baroque building were a memorial it might have quite straightforward norms for action despite its visual bustle. Complexity in a place has more to do with complexity of program than with spatial or visual effects, but complexity of place is not quite the same as complexity of program. A large city library, for example, will present a complex functional program for its designers to work with, yet may still house a fairly simple set of social norms and roles for its users.

In a complex place actions acquire more meanings and resonances, so that moves in the place are not easily summarized or simply presented. A complex place requires a long, many-leveled description to show the intricate relations among the parts of the place and the processes involved. Who stops to talk to whom, and in what location, could be a very complexly interwoven event in the corridors of a royal court or of the U.S. Capitol. Different norms and implications infect and influence one another. This opens the possibility of multiple identities in conflict.

On the other hand, sheer multiplicity does not necessarily increase complexity, since it could lead to social disarray and disarticulation.[8] As conditions changed in a city, a plaza could increase its place entropy—that is, become less organized—as it ceased to be a single place with complex interacting forms of life, and became a neutral arena for multiple uses that ignored one another, or did not respect its spatial organization or previous norms. In that sense the high entropy of a dirty urban square with trash blowing and people deposited here and there without any coordination of their roles would contrast with the low entropy of a plaza where roles and interactions were well determined and norms for the use of the place were mutually acknowledged even as they were differentiated and in tension with one another. In the degenerate high-entropy square, the social norms are more in Darwinian conflict than in social complexity.

Structural complexity involves discriminations and relations and tensions that provide occasions for lived awareness and linkage both within the place and to more remote forces and decisions. Complex social and spatial structure is less likely to be taken for granted as natural or isolated. Richer and more interconnected horizons of possibility encourage living norms and structures as socially produced and reproduced. Whether this makes remote forces amenable to change depends on more than such awareness, but the awareness aids efforts to change unjust conditions and structures.

PERCEIVING STRUCTURAL COMPLEXITY

Place complexity does not depend on psychological reactions. You have a rich emotional response to the color red; I barely notice colors; but we both stop at red lights because of a social norm whose force is different from the aesthetic or emotional impact of the color. The complexity is there (or not) in the norms and processes that define the place and its actions. These do not have to be always focally present, yet they shape the horizon of possibilities we move within, and they are available for explicit awareness of their content and their processes of formation. A brilliant social analyst might be able to show the background complexities behind an oversimplified place; this would be helpful, but it would not automatically make the average inhabitant perceive the place as complex. The place needs some explicit links and signs that allow inhabitants or users to experience the place in its larger context. That might be provided by media exposure of the analysis that made people more aware, but that perception would be fragile unless it could be inscribed into the architectural or spatial structure of the place, or into its habitual norms of action. Self-consciousness of social processes should not be just a momentary event; it needs to be anchored into the concrete place and its structures.

It would also be wrong to equate complexity with the capacity to surprise, or the capacity to keep revealing new information. Indeed, constant surprise would get in the way of the routines of living. Sheer informational complexity of learning what to do or how to get around gets reduced as actions and paths are routinized. A maze seems complex, but only for a while. Once you learn its pattern, it might be lived as a hallway whose spatial windings do not by themselves make it a complex place. A square room could exhibit far more social complexity.

However, a well-known building or place may have spatial or action routes that build in structural surprise even though you already know what is coming. Rereading a detective novel you know the ending already, but the structures of the novel still perform their indirection and buildup. A building could produce architectural effects, such as a transition from a dark cramped hall to a large atrium, that provide shocks of recognition rather than surprise. A place could bring us back repeatedly to the complexities within our identity and our values without needing constant novelty to do so.

What I've just noted about routines and surprise suggests an objection to the goal of increasing place complexity. Can complex inhabitation be sustained? Isn't the experience of complexity quickly eroded as it becomes habitual and changes to a background rather than a foreground experience? Walter Benjamin famously observed that "Architecture has always represented the prototype of a work of art the reception of which is consummated by a collectivity in a state of distraction. . . . Architecture [is] appropriated in a twofold manner: by use and by perception, or rather, by touch and sight. Such appropriation cannot be understood in terms of the attentive concentration of a tourist before a famous building . . . [Buildings are appropriated] not so much by attention as by habit" (Benjamin 1968, 239).

Benjamin was writing about buildings, but we can apply his idea to places. Although the structure and norms of a place influence us, we do not normally focus on them; rather we shape actions and goals in accord with the landscape of possibilities the place provides, looking not so much at that landscape as at the goals or objects seen across it.

Suppose a simplified place increases its complexity by creating more internal linkages and connections, by providing signs of the multiplicity of ways it is interpreted and appropriated into people's lives, and by building into the place explicit links to the other places and to the more remote processes that influenced its formation. These multiplicities and these links may be obtrusive at first, but won't the attempted complexity fade into the background as the place itself becomes background for the actions and goals we focus on? In urging more complex places am I demanding that places be lived in some constant state of direct self-awareness that cannot be sustained? Is lived complexity at most a temporary condition?

There are two responses to these questions. The first answer is that the objection wrongly presumes that complexity must always be experienced in a focal awareness. A place offers a spatialized landscape of social possibilities. Those possibilities do not have to be objects of explicit focal awareness. They are a kind of practical consciousness of what to do next, of how to go on. According to Anthony Giddens, "the continuity of the routines of daily life is achieved only through the constant vigilance of the parties involved—although it is almost always accomplished at the level of practical consciousness" (Giddens 1990, 98). A place's practical possibilities are the background against which things are presented. They are projections of past and future actions that give meaning to what is focally present. This happens in what Heidegger called circumspective concern, the kind of awareness that we have about what one does with a telephone or how one behaves in a restaurant. So lived place complexity does not demand a constant focal awareness, but it does enrich the background or horizon and change the sense of focal objects and activities.

That horizon of possibilities can become more focal when a tool breaks, when habits are challenged, or when experienced multiplicity forces a reconsideration of social norms. Works of art can also raise this horizon and its presupposed meanings into more direct awareness. I urge that the landscape of possibilities be as rich and complex as it can, and be lived as such; the goal is not some separate act of focused critical judgment, but rather a more complex horizon of possibilities together with more awareness of the processes of living within it.

The experience of complexity is temporal, with many different kinds of relations tying different moments of the temporal series together in nonlinear ways. Here is a spatial analogy: When I am hiking in the mountains, different contours of the land appear, and they include more than what is immediately visible to me. I imagine continuations that I cannot see. There should be a valley over that hill, and I imagine that this stream flows around that bend and widens. I estimate the distance to the summit. Those momentary projections extend tangent to my path. They relate this stage of a path to other actual and possible stages, and thus guide my actions and plans. The contour I perceive will be continually modified as I move, since the contour projects an overall landscape of what is possible. Many of my versions of this physical landscape will turn out to be mistaken. There is no valley, the stream divides, and that was a false summit. Still, I am surrounded by a projected contour of the land, and as I walk that contour changes.[9]

Places offer action contours, so as I walk about the cathedral or the government center or the school I perceive a changing series of contours in its landscape of social possibility and appropriateness. Actions that are doable here are inappropriate there. This is obvious when I stumble against social norms when trying to learn how to live in a new place, but there are changing contours of action even in a familiar place, for instance, the horizon of possibilities that changes within a university. The contours of appropriate action alter when you move from the faculty lounge to the student lounge. Sensing a place's possibilities and the influences on them needs more than the perception of positive data and straightforward qualities. I do not have to focus on these action possibilities; they are present as the horizon against which I perceive objects, in the social landscape I navigate toward my goals.

Dealing with oversimplified places, the goal should be, in Hegelian terms, to show that apparent immediacy is always mediated, more complex than it appears, linked and made what it is by its relations to others, and existing within an ongoing process that sustains and re-creates it. Complex places provide opportunities for such discovery, because their horizons of meaning for action show more of the underlying mediations of their social reality. None of this requires constant focal awareness, but it does require episodes of explicit discovery and self-awareness.

This moves into the second answer to the objection that awareness of complexity must fade. Complex places provide more occasions for explicit self-aware inhabitation. A complex place can provide more occasions when routines are questioned. The more complex the place, the more intersecting roles and social norms it has, and so also more opportunities for inhabitants to be jarred into focused awareness of those social norms. There are more chances to experience otherness, whether in different inhabitants, in different ways of inhabiting, or in collisions of norms that make one reevaluate one's own behavior. In the courthouse or the Capitol or the restaurant there may be situations where conflicting norms bring greater self-awareness of their multiplicity. There can also be architectural stimuli toward greater self-awareness. So complexity can increase the occasions for focal self- and social awareness.

Place complexity does not involve merely the contemplation of a social object. Inhabiting a complex place is not like looking at an intricate painting. Complexity is not a matter of observing a place's web of possibilities but of acting within that web, maintaining and reproducing it. In a complex place our ongoing process of interpretation and adjudication can be more obvious and self-aware. Inhabiting more self-consciously also means being more aware of the linkages and processes that have made a place what it is, and of the possibilities for intervening in those processes.

MODERNITY AND THE VALUE OF COMPLEXITY

Complexity can enrich places, but why should complexity be preferred? Place complexity can lead to a more self-conscious participation in the formation and reformation of places. This can increase the intensity of experience. The kinds of intensity available in a complex place are richer and more enduring, and bear repetition better than the intensities in simpler places.[10] Even if people have been conditioned to prefer intense simplifications—which require less effort to experience—they would be more fully human and alive to a different kind of intensity if they were more aware of their context and more consciously participated in their own activities of maintaining and interpreting the structures they follow.[11]

Through the "modern" social and intellectual changes that have been accelerating since the seventeenth century, social self-awareness and self-determination have become prime values, both for themselves and for leading to improved conditions and greater equity. Being more aware of internal and external multiplicities, divisions, and linkages can make injustices and oppressions more obvious to inhabitants, along with the intricate or blunt processes creating them. People can become more active as they perceive the effect of individual and social choices. "What is characteristic of modernity is not an embracing of the new for its own sake, but the presumption of wholesale reflexivity—which of course includes reflection on the nature of reflection itself" (Giddens 1990, 39).

It is wrong to presume that people long ago were unreflectively bound by their places, completely within their norms and rituals, with no internal distances. Humans are never in place the way we presume animals are in their environment, nor should we romanticize the premodern as a realm of immediacy. Inner division is part of what it means to be human. Imagined remote mountain villages free from tourism represent a modern fantasy of a life free from self-reflection and self-questioning. Although it is true that many premodern societies were less doubting about their values and customs and had fewer ways to contrast their norms to others than do modern societies, their imagined total solidity is an illusion fostered by different kinds and rates of change, especially in oral cultures. What is different in modern societies—and it is an enormous difference—is not the presence of reflection and questioning, but its unbounded extent and its public institutionalization (see Kolb 1990, ch. 7). Such reflection used to be peripheral, but now it is central to the processes by which modern citizens assure one another of their humanity and mutual regard. Nothing is taken for granted as fixed.

The social, intellectual, economic, and other changes in the last few centuries have brought new kinds of self-conscious complexity. Although intersecting multiplicities of norms are not new, we have new ways of dealing with social multiplicity. The tribal societies beloved of anthropologists are described as having elaborate social roles that prescribed what people wore, where activities were to be performed, and what behavior was appropriate for different genders, clans, and other groups. Such societies coexisted without a "modern" awareness of the social processes that form places and norms, though they could nonetheless embody conflicts and contradictions. Hegel's theory of tragedy offers insight into an earlier kind of complexity. He argues that in Sophocles' picture of ancient Thebes in the *Antigone*, the social whole there contains internal conflicts where there is no simple contest of right versus wrong. Antigone asserts the duties of family and the unwritten laws of respect for the dead and maintenance of family continuity, but she is also a citizen violating city law. Creon asserts the civic law, but he is also a father violating his duties toward his family. Each side is right, for each appeals to a valid norm, and each side is wrong, for each defies another valid norm. Destruction ensues, Hegel argues, because the social whole is not internally articulated and flexible enough to endure such conflicts once they become explicit. Individual self-consciousness is restricted to one or another of the competing roles, and there is no way to mediate the conflict (see Hegel 1977, ch. 6).[12]

Whatever the merits of Hegel's theory as applied to Greek tragedy, his point about society shows how a culture or a place might contain intersecting social norms where multiple roles relate to each other in a tension that does not reduce to right versus wrong, or to authenticity versus alienation.

There was another kind of ancient place complexity that looks at first more modern. Medieval Bukhara, Samarkand, and other trading cities of central and southern Asia were complex in a different way than Hegel's picture of traditional Greek society. As trade centers inhabited by people of tribal, Muslim, Hindu, Greek, Chinese, Christian, and Buddhist cultures, those cities contained a multitude of social groups. Each group's identity was in explicit contrast with other groups, but the group's identity remained based on religion and ethnicity. Social conflict was handled through negotiation among subcommunities and by generic mercantile social roles, but people's religious and ethnic identities remained primary.

Modern societies create mechanisms of participation that involve more generic roles that can be taken on by anyone in the society regardless of his or her religious or ethnic background.[13] This is a more radical change than simply juxtaposing one group's identity with another's. A citizen's political identity is now (in principle, at least) no longer mediated through naturally given facts about his or her history or family.

In modern society most facts about me and most social roles are supposed to be optional and should not impede the discharging of my economic and political duties. In earlier societies my definition would have had more substantial detail. My birthplace and my family and my gender and ethnicity and my father's occupation and religion would have largely defined my identity, and perhaps kept me from full participation in the economy or the political system. Modernization removed barriers to economic and political participation based on such givens. I may be of Italian heritage but decide that this will play no significant part in my life. Others are not required to deal with me on those ethnic terms, and I may be offended if they insist on doing so. Even gender may become a matter of choice in the technological future. As these aspects of my being become matters for voluntary association and cease to be as relevant to my definition as a member of society, my identity has fewer restrictions, but it may feel threateningly empty and fail to provide guidance and meaning.

Although complex places are not a recent phenomenon, modern societies can create both more simplified and more complex places than before. Some places, such as a parking lot, are more simple because they involve only a few thin social roles. Others, like modern cities, can be more complex because of the high number of intersecting roles and spaces, with fewer identities that are taken as given. So there is more potential for mixed identities and self-conscious participation in the processes of place and norm creation.

Designs and plans that acknowledge the complexities of places and selves may also increase people's awareness of their one-time mortality that cannot be measured by simple market norms. Then it becomes harder to go along with the oppressions that we suffer or perform. People can see better what is there and how it is maintained. This can loosen restrictions on our imagination and encourage action in all three dimensions of complexity and linkage.

THICK AND THIN PLACES

The next sections discuss two pairs of concepts that are related to the criterion of complexity. The first is the quality of thickness versus thinness. Thin places are those whose social norms involve only those slimmed down modern roles and identities discussed above. The social norms for a parking lot or an airplane trip engage people only as drivers or passengers. In such places the criteria for how people interact and recognize one another as equal participants demand only thin roles that abstract from most of the content of their lives. People may feel that their richer individuality is being repressed, because for the most part it is irrelevant to their role identity in such places. If all that is available are such thin roles, people may sense a loss of guidance from their social roles. An accumulation of thin roles may be complex but does not add up to a thick identity. Reaction against this can lead to a search for more substantive and content-ful roles. Premodern familial, gender, and other substantial roles can then seem more attractive even though they may embody many oppressions and limitations on freedom. The interplay between modern freedoms and thicker roles is a delicate balance, but the modern ideal has been that the richness and thickness of our social identities should be more our own creation than the result of our naturally given determinations.

Marc Augé discerns a class of thin places that he calls *nonplaces*. He uses the term because he restricts the term *places* to those studied by anthropologists, where, for instance, the spatial layout of a village might

assign each inhabitant a role and a rich identity tied to a shared cosmology and mythic history. Such places are "associated by Mauss and a
whole ethnological tradition with the idea of a culture localized in time
and space" (Augé 1995, 34). Many modern places do not offer such
thick identities and spatial closure, so he calls them nonplaces. He ties
nonplaces to what he calls *supermodernity*, the contemporary superabun-
dance of events and information, the acceleration of history, and annihi-
lation of distance.[14] "If a place can be defined as relational, historical and
concerned with identity, then a space which cannot be defined as relational, or historical, or concerned with identity will be a non-place. The
hypothesis advanced here is that supermodernity produces non-places,
meaning spaces which are not themselves anthropological places and
which . . . do not integrate the earlier places. . . . Place and non-place
are rather like opposed polarities: the first is never completely erased,
the second never totally completed. . . . But *non-places are the real measure
of our time*" (Augé 1995, 77–79, my emphasis).

Augé's typical nonplaces include "the installations needed for the accelerated circulation of passengers and goods (high-speed roads and railways, interchanges, airports) . . . the means of transport themselves, or
the great commercial centres, or the extended transit camps where the
planet's refugees are parked" (Augé 1995, 34). In these nonplaces there
are only thin social roles.[15] "A person entering the space of non-place is
relieved of his usual determinants. He becomes no more than what he
does or experiences in the role of passenger, customer, or driver. . . . The
space of non-place creates neither singular identity nor relations; only
solitude, and similitude. There is no room for history unless it has been
transformed into an element of spectacle, usually in allusive texts" (Augé
1995, 103–4).

Despite the negative-sounding term *nonplaces*, Augé is not condemning these places but commenting on the new kinds of identity they provide. I would argue that his examples of nonplaces are still concerned
with identity and relation, but in thin roles. Augé reserves the term *identity* for thicker combinations of roles. Could thin roles form an individual person's whole identity? Maybe so; whether this would be a satisfying
identity is a different question, related to the issue whether society as a
whole can exist with only thin roles. In Augé's view thicker identities are
necessary but are left behind when we enter his nonplaces.

In the descriptive passages that open and close his book, Augé pictures a traveler isolated in an airplane and takes this as the paradigm nonplace, isolated from ongoing social interactions. He summarizes this by remarking that "When individuals come together, they engender the social and organize place. But the space of supermodernity is inhabited by this contradiction: it deals only with individuals (customers, passengers, users, listeners), but they are identified . . . only on entering or leaving. . . . it seems that the social game is being played elsewhere than in the forward posts of contemporaneity" (Augé 1995, 111).

For Augé this produces "entirely new experiences and ordeals of solitude, directly linked with the appearance and proliferation of nonplaces" (Augé 1995, 93). His description of individuals in nonplaces as isolated and solitary may already be out of date, since that solitude is broken when other social roles and identities penetrate airport transit lounges and supermarkets that are linked to elsewhere by cell phones, pagers, and laptops. No places (or nonplaces) are purely themselves these days.

There is good critical use to be made of the notions of thick or thin places if these notions are changed so that they do not demand a return to premodern naturalized roles. In this revised sense, thick places would be those that engage more and richer aspects of our being. Whether those thicker aspects of our being were "natural" or not would be less important for this sense of thickness.

Thickness is not the same as complexity. Thickness refers to the quality of the contemporary roles in a place, whereas complexity refers to the multiplicity of those roles and the nature of their interaction with one another. A place can engage only thin roles but still be complex because of the number and interaction of those roles. For instance, though nothing in an airport shopping mall engages one's individuality in any thick way, various thin roles (shopper, traveler, expense minimizer, business employee) may come into conflict with one another and increase the complexity of the situation.

DENSE AND DILUTED PLACES

The terms *thick* and *thin* already appear in some discussions of contemporary places, though not always with the meaning I have given them here.[16] A new pair of terms, *dense* and *diluted*, can further our goal of appreciating and improving modern places. Historical density is a kind of diachronic thickness in a place. I call a place historically dense insofar as its social norms involve reference to a history that has been sedimented as people lived there and responded to it over time. Density is not a matter just of age but of how the marks and sediments of age are taken up into the contemporary texture of action in the place. Imagine a medieval English church located in a modern city. Under its placid, slightly decayed facade the church bears traces of centuries of usage and the swirls of divided community. Its history shows in the wearing down of the church floor and steps. This accumulation of use is different from an applied patina. Those grooves in the floor weren't designed to give an effect of history. The members of the parish have chosen not to repair the floor, because for them those signs of traditional use are more than accidental features of the place; they are normatively important. Part of what the members affirm in their dealings with one another is that they are part of a community that has endured all that history.

The example of the English church suggests that historical density has to do with a steady accumulation of detail around a stable identity. But density should not be confused with a demand for historical authenticity, which is a difficult notion to apply. The density of a place could record transpositions and recodings over the years, even if those changes depart from some idealized past. For example, in the small city of Tuscania, north of Rome, a 1971 earthquake damaged many houses in the medieval center, so the government moved people temporarily to newer housing west of the town center. After their original houses had been repaired, many of the owners preferred to stay in the more comfortable newer houses, and sold their homes for a profit, often to weekenders from Rome. The new uses for the houses were inauthentic, if by that is meant a continuation of the old use as primary residences for inhabitants of the town. But in another way the historical density of the houses increased with this new layer that self-consciously preserved traces of the earlier uses.

On the other hand, also in Tuscania a medieval monastery was restored in ways that diluted it. For several centuries, after the building ceased being a monastery, people had lived in apartments made by joining the original monastic cells. They parked carriages, then cars, under the arcades of the cloister. With the recent restoration, the monastery has become a museum. While it was being lived in, the stone and stucco of the monastery were in poor repair, but now that it is a tourist attraction, a guide from the town office announces that the building looks beautiful in its smooth perfection. However, with the elimination of all traces of its use as an apartment house, the place was diluted. After all, what was the monastery's "traditional use"? In the crypt of a medieval church outside Tuscania stand twenty-eight columns taken from Roman temples. There are more such columns in the nave above. People often esteem such medieval reuse as increasing the density of the place, while condemning or erasing more recent mixtures of old and new that also add to the historical density.

For an extreme in historical dilution, think of Planet Hollywood, the franchised theme club chain where patrons go to experience an energetic ambiance primarily created by the presence of mementos and objects connected to Hollywood. The building the club is in could have been constructed last week or it could have been an ancient building with signs of age, but this makes little difference since the social norms take no account of any historical traces except as a quaint backdrop for celebrity. Historical dilution and role thinness are related, since it is because modern social roles are less substantial that modern places get away with ignoring the weight of history.

A dense place is not all present at once, and its presence is not pushy. It is not coming at you; it was not aimed at you; it is on its own. You can take it or leave it without affecting its reality and purpose; you are not that relevant to its survival. This is not the way with a diluted place; Planet Hollywood has to come at you in order to keep its reality, which is in its attraction, a force that is real only when it is being felt. In such diluted places, too often your inhabitation is reduced to being the consumer, the victim, and perhaps the ironic observer.

DISTINGUISHING THICKNESS, DENSITY, AND COMPLEXITY

Neither thickness nor historical density is the same as complexity. Thinness happens as social roles become less substantial and more abstracted from other aspects of a person's identity. This is a separate issue from how complex a place is, since the place could still be complex if it contained multiple thin roles interacting in intricate ways. Density concerns the way history remains and is taken up, but this need not be done complexly.

I argued in chapter 2 that for an area to be a place it is not strictly necessary that it be associated with personal or social narratives, memories, and feelings. What is essential is the presence of social norms for inhabiting the area. But places gain in richness and atmosphere from associated dreams, narratives, and feelings. What I have here called historical density involves traces and narratives and memories. However, for density these are not just associated with the place but are taken up into social norms that demand explicit attention and recognition of the history as shaping the identity of people and the social roles in the place. Density and thickness provide a richer texture to anchor associations than do thin and diluted places with their thin roles and irrelevant histories. Place complexity, too, provides more angles for association and memory. So it is fair to say that as complexity, thickness, and density increase, more personal and social narratives and memories will likely attach to a place. Complexity, though, is likely to lead to multiple associations that are not so consistent with one another. The following paragraphs provide examples that give us a common basis for understanding the distinctions among thickness, density, and complexity.

For density without complexity, consider the Carceri, a beautiful hermitage above Assisi used by Franciscan monks since the thirteenth century. The Carceri's seclusion and forest location allows contemplation and prayer away from the bustle of the city. This is a historically dense place, both from long endurance and from the currents of church history that have swept over it, but it is not a complex place because its norms enjoin straightforward actions involving only a few (albeit thick) roles.

For density and complexity combined with thinness, consider the Irish town of Killarney. The place is historically dense in the sense of having a long history inscribed in its material existence and celebrated in its self-presentation. However, while the historical traces are celebrated, they are presented as a nostalgic experience of Irishness that hardly does justice to the historical hardships of Irish existence nor to the new Irish economy. The place is historically dense yet thin, since most of the social roles enacted in the town are relatively thin. The place is still complex, though, because multiple roles interact, especially in the lives of the inhabitants, so that, for example, being a shopkeeper is only part of a townsperson's life. So, complexity, density, and thickness do not necessarily imply one another.

There can be absolutely diluted places where what traces history has left have no normative bearing at all on the texture of contemporary action. There cannot, however, be absolutely thin places, whose social roles have no substance whatever. Even the thinnest of economic roles—supermarket shopper, ticket vendor—cannot be extracted from the wider contexts of the economy and biological and political life. Roles that are defined by thin institutions still stand in other contrasts and relations. Though most institutions that form that larger context may be thin as well, there remain issues of priority among values and the relative distribution of costs and benefits that can lead to a politically thicker community.[17]

Can a place be very old and still be thin and historically diluted? History tends to cling to places, but it can be resisted. Imagine a McDonald's restaurant that had been running for two hundred years, with changes of menu as tastes changed, so that it would be as up-to-date then as it tries to be today. The building might have abundant historical traces, but the normative texture of the place might ignore them. So, despite the place's history, its normative use could have kept it a diluted place with thin social roles.

Can a place be very new and still be thick? Thickness comes from substantial richness in the roles and patterns of life embodied in the place. A newly established legislature in a newly democratized region would be a thick place from its very first day. Its roles and expectations might even be thicker on that first day than they will become later when it becomes more bureaucratized. The legislature would also be a complex place, because from the start there would be a swirl of community norms and thick social roles interacting and competing. That complexity would likely increase as time went on. However, although thickness is not the same as complexity, the two are related in that thick roles are more likely to facilitate the internal multiplicity that brings complexity.

Can a place be very new and still be historically dense? This is strictly speaking impossible, since density refers to the inclusion of history in contemporary social norms. But today there are new places designed to look old. Many older centers in northern European cities were rebuilt after being damaged in the Second World War. The rebuilding used modern methods but produced facades and civic spaces nearly identical to those from the earlier time, and people resumed older habits for using the public spaces, though the interiors of the buildings might have new uses. So even though the buildings were new they were historically

dense. One could also imagine that at great expense Disney could produce a castle with all the traces of age. If it were then lived as old, and
not in an ironic mode, it would have a sense of historical density. But
it would have to be lived as more than a sample or illustration. In the
English church example earlier in this chapter, the parishioners want to
foreground the historical quality of their building, but it is crucial that
this is not the sole purpose of their activities. The historical density adds
to the atmosphere of the hymns and services, but the hymns and services
do not exist in order to push the historical traces into the foreground, as
they would in a staged Disney replica.

Are thin and diluted the same as commodified places? These qualities
too can be distinguished. A place could be both thin and commodified
(New York's South Street Seaport). Or, thin and not commodified (an
efficient market where corporate agents deal with one another only as
buyers and sellers). A place can be thick and not commodified (a monastery). The problematic case is whether a place can be both thick and
commodified. Thickness resists commodification, but it cannot completely fend it off. For instance, there are places that sell experiences
or training in thick roles (a place where you pay to live as a farmhand,
or the school in London for those aspiring to become butlers for rich
families). So thickness and thinness are distinct from commodification
and also from complexity.

Analogous points apply to historical density. The English parish church
we looked at earlier is historically dense and a new church would be historically diluted, but as places of worship neither would be commodified.
A new video arcade would be both historically diluted and commodified
as it sells "experiences." The problematic case is, again, whether a place
can be both historically dense and commodified. Commodification is
not the same as historical dilution, but commodification will tend to cor-
rupt historical density because commodification tends to sell the experience of historical traces rather than letting them remain as qualifiers on
other normatively central activities.

Density and thickness are not automatically positive values. They describe the nature of roles and historical inscription, and those by themselves do not settle the value of a place. The next chapter discusses the
fear that all places will become thin and historically diluted as they are
commodified. No place can be completely thin, but places can go far in
that direction. Whether a fear of total thinness is justified depends on

what causes are operating to thin places down, and whether those causes are universally operative. Too many of the critics mentioned in chapter 4 assume without proof that such is the case.

COMPLEXITY EVERYWHERE

Urban planners, architects, urban theorists, and others who criticize contemporary places sometimes conflate the qualities I have been considering, but these qualities are separate though related. A place may be complex or simple, commodified or not, thick or historically dense or not, independent of the other qualities. New places today cannot be automatically classified by one side of these dualities just because they are new. Nor do the various dualities necessarily parallel one another, though they often do.

Complexity, however, remains a special case. There could be market-free tribal societies where commodification would not be a relevant description, but complexity is a relevant measure for any place in any society. Any place will be more or less foreground, offer more or less linear spatial and social routes for action, and embody one or more forms of life, have more or less self-awareness of its social processes, and so on. There are and have been societies in which the modern value of self-conscious participation is not operative, but even there complex places can still provide opportunities for a more aware participation in the creation and maintenance of place norms and structures.

Do we then conclude not just that the pair complex/simple is relevant to every place, but that every place is to some extent complex? Yes, because every place contains the seeds of complexity in the temporal dispersion and the spatial differentiations implied in its having any place norms at all, and in the context and larger processes it links to.

There are no theoretical limits on how complex a place can be, but there are practical limits, for instance limits on memory and decision-making. However, there are theoretical limits on how simple a place can be and still be a place. An absolutely simple place would be totally foreground and completely linear, offer routes of action composed of stages with no second-level connections or references among them, and embody only one form of life composed of the thinnest possible single-ply role, lived in a totally immediate way with no self-awareness of social processes. There can be no such place, because places always contain some discontinuities unified by rules and norms and are always enmeshed in larger social processes. Discontinuity and possibility imply potential complexity, since possibility and meaning cannot be completely controlled.

If complexity is always possible, then a strategy for dealing with the bad aspects of contemporary places will be to reveal their underlying complexity and to take steps to make those places even more complex; here are five general tactics that might be employed.

The first tactic implementing this strategy would be to stimulate greater attention to the place's wider contexts in its linkages to other places and to political and economic policies and systems. Architectural and planning interventions can increase the salience of the context and its processes. Even an oversimplified place can be attended to for what it is and what has produced it, and it will turn out to be more than it seems. No matter how simplified its norms, the place can be seen within the context and processes that make it possible.

A second tactic would be to show how beyond the standard routes of action, a place's internal landscape of possibilities will always be surrounded by a penumbra of stranger possibilities. As places are maintained and reproduced by local interpretive processes, they can mutate in unexpected ways.

A third tactic for dealing with the bad aspects of a contemporary place would be to note or create more reminders of the place's history, its formation, and the forces shaping it. The reminders could be symbolic, pieces of the past left in place, or signs of prior or ongoing conflict. Public art has traditionally been used for such purposes, though usually to celebrate an illusory image of past harmony. But art in public places could be used instead to remind inhabitants of disruptions and debates.

A fourth tactic would be to increase the nonlinearity of the place. This can be done by emphasizing latent multiplicities and the discontinuities and joinings across space and time that are built into any place. More complex places show their complexity in the nature of the transitions and temporal interrelations within trajectories of experience. Creating architectural or symbolic opportunities for expressing and increasing such relations in simpler places could render them more complex.

A fifth tactic would be to increase the multiplicity and interaction of roles and patterns of life within the place. This means changing or multiplying the norms for the place. There are barriers to this in many places:

design and behavior codes, corporation policies, and enforcers of atmosphere in privatized public spaces. Increasing the number of roles normatively appropriate in a place, or increasing the interaction of roles,
resembles the recipes for denser urbanity given by writers such as Jane
Jacobs and Richard Sennett. Those tactics can be applied to suburban
sprawl as well.

Such means for encouraging structural and lived complexity have
some similarities to Kevin Lynch's ideas about the legible city. In his classic work, *The Image of the City*, Lynch discusses spatial navigation, visual
versus tactile appearance, and ways to have parts of the city show how
they relate to the larger civic whole. In later works he broadens the discussion beyond these modalities: "So I risk a general proposition: a good
place is one which, in some way appropriate to a person and her culture, makes her aware of her community, her past, the web of life, and
the universe of time and space in which those are contained" (Lynch
1981, 142).[18] However, Lynch insists very strongly on clarity and coherence rather than complexity. "We have the opportunity of forming our
new city world into an imageable landscape: visible, coherent, and clear"
(91). He seeks "a simple and patent first order structure" that will offer a
sense of "overall certitude" (144). This does not fit contemporary places
that are intricately linked to distant locations, nor to the complexities
that arise from multiple and intersecting place norms. However, self-
aware place complexity agrees with Lynch's sense of the importance of
alertness and navigation, though in a landscape that may be more laby-
rinthine and multiple than he would like.

This chapter began with the claim that complexity could be a more useful normative criterion than authenticity when dealing with contemporary places, which show interacting dimensions of complexity without
demanding a unique authentic core. In a way, though, self-aware place
complexity asks for a second-level authenticity to the process of living
fully all the dimensions and processes of place-making.[19] The next chapter examines those processes in connection with the criticism that today
we have only commodified simulacra of true places.

CHAPTER FOUR

Commodification, Systems, and Places

*The universal Megalopolis . . . intends . . . the reduction
of the environment to nothing but commodity.*
(Frampton 1983a, in Nesbitt 1996, 482)

*I'm troubled that Brooklyn is being regarded as an
opportunity [for profit] rather than a place.*
(Jacobs 2005, 78)

*The struggle of a bewildered and put-upon generation to
speak authentically in an era whose central directive is to
reduce all art and all life to an infinitely replicable commodity,
to turn Kafka into a T-shirt and Havel into a carny attraction,
to shrink-wrap cultures as pasteurized package tour exotica, to
make art a bogus knickknack and heritage the hottest-selling
market segment of the Museum Economy.*
(Sterling 1995, 158)

THIS CHAPTER EXAMINES place complexity in relation to the claim that contemporary places have become overly commodified. With attention to the second and third dimensions of complexity mentioned in chapter 3 (complex processes of local interpretation, and complex relations with remote systemic and political processes), I argue that today's places are more complex than writers such as those quoted in the chapter epigraphs realize, and that their complexity might be further developed to combat commodification and other bad features of contemporary places.

Many who argue that today's places have been denatured would dismiss my proposals as superficial or even dangerous. They would say that the forces involved in modernization have so weakened the sense of place that suggestions about complexity and linkage and new kinds of unity either sell out to the enemy or offer superficiality when deep therapy is needed. With obligatory reference to Disney and tourism, places today are said to have become thin commodified simulacra of their former selves. While I concentrate on the commodification critique, it is representative of other attacks on today's places as insubstantial spectacles, emptier than in the past and more the tools of larger economic and social systems of control. Like most contrasts between a rooted past and an uprooted present, such complaints overstate both traditional fixity and modern mobility. But the issues are real and need discussion in the context of the processes of place making.

Some of these criticisms come from conservatives who want to return to traditional unities and naturally defined social roles, but criticisms also come from radicals seeking to increase modern self-creation or postmodern fluidity. The first group sees today's places as too loose and lacking in substantial thick identities. The second group sees today's places as still too tight, restricting free self-creation and imposing limits on people's identities as they are thinned down. Such criticisms do provide useful diagnoses and important issues, but they are often used as totalizing essences for the entire being of today's places, becoming one-factor explanations for all ills. They fit into narratives about global capital and other unstoppable forces. Those who tell such stories often feel frustrated and outflanked by the processes they are criticizing. The frustration is genuine, for it is hard to enrich the lives of people who inhabit thin places and receive mostly hollow cultural nourishment.[1] Although there is no denying that commodification is a problem, commodification is never total, and it is located within the wider complexities of place structure and process that can be mobilized against it.

Commodification and global media can seem to be creating a universal place that digests local particularity and transforms it into lifestyle products. There seem to be both a global leveling and a sometimes confident, sometimes frantic reassertion of localities. The global market spreads identical products and tools. The modern movement in architecture sought globally valid standards for a short list of functions that all buildings were to follow at the expense of local functions and norms. Those standards combined with the efficiencies of modern construction techniques to produce buildings and cities that more and more resemble one another, although lately the anonymous boxes have acquired local decorations. This world can look more and more like a gray totality of efficient production and consumption covered over by a multicolored screen of artificially intensified salable localities, fads, and identities. A heartless universal offers rootless freedom to resentful locality.

These options seem bleak, but that is because this way of framing the situation envisions that people must choose either a universal or a particular identity. The second dimension of place complexity, local interpretative process, refuses to be confined to that either/or. Complex place identity refuses both closed particularity and easy universalism. As described later in this chapter, people come to themselves within the processes out of which both universal and particular emerge. They cannot finally identify themselves with either side of this duality, even though they are pushed to do so.

PLACES AS COMMODITIES

Modernization brings thin places and social roles, and loosens the tie between thicker roles and specific locations. The commodification critique claims that the decline from classic places has gone even further: Places have lost their power to locate and shape our lives.

Discussions of commodification derive from Adam Smith and David Ricardo, as taken up by Hegel and Marx. They all insist on the distinction between use value (you wear the shoes) and exchange value (you trade the shoes for some food, or for money, the universal commodity). The essence of a commodity is that its exchange value trumps its use value. To turn a place into a commodity is to turn something definitive into something exchangeable. A place that has become a commodity no longer locates you within its norms and perspectives. You now position the place within your goals and activities of exchange. One way to convert a place into a commodity is to sell the area for redevelopment. More subtle is to make it a stage for the marketing of experiences, a commodity that is itself, which competes against other places offering rival experiences. The place becomes expendable and can be traded for others, or consumed by pay-per-view. The norms of the place and its rituals of inhabitation become spectacles ready to be exchanged for the latest version. You cease to be a thickly defined inhabitant and become a perpetual visitor or customer trying to patch together an identity by purchasing a series of the right experiences and products.

The most blatant architectural effects of commodification occur when the reasons for building become subordinated to considerations of profit and capital flow. Localities are devastated by outsized or inappropriate developments that disrupt the community, or by projects that are suddenly abandoned because the tides of capital have turned. Local ways of shaping places and constructing buildings are pushed aside or mutate into loud imitations of themselves. Commodity places are structured for efficiencies that care little about human welfare or local peculiarities except to market them as images. This simplifies them for quick recognition and persuasion. "Social space and practices tend toward complete homogenization and architectural experience risks collapse into an all-encompassing, generalized media experience" (Hays 1999, 50). Form and meanings weaken as surface effects become primary and places become items to be collected and consumed. Resale value can become more important than the current use of the building.

A commodity culture offers wide arrays of alternatives but manipulates consumers into wanting only the predefined options. People may come to believe that superficial abundance is the totality of a full human life. A fundamental passivity may be smeared over with shallow busyness. Public space and public participation decline when all social interactions are reduced to buying and selling. Citizens allow themselves to be turned away from the complexities of their situation and their eyes to be averted from areas without abundance and freedom. "The embrace of the perceptual apparatus given by mass media risks simply repeating a mode of reception that is more properly called consumption, challenging nothing of the conditions of our consumerist life and making it possible for everything to comfortably remain in place . . . the system as a whole can remain unchallenged" (Hays 1999, 55).[2] The freedom to buy can co-opt difference and resistance and hide oppressions and inequities. Does this make us freer, or homeless, or both?[3]

The theories that propose universal forces of commodification (and related critiques) are not well founded. Claims about universal forces and total changes should require strong backing, yet many critics seldom do more than cite a few striking examples. Taking as the key to everyday places extremes such as Disneyland or tourist resorts falsifies what ordinary places are and how they are lived in. The extreme examples do point out dimensions that exist in other places but are not their entire being. Universal totalizing claims that have been proposed either lack sufficient empirical backing for their claims, or illicitly make empirical generalizations into a priori or transcendental laws.[4] They may appeal to large-scale theories such as Foucault's analysis of power and subjectivity, Marxian ideas about capital and ideology, or Heidegger's history of being and the technological essence of modernity, but each of these has its own weaknesses when pushed too far.[5] It is worth recalling that the last time there were claims about total social changes, in the post–World War II large-scale theories of modernization, it turned out that there were surprising survivals and mixtures that weren't easily accounted for by the theory. That is true today as well.

Although many places today have become commodified, it does not follow that their entire being is taken up in their commodity role. Places are not items that can be put into bags and sold. They have many dimensions and links. Tourist being-in-a-town does not exhaust the town as a place. A book touches a desire and Provence suddenly becomes the rage. A few years later it is Tuscany's turn, and other regions vie to be next in line.[6] The influx of tourists resembles the flow of international capital, and is similarly fickle, though each wave may leave behind some new infrastructure, as well as some locals suddenly without livelihood. Tourist demands can denature a place for its native inhabitants, forcing them to live a simplified imitation of their own lives. "Conforming to the requirements of being a living tourist attraction becomes a total problem affecting every detail of life. . . . Any deviation from the touristic cultural ideal can be read as political gesture that produces conflict not between groups but within the group" (MacCannell 1992, 172). Such conflicts are real and painful, but the conflicts complicate rather than simplify people's lives. For its inhabitants the place can become more complex because the norms and patterns of tourism are added on to their lives. Even for the tourists the place is not as simple as it might seem, since when tourists consume it the place is inserted into the circulations of the tourists' own lives with their own contrasts and goals.

Nor is simplification a necessary consequence of tourism. Most towns do not become Colonial Williamsburg—and Colonial Williamsburg is only a part of Williamsburg, which has other economic and institutional resources, such as the College of William and Mary.[7] Commodification taken up into place norms can force a place to become more concentrated, themed and self-conscious. Yet unless the place is hollowed into pure show (and some approach that condition), it will not be totally occupied by its own spectacle. Commodification is only one aspect of a place, and it can actually make the place more complex.

For instance, in the town of Chemainus, on Vancouver Island in British Columbia, the sawmill that supported the town's economy went out of business. Seeking economic survival, the citizens decided to memorialize their past as a lumbering town. They painted on the sides of buildings large murals of log drives, timber work, loggers in the forest, loggers coming out of bars, and, in many cases, images of the building's own earlier conditions and use. The ploy worked: tourists came, and the town prospered so much that when the sawmill eventually reopened, it was no longer the center of the town's economy.

This is not, however, the Baudrillardian simulacrum in action. It is true that the town did turn itself into an image of itself exactly when the conditions that would support that older self disappeared. The town now sells that image in the tourist economy of exchange, visibility, and quick interaction. Tourists buy a conveniently wrapped experience of a way of life that no longer exists. The town turned itself into an image in order to survive on the rough seas of international business. But it was not Disneyland surfing a wave of capital. People who live nearby are proud of the way Chemainus saved itself by inventing a business. The tourist business is just a business—it's not a way of life. Vancouver Island's economy seems to be mostly forest products and tourism, and Chemainus had managed to move its economy from one emphasis to the other.

A postmodern image trade is from one point of view just a business, and there is a legitimate point to asking, What is a business today? What is being sold? To whom? What is stimulating or fulfilling what desires? But we should be wary of the tempting simplifications suggested by such questions. The people in Chemainus now have an oddly doubled life. It is unclear whether and how their rhythms of work and leisure, their topics of conversation, and their modes of socializing with one another have changed. With the mural business Chemainus has become more complex, not less so. Some of its social roles have become thinner, but bear in mind that complexity and thinness are not necessarily opposed.

Could there be absolutely commodified places with no other normative aspects to their structure? Disneyland is frequently cited as an example. Yet for its employees it is not a commodity but a workplace that develops its own subcommunities and rituals that go beyond what is sold to the public. For its customers, at least for repeat customers, it can become integrated into rhythms and activities that are not those of simple consumption (see Raz 1999 and Watson 1997).

A completely mechanized Disneyland with no human staff might be closer to a pure commodity. Yet would a completely mechanized Disneyland be a place? Instead of mutual expectations and accepted norms it would have instructions for use. It would be a large machine whose use is purchased and enjoyed in common with other people. But joint and coordinated use of an object does not automatically create a place. It could *become* a place, especially through repeated use and integration into shared rhythms and rituals of the users, in the way a McDonald's or a mall can be taken up into new sets of norms when teens use it for their own purposes and rituals. But if that happened, then, like the McDonald's, the mechanical Disneyland would no longer be only a commodity; it would be a scene for actions with a social meaning beyond consumption.[8]

We can reverse the question: Could there be an absolutely noncommodified place? We imagine a remote village unvisited by tourists, where people go about their lives in peace and harmony. But the tourists might arrive any day. So the real question is whether there could be places that were in principle immune to commodification. Since all places involve spatial extension, they will always be approachable from the outside, able to be seen and used in "inappropriate" ways, and besides tourists there are many different outsiders who observe and twist places: salespeople, spies, missionaries, government functionaries, and the like.[9]

One difficulty with the commodification critique is that it can be unclear what kind of inhabitation of a place would count as *not* consuming it. Either every possible relation to the place counts as consumption, in which case the critique has no validity, or there are particular relations that are consumptive and others that are not, in which case the issue again becomes one of deciding empirically what forces and influences are at work and which can be mobilized to influence the place for the better.

Such critiques often offer no choice but complete escape from the tyrannical totality. Such theories see capitalist culture (or technology, or the media, etc.) as outflanking all attempts to get beyond its reach. Those seeking to avoid commodification search in vain (in the primitive, in the unconscious, in the avant-garde, in various Others) for outside critical positions, which are soon co-opted by the system. What is there that could never be converted into a commodity? The answer cannot lie in finding some magical object or infinitely distant metaposition. It has to be found in a better understanding of the discontinuities, distances, and spacings already present in the embodiment of the current condition.

SYSTEMS AND PLACES

Dimensions of complexity remain even in highly commodified places. The forces and effects are not as total as in the rhetoric of the attacks on commodification. But granted that these forces are not totally dominating, there remains the question whether they are still strong enough to cripple attempts to improve contemporary places. Facing this issue calls for us to look more closely at the distinction made earlier between a system and a place. An extended analogy with two kinds of form for a building illuminates the distinction between the two. Applying the distinction to places will show no simple dominance in either direction. The system restricts place making, although place making gives meaning to the system. We live within that interplay.

Imagine, for the analogy, an office building. How is the building unified? Aristotle says that a house is a house because of its form and purpose, not because of its bricks. However, although the office building has a current purpose, buildings can last a long time and their purposes can be changed. The office building could become an apartment house, and in that conversion some elements of the building would not change: the walls would still support the roof, the windows let in light, and the heating system warm the spaces. These elements, and others, make up what I call the operative form of the building, which includes the physical systems that move air, resist gravity and wind, provide heat, and do other tasks of this sort (Kolb 1990, 122–24). This is not the same as the functional unity of the building: the function sets goals, whereas the operative form organizes causal interactions as means. The operative form is how the means work, even if the goals change.

Operative form has its own kind of loose unity. Even if one wanted to create a building that expressed an avant-garde disdain for goals and resisted any wholeness, the building would still need an operative form that would be a kind of whole. There would be structural members, heating and air circulation systems, electricity service, and the like, and these would be most efficiently planned as integrated systems. The operative form might be less unified if the place were a conglomeration of parts from different periods such that different heating and circulation systems were cobbled together as the building evolved. If one were de-signing it anew, however, no matter how deconstructive or fragmented it might be designed to "be," economic considerations would probably lead to a highly integrated operative form.

The systemic operation of a building differs from its role as a place. These two different kinds of unity can vary independently of each other. You can change the operative form by replacing the heating system, without changing the purpose of the building or the norms of the place. On the other hand, you can turn the building into a new kind of place without altering the way its roof is supported.

Operative form may be shown or hidden. A building supported by steel beams may appear to be supported by stone pillars. The modern movement in architecture wanted buildings to show honestly their op-erations of resisting gravity, letting in light, circulating air, and so on. But presenting the operative form of a building puts that form into a new context where it is contrasted not just with other possible opera-tive forms (other ways of heating or other ways the ducts could have been mounted), but also with other possible aesthetic effects and with other strategies of presentation. What was a matter of causal links and efficiency gets considered in terms of meaningful norms and aesthetic contrasts. The interplay of system and aesthetics makes the architect's task more challenging.

Using the analogy of the office building, we can see a similar distinc-tion with regard to places. The scope is wider, but there is still a distinc-tion between operative causal effects and normative issues of meaning. In what I call a system, events in one location have effects in another. If I make this window larger I may weaken the wall and cause the ceiling to collapse. If I attach this air conditioner I may overload the electric wiring. If the bank in Boston puts money into this housing development it will have to reduce its investment in that shopping center. If you run that smelter these cities a thousand miles downwind will be subject to in-creased air pollution. Such links are causal, not normative. They happen whether or not they are intended, and no change in place norms can by itself keep them from happening.

Systems produce chains and networks of causal effects, often rein-forced by feedback loops. The effects may occur in remote locations, especially with ecological or economic systems. The connections in feedback systems are not the same as those made by norms in places.

Place norms require creative interpretation. For instance, when multiple norms are engaged within a place, they can conflict in ways that demand judgment and decision. The right of public access to an office may conflict with security concerns; a court may have to rule on what degree of access must be allowed. In systems, competing forces come to a causal resolution. Systems can be said to conflict, for instance in a room where one system is trying to cool the space and another admits sunlight that is heating the space. This is unlike a conflict of norms, however: the temperature of the room may oscillate or it may be stable, depending on the details of the systems involved, but this will happen without any interpretation about the priority of one norm to another.[10]

So system patterns and place norm structures are not the same. The efficiency of a system is not the ritual of a place. A functional role in a system does not of itself make a local "we." Our actions function within more elaborated systems and economies than we can be aware of, but these functions are not automatically social roles. A system is not a place.[11]

With this distinction in hand we can avoid confusing the reach of systemic effects with the presumed creation of a universal place. There is no universal place that has swallowed all particularity, but there are widespread flows and systems. Local inhabitations are under pressure from systems of interaction that link events and consequences in ways independent of the norms that define places. There are vastly accelerated flows of capital, of signs, of people and products and chemicals and biological effects. We are not in any of these flows as in a place, though places are deeply affected by these flows.

Having made the distinction I now must complicate it, for although it is useful to distinguish systems from places, the two intermingle. Place norms must take systemic effects into account. Systems influence which norms and expectations are livable. With fewer culturally imposed restraints on economic interactions and with increased power to influence biological events, today's economic and biological systems put new pressures on local places. Resource ebbs and flows are rapid, technology changes quickly, and economic fluctuations can have almost instant effects. These all influence local social norms, not by directly changing them but by altering the resources for places and the effects of possible patterns of action. In his discussion of "the practico-inert" Jean-Paul Sartre discusses the ways in which system effects and norms can become entangled and jointly reified to constrain future possibilities (see Sartre 1991).

Also, just as architects might want to reveal a building's operative form, large-scale systematic effects can be given normative roles. For instance, environmental effects have become normatively important in ways that they were not before. Normative social roles are created that are dedicated to the use and control of such systemic effects. There can be places that ritualize systemic functions—stock exchanges, banks, financiers' clubs—though there remains a difference between the system interactions and the norms for those places. The difference becomes obvious when such institutions continue even though the systemic patterns have changed. Another mixture occurs when a system effect changes the local horizon of meaning. For instance, when a corporation in search of profit beams images and symbols by satellite TV into remote areas, it puts local norms into new and unintended meaning contrasts.

Third, system effects and social norms may be used by each other. System effects can be manipulated to bring about changes in social norms, for instance by deliberately shifting resources so that certain activities become possible or impossible. Economic actors can manipulate system effects to put pressure on laws and social roles. Or laws can be changed to try to alter economic feedbacks. Social norms can be changed to influence the distribution of system effects, as with new social norms about the environment. There are always larger games and systems to be influenced by changes in local arrangements.[12]

Lefebvre's notion of social space shows that normative and systemic effects can combine. For example, what he would call the space of the U.S. interstate highway system was produced by political decisions dealing with the causal realities of transporting goods and troops, and the perceived needs of the post–World War II economy. Once produced, that network of highways had causal effects on the speed of transport, but it also gained normative status as the expected mode for some kinds of travel. This produced intended and unintended systemic effects that altered resources for the development of small towns, affected the tourist industry, caused air pollution, and so on, and these effects were then taken into account by new social norms and roles. Such a large-scale network is "simultaneously, both a field of action (offering its extension to the deployment of projects and practical intentions) and a basis of action (a set of places whence energies derive and whither energies are

directed) . . . at once actual (given) and potential (locus of possibilities)"
(Lefebvre 1991, 191).[13]

Manuel Castells structures his monumental study of the Information
Age around a duality that resembles the distinction between a universal
open system and closed local places. He analyzes "a fundamental split
between abstract, universal instrumentalism, and historically rooted, par-
ticularistic identities. Our societies are increasingly structured around a
bipolar opposition between the Net and the Self" (Castells 1996, 3). We
live in the intersection of local places and "the space of flows." These
have their own separate logics.

> There is no longer continuity between the logic of power-making
> in the global network and the logic of association and represen-
> tation in specific societies and cultures. The search for mean-
> ing takes place then in the reconstruction of defensive identities
> around communal principles. Most of social action becomes orga-
> nized in the opposition between unidentified flows and secluded
> identities. (Castells 1997, 11)
>
> [There is no bridging] the separation between the market logic
> of global networks of capital flows and the human experience of
> workers' lives. (Castells 1998, 366)

As these quotations indicate, Castells's notion of system is more historically specific and includes more components of intentional behavior
than does the concept of system I am using. For him systems have become networks in the "space of flows" of linked exchanges. This network
is partly automatic feedback and partly intentional design in the service
of elite groups. "Global networks of instrumental exchanges selectively
switch on and off individuals, groups, regions, and even countries, according to their relevance in fulfilling the goals processed in the network, in a relentless flow of strategic decisions" (Castells 1996, 3). The
disengagement of the system from any local meaning production is a
strategic move in favor of dominant elites. "Articulation of the elites, segmentation and disorganization of the masses seem to be the twin mechanisms of social domination in our societies. . . . Elites are cosmopolitan,
people are local" (Castells 1996, 415).

Without trying to deal with the whole of his remarkable analysis, I
point to two conceptual issues that are relevant to my discussion. The

most important is that Castells views places as basically closed. "A place is a locale whose form, function, and meaning are self-contained within the boundaries of physical contiguity" (Castells 1996, 423). This puts all linkage on the side of the systemic networks. But places are linked and complex in ways other than through systemic connections. Meaning refuses to be confined to a local horizon, and the meaning and function of many places depend on normative relations and cognitive references to other places far away. Castells seems to be working with a monadic notion of local cultures that stems from older anthropological conceptions. But cultures stand in self-conscious as well as systemic relations to others, and their places do not form closed horizons.[14]

Places are not just meaning givers; they themselves take on meaning within wider webs of action. It is unrealistic to treat places as final horizons, as unlocated locators that give closed meaning to what lies within them. Such theories often refer to anthropological descriptions of primitive tribes whose social rules structure a closed world. Their world has no effective contrasts with other possible cultural worlds, so the social norms seem just a natural fact. Tribe members perceive neither their world's horizon nor its closure, but only the items classified and located within their world. Whether there ever really were such tribes could be argued, but modern people live in multiple worlds. Social norms and places are revealed in contrast to other norms both actual and possible. This liberates us from a confinement we imagine in our ancestors, but it also enforces a homelessness — *if* being at home is defined according to that closed model. Although no set of local meanings can close totally, there are many ways to make it appear that it does so, and to enlist people in the efforts to hold the horizon closed. That effort requires a certain bad faith, to be warding off other possibilities constantly while denying they are there. The usual form this bad faith takes in political and religious and scientific fundamentalism is to label the other possibilities (of belief, behavior, or place norms) as illusory, evil, or lacking a true foundation.

Because he sees places as closed, Castells offers only a nondialectical relation between system and place, global and local, universal and particular. This can be seen in his reaction to Anthony Giddens's views on modern reflexivity. Giddens proposes that "the more tradition loses its hold, and the more daily life is reconstituted in terms of the dialectical interplay of the local and the global, the more individuals are forced to

negotiate lifestyle choices among a diversity of options . . . reflexively organized life-planning . . . becomes a central feature of the structuring of
self-identity." Castells opposes Giddens's idea. He says, "While agreeing
with Giddens' theoretical characterizations of identity-building in the
period of 'late modernity', I argue . . . that the rise of the network society
calls into question the processes of construction of identity during that
period, thus inducing new forms of social change. This is because the
network society is based on the systemic disjunction between the local
and the global for most individuals and social groups. And, I will add, by
the separation in different time-space frames between power and experience. . . . Therefore, reflexive life-planning becomes impossible, except
for the elite inhabiting the timeless space of flows of the global networks
and their ancillary locales" (Castells 1997, 11).

However, Giddens is right about the possibility of constructing identities through the interplay of the local and the global, particular and
universal. The more self-aware people are of their inhabitation of places
today, the more they are doing what Giddens describes, and that awareness is not restricted to cosmopolitan elites. When there are pressures
aiming to separate and segregate local cultures there will be ways under
and around those pressures other than sheer resistance. Castells admits
as much in his description of new social movements that have developed a "project identity" that goes beyond pure defensiveness (Castells
1997).[15]

The distinction between system and place connects to commodification critiques through the worry that normative frameworks have been
pushed by systemic pressures to measure everything in terms of the instrumental values of efficiency and velocity of exchange. "Economic vi-
ability is not a new need; not much ever happened without it; but somehow it has become the purpose, rather than the means, of civilization"
(McCullough 1997, 71). Economic efficiency and velocity are systemic
parameters, not social norms. Their translation into values and norms
does not happen automatically but comes about through social processes. In those processes, optimizing market efficiency will not be the
only norm, though there are many pressures to make it so.

The more voices that can be heard, both socially and within individuals, the less can any simple optimizing function dominate social priorities. Democracy tends to increase the complexity of factors that need
to be considered, and encourages repressed groups and ignored parts

of ourselves to find their voices. So increased democratization is one way to counter oppressions that arise from attempts to make everything respond to a single norm of efficiency. Democratization, however, is not enough if all the place norms and social roles available are thin and abstract. Then people's identities will have few resources that can resist the dominance of cultural goals defined by pressures toward system efficiency.

Lefebvre's account of space emphasizes the ways that the power of the state or other agencies shapes us through influencing habitual bodily movements and "immediate" perceptions. He describes how networks are set up to distribute activities and resources and identities. This is not so different from my discussion of place norms and systems influencing changes and linkages in spatial areas. But, perhaps because of his revolutionary intent, Lefebvre's account of social spaces tells of holistic larger spaces that dominate local areas. This ignores the ways in which local place norms can be created askew from larger spaces and stand in opposition to them, or reinterpret their influences. Lefebvre tends to paint a totalizing picture that misses the complexity and linkage of local places.[16] I am not saying that Lefebvre's postrevolutionary differential space already exists, only that existing place norms have more complex relations to larger systems and places than Lefebvre's account of domination and ideology suggests.[17] We see in the next chapter how a theme park that seems only a spatial machine for mindless thrills and caricatures of otherness in fact depends on complex contrasts and reflective divisions that can be made more self-aware. We will consider in chapter 7 how tidy New Urbanist villages that look disconnected from the rush of the contemporary market and media are nonetheless penetrated by them, and yet the villages can promote a form of community that goes against the system's pressures to thin out social roles.

ACTIVE COMPLEXITIES IN PLACE MAKING

The question remains whether we can resist the forces of commodification. It is important to realize that awareness of place complexity is not passive contemplation: we are active in the interpretation and reproduction of social norms, and awareness of our activity can lead to innovations that change the social game, such as organizing to bring new agents with new voices onto the social scene.[18] It is here that the

worry reappears that even though system effects and the forces of commodification cannot be in total control they might be strong enough
to block efforts to improve today's places. Lefebvre rightly argues that
the simplifications enforced by thin functional place norms need to be
fought by finding gaps and opportunities for more self-conscious inhabitation and creation of places. Commodification tries to stuff those gaps
with intense repetitive choice among thin places and thin identities. It is
an empirical question whether or not this can succeed in destroying the
possibilities for richer inhabitation and intervention in any particular
place. The next chapters look in more detail at possibilities for self-aware
complexity in themed places and in suburban sprawl. Here, though, I
discuss how in general the three dimensions of place complexity might
reduce the hold of commodification.

We have already seen that the first dimension of complexity is in the
structure of norms and spatial arrangements. The interplay between a
place's spatial features and its social norms may be loose or tight, and
one side can suggest changes in the other. Noticing the architectural
features of a mall may bring people to question the social norms active
there. Often there are multiple sets of norms, so local norms of polite-
ness or ethnic identifications might disrupt the norm of consumption at
the mall, or cause one to question its spatial arrangements. Sometimes
the same spatial area can be several different places at once. A visit to
Washington Square in New York reveals several communities making different divisions and usages of the park at the same time. Children playing, elders relaxing, students reading, people making drug transactions,
all follow different norms for the use of the square. Sometimes these
peacefully coexist, sometimes not.[19] Their multiplicity offers opportunities for the cooperative or contentious creation of new social voices and
agents.

Place structures are spread out in space and time and cannot fully
dominate their medium. To be spread out and embodied in a particular
area at a particular time makes it necessary to carry forward and continually reproduce the place's norms over time. That process can introduce
new connections and new interpretations. Also, to be spread out is to be
in a shared medium, to have blind sides, and to be among meanings and
possibilities that are beyond control. The norms and the place can be
approached from unexpected angles; they can be encompassed, quoted,
resegmented. That exteriority is neither created nor dominated by the

norms of the place. Having this outside is not a contingent feature in the structure of a place; it is a condition for there to be a place at all. This means that no set of norms, whether thick and substantive or thin and commodified, can totally dominate a place; there are always other connections and strange possibilities.

Michel Foucault suggested that the continuity of imposed norms gets twisted and broken in those places he called heterotopias. A heterotopia is not a breakdown of social norms but a place that shows how systems of social norms include their own incompleteness, inconsistencies, and openings. For instance, a place might present standard roles in ways that call them into question (retirement "homes") or present skewed miniatures of the whole society (ships at sea, military camps). Heterotopias are not structureless moments free from control, but places that show how that control is not all what it appears to be. Foucault presented his notion of heterotopia in a widely circulated 1967 lecture, "Of Other Spaces," but he never developed it into a lengthy discussion.[20] The examples he offered in the lecture are difficult to gather into a consistent notion. Those who have taken up the term often move it toward avant-garde or Situationist International moments of transgression, or toward the breakdown of structure, rather than the self-constructive-deconstructive places that Foucault seems to have had in mind. Some of his examples are permanent institutions with their own social norms. Their significance arises from the way their norms interact with and throw light on the content and processes of the larger society, and on the way those processes can provide their own self-commentary and new openings.

Place structure exists amid an excess of possibilities. There is always spatial excess; the textures of space and architecture are richer than any particular social norms take note of. There is an excess of meaning as well. Any set of distinguished aspects can acquire other meanings, can be used metaphorically, can be extended, quoted, reused, put into new context, crossed with others, and so on.[21] Inhabiting a place is not a simple submission to a permanently fixed and totally clear set of norms. The borders are not so definite.

Places prepare the way for their own changes by providing a field of possible combinations that exceed current practice. The distinctions of areas and actions made in a place can be combined in many more ways than those that are expected. In a courthouse there are distinct areas for different activities, but precisely because these areas and activities have been distinguished, they can be imagined in other combinations. Have the trial on the courthouse steps, have the jury use the judges' chambers, make the lawyers address the court from the top of the judges' bench, or appoint a panel of judges by lottery from passing pedestrians. Normally, as a matter of course, such wild possibilities do not occur—that's what makes the normality normal—but those possibilities and others continue to haunt the place structures, which exist by excluding them. Neither the borders nor the internal differentiations of a place are as naturally firm as they appear to be. They are reinforced by social repetition, but that process can also change them, in the interpretive work necessary to continue a place through time.

So the first dimension of complexity, place structures, can provide openings for new norms and new kinds of activities and social voices. Place structures exist within the process of their own interpretation and reproduction, so new possibilities can be realized through the ongoing process of active interpretation and reproduction.

The second dimension of complexity is in those ongoing interpretive processes that sustain and reproduce social norms and places. The processes of global capitalism, technological change, and the media affect all places today, but they are not irresistible forces. Global markets and the mass media cannot be avoided; they influence even places that are "unwired" and "off the map," because systems shift allocations of resources and change flows of people and information, altering the range of what is possible in a place. These effects, though, do not fully decide their own meaning and impact on place norms. These involve active local reception and reinterpretation and innovation as well as flows from hegemonic centers.[22]

> As rapidly as forces from various metropolises are brought into new societies they tend to become indigenized in one or another way: this is true of music and housing styles as much as it is true of science and terrorism, spectacles and constitutions. (Appadurai 1966, 32)[23]

> At times . . . the depictions of the postmodern age deserve some of its own incredulity. When it is claimed, for example, that identities become nothing but assemblages from whatever imagery is for the moment marketed through the media, then I wonder what kind of people the commentators on postmodernism know. . . . It

is a problem of postmodernist thought that as it has emphasized
diversity and been assertively doubtful toward master narratives, it
has itself frequently been on the verge of becoming another all-
encompassing formula for a macroanthropology of the replication
of uniformity, like any other conception of a Zeitgeist, or of national character. (Hannerz 1992, 35)

Place creation is not some metaphysical machinery churning away behind the scenes. It is in the behavior and expectations of people as they
live day to day. It is neither willfully arbitrary nor just random, for it
develops in relation to earlier beginnings and ongoing projects. It is the
process of living and moving, in which concepts and particulars, norms
and things normed take up their relations to one another amid the development of habits and routines reflected upon in our practical awareness of how to go on with what we do. "The reflexivity of modern social
life consists in the fact that social practices are constantly examined and
reformed in the light of incoming information about those very practices, thus constitutively altering their character" (Giddens 1990, 38).[24]
Social practices are reflective and therefore changeable. "The point is
not that there is no stable social world to know, but that knowledge of
that world contributes to its unstable or mutable character" (Giddens
1990, 45).

The process of creating and continuing place norms is not something
we all direct from outside, but neither is it something that simply manu-
factures us. We exist within the separation and combination of the moments of time, opening the tensions between universal and particular,
self and context. Historical location and ongoing projects are not neutral data manipulated from a detached position. We are not the lords of
meaning, standing above it all and decreeing social patterns in sovereign
independence; instead, we are ourselves shaped within the process of
meaning creation. Yet if we are not totally active, neither are we totally
passive.

Place norms are not possessed the way a rock holds its shape. Nor
do they exist as a simple possession plus added layers of distanced self-
reflection. The process of active embodiment and interpretation is not
totally under our control, and yet it is in that process that we can be said
to exercise our modern freedom.

At least from the time of Rousseau and Kant that freedom has been conceptualized as self-legislation. Modern individuals and communities are supposed to set up their own criteria and patterns of action without relying on natural impulses or desires that have not been reviewed and judged. The standard modern dilemma is to find ways to hold together both the self-defining activity of individual and community as well as their belonging in history, language, and place that they do not totally control.[25]

Language and social forms of life resist our will and can resist commodification and other pressures from larger systems. Habits cannot be undone in an instant, meaning cannot be controlled, and the past is always already active. Social content has its own tensions, dynamisms, and inertias.[26] People awake to themselves as already involved, carried along by ongoing projects in a network of language and social habits, but at the same time they sustain and rework those projects. They act in time amid histories they did not create but which they must take up. They remake and change those histories and norms and concepts as they act and move and pass them along in time, but without possessing any absolute point of view.[27]

In individuals and in places there is no central point source of creativity or resistance to rally around; our selves are woven amid the tensions and complexities of multiple forces and processes.[28] But then, neither is there in individuals or places a central fortress that can be captured by outside forces of commodification that can thus take over the whole. There is nothing solid and simple; everywhere there are intersections and complexities. Neither the structure of places and norms nor the processes that create and sustain them are single-ply.

So criticisms of modern places are wrong when they depend on simple identifications. Some picture a battle between creative place makers and the forces of oppression. Some see us as completely shaped by where we dwell, but now exiled from where we belong. Some see us as helpless pawns of commodifying or other totalizing forces. But neither individuals and communities, nor the processes that sustain them, nor the outside forces that try to shape them are pure and unified. Space for criticism and resistance is available within the internal differences and spacings that make places.

We are more than commodity pressures want us to describe ourselves as being. Room is opened by the temporal divisions and processes necessary for there to be any meaning at all, and by the excess that is a condition for any meaning to be definite. These factors keep us from being rigidly confined and dominated. Indeed we slide around on these factors even when we are trying to make ourselves rigid and confined.

Still, the worry about commodification can be restated yet again. It is true that people are neither the simple products nor the lordly directors of meaning. But because people are in that middle condition we are vulnerable. Through distraction or mystification, people can lose touch with our activity in the creation and the reproduction of social norms. This moves the discussion into the third dimension of complexity.

The third dimension of complexity is the multiple remote systemic and political processes that influence places. Commodification and other totalizing criticisms often imply that the processes they describe are unstoppable by anything short of global revolution.

Inherent in the first two dimensions of complexity are possibilities for active interventions to reduce the impact of commodification and other system pressures. Some are interventions in the structures of a place: creating new social norms or twisting old ones; letting complexities and multiplicities in the norms become more explicit, marked, and celebrated; and creating alternative divisions or nodes within the place. Some are interventions in a process of interpretation that cannot be controlled from the outside, making that process more self-aware and internally multiple, creating new occasions for dialogue.

There are also interventions in the third dimension of complexity, which deal with relations to larger outside forces: spreading knowledge of those forces and recognizing their multiplicities, locating or assembling countervailing forces, seeing outside pressures as resulting from decisions or policies that might be changed, creating new social agents, and organizing to represent oppressed or invisible groups and interests.

There are always other flows and forces. Any relatively stable biological, cultural, or economic system exists within a wilder flow of events, energy, and resources that can disturb it. Within this flow systems and protosystems interact with all the Darwinian possibilities of mutation, symbiosis, parasitism, cannibalism, and the like. This is a systemic analogue to the always-present excess of meaning around norms and roles. In both cases the excess allows for more maneuvers than the current systems or norms define. There are wide-ranging events such as the accidental discovery of a technologically important new scientific law, and significant local events such as the organization of a new political voice.

The speed and linkage of contemporary systems and lives can be worked with in ways that do not favor monopoly control and the forces of commodification. "The new global cultural economy has to be seen as a complex, overlapping, disjunctive order that cannot any longer be understood in terms of existing center-periphery models (even those that might account for multiple centers and peripheries). Nor is it susceptible to simple models of push and pull (in terms of migration theory), or of surpluses and deficits (as in traditional models of balance of trade), or of consumers and producers (as in most neo-Marxist theories of development)" (Appadurai 1966, 32). There is no solidity outside the processes that could be a firm point of resistance, but within the processes there are complexities and openings for a strategy of multiplying and twisting flows. Movements and linkages can be used for more than their standard purposes, and local connections and networks can be made within and around larger networks. Attempts to create local communities on the Internet are an example: the results are not outside of but are enabled by the larger forces, while working to turn them in different directions. No firm solidity can be gained this way, but there can be effects and interactions and practices that go beyond commodified expectations.

FIGHTING MONOPOLIES

It is also important to become aware of all the flows and processes, even those that commodification would make invisible: poverty and injustice, death, and the nonexchangeable qualities of sheer temporal and material presence.[29] Let what is often rushed over be apparent, instead. This may mean slowing down, but doing so is not abandoning the flow; it is seeing more of it than usual.

All this means fighting monopoly, both corporate attempts to narrow choices and dominate the means of communication, and also individual or group attempts to impose monopolies of meaning. When social norms and place structures, the first dimension of complexity, are seen as maintained by the second and influenced by the third kinds of complexity, there can be more space for maneuvering. Discontinuities can be bridged by links that create new kinds of places and groups.

Commodification can become just one of many pressures. Even current capitalism can be seen as a particular configuration that is not the only possible realization of the ideals of market exchange. Property and ownership are a bundle of rights and regulations that might be influenced and recomposed in new ways. This is already happening as the relative importance of different kinds of ownership shifts in the era of globalization. It could happen more consciously. Here too the issue is fighting monopolies of meaning and practice while finding ways to take system pressures into account without being defined by them.

As Castells points out, in an age of linkages and flows, one has to maintain space for more kinds of nets and associations.

> In this network society . . . power does not reside in institutions, not even in the state or in large corporations. It is located in the networks that structure society. Or, rather, in what I propose to call the 'switchers'; that is, the mechanisms connecting or disconnecting networks on the basis of certain programmes or strategies. For instance, in the connection between the media and the political system. . . . Power is exercised by specific configurations of these networks that express dominant interests and values, but whose actors and forms can change. . . . That is why to counter networks of power and their connections, alternative networks need to be introduced: networks that disrupt certain connections and establish new ones, such as disconnecting political institutions from business-dominated media and re-anchoring them in civil society through horizontal communication networks. Networks versus networks. (Castells 2004)

The generalities I've offered in the last few paragraphs lead to strategies that multiply voices and social actors, create new networks, use places in new ways, and question laws and practices that encourage large scale control and monopolies. Although this book is not intended to be a detailed handbook, the next three chapters provide examples dealing with theme parks and suburbs.

Places should be inhabited with more lived sense of their complex internal multiplicities and linkages, and with more self-consciousness of the multiple forces and pressures at work. Aiming for this increased self-awareness of place complexity resembles the strategies of unmasking and defamiliarization so prominent in modernist art and in theories of culture influenced by Freud and Marx. Those artistic and critical strategies try to make fluid what is taken as static, and try to reveal as socially constructed what is taken as naturally given, so as to break through ideological constructs and remove false consciousness.

Stan Allen describes these strategies this way: "The available conceptual models for the project of resistance—from Frankfurt School Marxism to deconstruction—depend in one form or another on a modernist idea of making difference visible through operations of unmasking (or related strategies of demythification, deferral, or negation). For all their significant differences, they share the assumption that the task of critical work is to uncover the artifice in that assumed to be natural" (Allen 1995, 53).

Such maneuvers aim to help people see the forces shaping their lives, and to realize that norms and relations constructed by one artifice could be reconstructed by another. I share the ideal of a more active self-relation for both individual and community, but the strategy of increasing complexity is broader than strategies of unmasking. Trying to increase complexity works to undo the illusions of simple immediacy. Ideology and false consciousness are only one kind of immediacy, and aiming to increase complexity can be appropriate in cases where there is no false consciousness in the Marxist sense.

Increasing place complexity will always mean less isolation, more connection and mediation, and more intertwined self-relations. It does not, however, mean the maintenance of a constantly detached critical attitude. Allen argues that in the case of architecture and place, strategies of unmasking that encourage critical detachment suffer from the problem cited in chapter 3 from Walter Benjamin. Architecture and places are lived without direct attention to their qualities because people are rightly distracted from the architectural object when they concentrate on their goals and activities in the place. "With regard to architecture and the experience of urban space, if we first stipulate the predominance of distraction and, second, recognize that this implies a model of reception other than the linguistic . . . it seems to me self-evident that unmasking operations, which assume a degree of critical consciousness on the part of the spectator, will be of limited effectiveness" (Allen 1995, 54).

Allen's objection has the most force when a model of critical consciousness demands a detached observer, which in turn demands focal awareness. The strategy of complexity does not depend on detachment. Overcoming the self-declared immediacy of an oversimplified place will reveal the complex mediations that were there all along. Making the horizon of activity more complex because a place's links and context are now more present can make new moves possible within a more complex set of norms for the everyday. This enrichment of the horizon of possibilities changes everyday meanings without demanding a detached critical stance (see Kolb 2002).

Fuller inhabitation is not a combination of naive absorption plus a detached critical view. It is a broadened practical awareness of the possibilities of things and places, more like an artist's altering a work in progress than like a critic's detached evaluation. The artist sees possibilities not obvious in the immediate appearance of the work.[30]

Richer inhabitation of, for instance, a themed place or a suburb involves a kind of doubling that is not a critical or ironic detachment.[31] One can appreciate the surface of the suburb or the mall or the themed place, enjoying the sheen of its immediacy as part of what the place is trying to do and be, but at the same time seeing this surface effect for what it is. One can experience the game while realizing that it is itself a move in larger games. The enlarged awareness becomes active when one refuses to be defined by surfaces, games, or norms that try to enclose and limit the place's connections and possibilities to what is standardly available. This may require gestures that accentuate or alter the processes or point out linkages and context.

When the immediacy of a place obscures injustices and inequities or tries to make them seem natural and inevitable, one must be aware of the attempt and yet move beyond it. When explicit action must be taken to change or resist unjust place formation, then explicit critical consciousness may be needed, but that still relies on a wider sense of the place's internal complexity.

Seen in their full concreteness and context the commodified, thin places produced by modern and postmodern forces have a complexity that can be mobilized and increased for a richer inhabitation. Tactics other than increasing traditional deep rootedness are available to counteract the bad aspects of newer places.[32]

What I recommend here resembles what Stan Allen finally urges, that "the radical gesture today is not to unmask the simulacrum as a lie, but rather to require the simulacrum, against expectation, to function as the real" (Allen 1995, 53–54). Some of the tactics I suggest in the next chapters to improve suburbia and themed places by making them "function as the real," that is, to function fully as the more complex places they are rather than the simplified places their self-definitions and architectural form claim them to be.

CHAPTER FIVE

Full Theme Ahead

*A theme park is much more than a simple location. It is a shrine
to its message and to succeed must be bounded—isolated from
the ordinary landscape . . . . If a distinction between special and
ordinary does not exist, the former offers no control over the
latter and fails to be a pilgrimage site.*
(Young 2002a, 6)

THEMED PLACES SEEM EMBLEMATIC of the worst of contemporary
places. A student once remarked that she had enjoyed Disney creations
until at architectural school she learned that Disney was the Evil Empire.
Themed places sin against modernist canons of honesty. They also
reek of the commodification that offends postmodernists who would
otherwise approve of fantasy. For almost everyone themed places show
life in a fast-paced, image-drenched society that seems to leave unsatis-
fied a basic need for contact with reality, even though the themed places'
obtrusive reality assaults us at every turn.[1]

According to the criteria given in chapter 3, themed places seem thin,
diluted, and simplified in their social norms, no matter how spatially
complex they might be. They are by design almost entirely foreground,
and they encourage linear routes of action through scripted simplified
thin roles that don't interact much with one another. In this chapter I
discuss the nature of themed places and the tactic of finding or creating a complexity that exceeds the official self-definition of a place. For
themed places, all three dimensions of complexity are relevant. Themed
places structurally depend on contrasts with other themes and with everyday life, they are maintained by explicit cooperative interpretation,
and they are blatantly inserted into larger economic and cultural systems. I argue that the complexity of a themed place is at the borders
of the place, but those borders must be kept present everywhere in the
place in order for the theme to function.

These are themed places: Disney and Universal Studios parks, a park in Japan that reproduces a miniature Netherlands, another Tokyo park that celebrates the Hello Kitty brand, and all those Wild West parks, Santa Claus Villages, and their kin. Then themed restaurants, such as the Medieval Times chain of castles with jousts during dinner, and neighborhood Irish bars, opera-singing Italian restaurants, themed malls with local regional decor, and festival markets with a historic theme, such as New York's South Street Seaport. Themed resorts and hotels. Historical reconstructions such as Colonial Williamsburg and its cousins. Towns emphasizing a theme, such as Fredricksburg in Texas that emphasizes its Germanness, or the mid-America towns along Interstate 80 that try to attract drivers by presenting a historical theme. Themed residential areas such as Battery Park City in New York, and themed suburban housing developments. More and more, places try to attract and hold attention by offering themed environments.

> "You'll see themed hospitals and doctor's offices, themed automobile dealerships," says entertainment consultant Joseph Pine. . . . "I've heard of a dentist in Scottsdale, Arizona, who has installed a Native American motif in his office, done by a company that worked on the Forum Shops in Las Vegas." . . . Increasingly, any institution that wants to woo or captivate the public will need to compete with Net- and home-based entertainment, and with themed retail, dining, and park-in-a-box concepts like Sony Metreon and DisneyQuest. (Kirsner 2000, 188–90)

Themed places can be for consuming the fantasy, for "escape," for buying ethnic goods, for vacations, for thrills and adventure, for learning, or for adding some atmosphere to your dining, or your shopping, or your home life.

Themed places must be taken seriously not just because they are increasingly common but because, despite their frequent tackiness, they show the self-conscious interrelation that is needed as contemporary places become more complex. I claim in this chapter that the reality of themed places depends on self-aware difference. We can learn from themed places how to deal with other contemporary scenes and how to keep self-awareness and cross-references from being smoothed down to a commodified norm. The illusions and self-presentations of themed places can be enjoyed within larger fields and processes than their official self-presentation admits.

It helps us understand everyday theming to look at more extreme examples such as Disney parks and festival malls, but it is important to remember that theming is a wider phenomenon than theme parks. It is a standard critical routine to dismiss themed places. For instance, Ada Louise Huxtable says

> Today's themed creations are not, and never will be, real places; they are not meant to be. They are made for the moment, instant environments intended to serve only as temporary substitute events, conceived and carried out as places to visit in which novelty, experience, and entertainment are sold for immediate profit and a short period of time. . . . To embrace their limited and exclusionary objectives is to forfeit the large needs of place and society. To imitate their poverty of reference is to lose all we know about the past. To think that American cities can learn from them is to embrace the most dangerous illusion of all. (Huxtable 1997, 69)

To discuss themed places more carefully than do such blanket condemnations, we need concepts that will let us see that theming is not an alien perversion but one modulation of the conditions that make places possible at all.

WHAT IS A THEME?

Some preliminary distinctions are necessary before we take up the question of what is a theme. Here is a distinguished writer using the term *theme park* carelessly:

> Major European cities lack massive, structured, touristic consumption, a shortcoming that is remedied by their conversion to theme parks such as the Parisian Louvre. However this addition ends up taking the place of the previous city, which in turn is integrated as part of the theme parks or as neutral picturesque or invisible background. (Gandelsonas 1999, 37)

Mario Gandelsonas here claims that the Louvre and Paris have been turned into theme parks. Yet Paris has not made presenting or selling itself into its total occupation, as does Disneyland. A theme *park* contains only staff and customers, whereas a themed *place* has residents or users for whom its theme forms a background to other activities than showing or consuming the theme. Manhattan's Battery Park City themes the New York of the 1920s, but people live and do other work there; they don't just consume or sell the theme.

This distinction can be sharpened if we consider another careless statement.

> In the 1970's [Boston] chose to redevelop the Faneuil Hall area. . . . Demolition was out; restoration was in. . . . the city desired a colonial theme park. The Rouse Corporation created the 'festival mall' concept. (Star 1999, 120)

Boston's Faneuil Hall and Quincy Market area has only staff and customers, yet it is not a theme park. Disneyland sells fantasies and experiences, with its retail goods supporting the fantasies. At themed festival malls the fantasy supports the retail. You don't need to go to Disneyland for the retail goods sold there; you can buy them at a Disney store in your local mall. But you do go to Quincy Market for its products, and secondarily for its atmosphere. So, though both have no inhabitants, we need to distinguish them on the basis of the relative priority of immersion in fantasy versus retail sales. Themed residential areas might be divided in a similar fashion; in some the theme might be a primary goal, but in most it provides only a supportive atmosphere for activities that people would be doing anyway.

But these distinctions do not explain what a theme is. When does decor become a theme? Is St. Peter's in Rome a themed place? The Seagram Building? The U.S. Capitol? We need to distinguish themes from related notions such as decor, unified design, atmosphere, and ambience, and from allusions and references. Just what it does it mean for a place to have a theme?

Consider a restaurant in Kraków located in a high-vaulted basement. It has candles in sconces on the walls, wooden trestle tables, and objects on display that give the place a distinctive and pervasive character. The atmosphere is stimulating, but it does not create a theme. For one thing, the waitstaff is not on view in the same way the walls are. If, on the other hand, they were costumed to fit the decor, and acted in special ways, then the restaurant might be themed rather than just atmospheric. (I say "might be themed" because there are additional conditions, as explained below.) By contrast, consider a themed Elizabethan banquet held in the actual dining hall of the English castle where Queen

Elizabeth I spent her youth. The staff is costumed and behaves in what is deemed an Elizabethan manner, there is an actress playing Elizabeth who leads various participative events during the dinner, and the guests are instructed how to eat in the appropriate fashion and how to treat the staff imperiously.

Whether or not a place is themed does not depend simply on its decor, nor on how it is received by the visitor. Rather it depends on the place's institutionalized mode of self-presentation. What is important is the source of the unity of the decor and atmosphere. Suppose a bar is to have an Irish theme. It will likely use the color green (rather than blue), and probably include certain styles of windows, representations of shamrocks (rather than roses), and so on. The bar will probably serve certain kinds of beer, and the waitstaff will dress in particular ways and encourage certain behaviors among the customers. The Irish restaurant does not just happen to have all these features because the owner likes green and Guinness. These features are not just randomly combined, nor are they there because they seem aesthetically harmonious: the explanation for their combination is found elsewhere, in an established "Irishness" that provides a unified meaning and narrative for the multiple details.

The character of a place is distinct from its place norms, as we know because there can be social norms creating places that lack unified character, as well as locales with character that are not social places. In themed places, however, the norms for the place decree that it should feature a unified character, which is to be controlled by an unusually detailed set of prescriptions for actions and decor. The unity of these norms is found in an already established meaning.

But there is more. Not only is a themed place influenced by social norms, it self-consciously presents itself *as so influenced*, and this self-presentation is itself on display. In the Irish bar the unity of the place's Irishness is being self-consciously displayed *as being self-consciously displayed*. The norms for the place demand self-conscious display of the controlling normative meaning for the place. There is a norm of presenting the norms *as* presented norms for the customer to encounter as such.

There is still more. We should be able to distinguish between a themed place and other kinds of self-conscious places. Rome is flamboyantly Italian; is it then a themed place? The Paris that Gandelsonas criticized presents itself explicitly to the tourist; does that make it a themed place?

There are many kinds of self-display, not all of them the same as theming. In a themed place the social norms are self-consciously presented *as other* and *as different from the local everyday* expectations.

If a place does not put itself forward as representing something other, but is just a place where people live in a different manner, even quite self-consciously so, it may still be a tourist destination, but it is not a themed place. *Having* a different mode of life is not the same as *representing* a different mode of life. Being a *piece* of another culture is not the same as being a self-consciously presented *representation* of that culture. Boston's North End, or Chicago's ethnic neighborhoods, offer visitors a chance to encounter a different way of life there—in the behavior and body language of the inhabitants, in their use of public areas, in food, and so on. This is more like visiting another country than visiting a themed replica.[2]

A themed place, then, involves the self-presentation of the place as a self-conscious representation of something else. More precisely, a themed place has a unified normative meaning and narrative that controls the details of its decor and character, and a themed place self-consciously presents that meaning and character *as* self-consciously presented, as influencing those details, as *different* from the norms and character of local everyday places, and as based on a unified ruling meaning that is already established elsewhere.[3]

This means that the reference to what is outside the themed place is a constitutive element in the place. Though they pretend to offer total absorption in their themes, themed places rely on a continual awareness of the outside and their difference from it.

Theme concerns not just the character of a place, but also the relation of a place's character to its social norms. A theme can affect a place's norms and function to varying degrees. In a theme park consuming and enjoying the self-consciously presented character becomes the major function of the place. In themed restaurants or malls, other activities are the main functions but are qualified by thematic unities.

In a themed place the social norms reach far into the details of the place's atmosphere and decor, and enjoin a peculiar doubled mode of self-presentation. A restaurant may still be a restaurant when a theme is added, but it will have a new kind of relation to itself.

Though themes employ symbols, a theme is not a symbol, but rather a unified meaning or identity that controls the use of symbols. Similarly, a theme is not a single route of action, though in some themed rides and themed tourist towns there are routes along which you are hauled. The theme is not the route but the normative identity of the world of possibilities through which the routes move. Themes define norms for social practice; they are not accidental products of audience reactions but are norms for social practice. In principle a theme has to be recognizable, but it also explains how we may know that a place is themed even though we do not recognize its particular theme, because we feel the unity and intensity of the place's self-conscious self-presentation.

The definition of a themed place requires that the theme present itself as referring to an established unity of meaning or identity. Strictly speaking, that unity does not have to be oversimplified, but everything in the process of theming encourages simplification, since the real identity of, say, Irishness or the Wild West would be more contested and complex than is convenient for a place where the theme must be clearly available.

There is also a distinction between being a sample of an identity and being a themed replica of that identity. A cathedral in Europe can be an example of Gothic architecture without having a Gothic theme. The church is not a themed place just because it is an object of the tourist gaze. A place that is a sample, in Nelson Goodman's sense (N. Goodman 1976), may or may not also be a themed place; this depends on its institutional setting and normative mode of self-presentation. Theming's doubled self-conscious presentation *of* its self-conscious presentation of otherness explains the difference between a European cathedral and its Las Vegas replica. Even if the Las Vegas cathedral were an exact duplicate, even if the whole European town were replicated, it would be presented *as* being presented as a European town *in* its otherness.[4]

Themes weaken if they come to be accepted as part of the everyday. For instance, the decor in the average Chinese restaurant in America may have once had a theme effect, but now it is taken as a sign of an everyday sort of restaurant, so giving a restaurant a Chinese theme now requires much more extravagant gestures than before.

Some themed places are multithemed. Disney's Magic Kingdom fantasy areas or Epcot national areas have no closed borders, so sound and sight overlap, clashing and enticing you, as well as providing occasions for complexity and psychic distance. Most themed places are monothemed, as all those Frontierlands, Santa Claus towns, and the like.

Monothemed places are more numerous, and more problematic from a critical point of view, since multithemed places increase one's awareness of theme fantasies as such.[5]

THEMES COMPARED WITH OTHER UNITIES

There are many kinds of normative and design unity, and theming is only one type. Consider the unique architectural character that might be created when an architect plans a house or remodels a restaurant with repetitions and details invented by the architect. The architect's design might be based on his or her ideal of how people should live, but such a design would not offer the kind of meaning based on a social "elsewhere" provided by Irishness or the Wild West.[6] A theme provides a ready-made normative identity, so theming is easier than creating a unique architectural character.

No matter how strong they may be, decor and atmosphere by themselves do not necessarily create a theme that refers to an established cultural meaning elsewhere. But it is important to note the ways in which decor and atmosphere, as well as spatial and architectural effects, can work on us independently of place norms. Designers and architects can create such effects without creating self-conscious themes. Heights and massing and proportion and color, the location of entrances and transitions between different spaces all have effects on us in ways other than as signifiers. Themed places may then use these effects as signifiers, but the theme and the architectural effect are not the same.

For instance, Michael Graves's Dolphin and Swan hotels in Orlando have strong identities involving repeated images and colors and fabrics, together with dramatic spatial modulations, but they are not themed places. There are a number of themed hotels nearby: Wilderness, Caribbean, Western, and the Portofino Bay Hotel. The Dolphin and Swan are arresting because of their dramatic architectures. The other themed hotels are mostly so predictable that the eye passes quickly over them. Their themes are communicated by visual clichés. Whereas the Dolphin and Swan have unusual shapes and sudden changes of scale, the other resort hotels are familiar boxes with surface decorations. The Portofino Bay Hotel differs because the hotel is designed to resemble a cluster of differently sized buildings in the Italian port town, but even there the effects are mostly scenographic rather than spatial.

Although themed places are certainly stagy, they are not the only kind of places designed to produce emotional and behavioral effects through architecture and decor. There are many kinds of immersive environments designed for unified character and maximum effect. These include high-design retail and restaurants, but also fast-food franchises and low-budget outlets offering meticulously designed cheap atmospheres. Such environments are not always themed places, because their place norms and character may not refer to some normative cultural image or meaning located elsewhere.

Imperial capitals such as Rome and Paris were designed to produce feelings of grandeur and submission. These, and religious places, were and are very manipulative in their architecture, but they are not necessarily themed places, for the normative meaning that they self-consciously display *is* their everyday life. They are emphatically not about a different elsewhere (though the daily life they present may itself include powerful references to a hereafter or a total cosmology or a far-flung empire).

Themed places carry to extremes the tendency to scenography and surface effects found in so many places today. But we should not call all scenographic places themed, for doing so lessens our capacity for critical distinctions. In the eyes of many architects all such places sin because they work through clichés and rely on easy emotional reactions rather than on good creative design. Still, it is important to distinguish these complaints about oversimplification from the questionable modernist ideal of the honest architect who always creates a novel form.[7]

Next, a theme is not a style. In Art Deco or International Style buildings, it seems directly perceptible how this color and these shapes go together aesthetically. We can sense why modernist flat roofs have been combined with ribbon windows and open plans. We perceive an appropriateness, if not a necessity, in the combinations. On the other hand, in an Irish bar the greens and the beer and the accent have no perceptible reason why they should be combined, except that they refer to a pre-established identity. However, it is no accident that the easiest examples of perceptibly unified style are recent and familiar. We have become accustomed to those unities. Appropriateness in complex historical styles such as the Baroque is not so easy to sense. Also, the more historical and the more elaborate the style, the more the unity of the style will refer to earlier precedents. Should we then say that historical styles are actually themes? A Baroque or Gothic building can be a sample without being themed. In addition, styles need followers, whereas themes do not. If a style is not picked up by others, it is at best an attempt at creating a style. Repetition opens the difference between the paradigmatic example and the style itself. But a theme can be created without needing a following. The distance between the themed place and its theme is built into the act of thematic reference.

Finally, a themed place is not deceptive. Some find the experience of themed places demeaning, feeling that something is being put over on them. However, a theme is not a put-on or a fraud, because a theme will not work if it is presented as straightforward reality. Themed places depend for their attraction on a display of their otherness from the everyday. In a themed restaurant you are not being fooled into thinking that you are in 1920s New York. You are enjoying the complexity of being in a Texas restaurant and having the identity of 1920s New York playing about you.

There is, though, a type of deception that does involve theming. Consider again the difference between a place that is a sample of another culture and a place that is themed as another culture. A family restaurant in a large Chinatown is not the same as a Chinese-themed restaurant in a suburban mall. In the Chinatown restaurant little signs in Chinese announcing various dishes may be posted on the wall; this is not for touristic effect but for the convenience of patrons accustomed to the Chinese way of displaying menus. Other patrons receive a more limited menu in English. A suburban Chinese restaurant may have much more elaborate and stereotypical Chinese decor than the Chinatown restaurant, and any Chinese characters on the menu or menus on the wall will be there mostly for touristic effect. The Chinatown restaurant is a piece of Chinese culture, the suburban restaurant is themed Chinese. Given that distinction, there is a deception possible, if we are led to think that entering the suburban restaurant puts us into a piece of China. The deception lies not in being themed but in claiming to be more than themed.

Themed places refer to established meanings and narratives. If you are creating an Irish bar, you refer to an Irishness established by a normative selection from the myriad details and variations of Irish life. Such unities may be assembled out of history, as when Sir Walter Scott and others made the Highlanders central to Scottish identity. Or the unities themes refer to may accrete by selection and combination of existing

and invented traits and paradigmatic places. This process of canoniza-
tion is seldom peaceful or consensual, and there may be competing versions of theme unities such as Irishness or Parisian life.

However, a themed place could refer to a unity of meaning that was
being established at the same time as the place. For instance, if a national identity was in the process of being created in a newly independent region that was trying to enforce unity upon a diverse population,
the government could establish a theme park that represented and in-
culcated the national character it was trying to create. The government
would likely combine some items and repress others from the subtradi-
tions it was trying to unify. Self-establishing themes can also be created
from scratch. For instance, a corporation might create a theme when
designing a building that it hopes will instill a certain spirit in its employees. Or, a theme park might be created to celebrate and sell a set
of products that were launched at the same time as the park. Puroland
park in Tokyo celebrates Hello Kitty, which is a general brand, a cute image that almost any product can license. The brand was established before the park, but they could have originated together in a giant marketing extravaganza. In these cases the place would be set up as referring to
the theme as if the theme were long established, but in fact the theme
and the distance between the place and the theme would be created
along with the place. It is the act of referring to the theme as already
established that establishes it, widening the gap between the theme and
the local instance.

Throughout this discussion I have been describing themes as if the
notion of representation were unproblematic. Though this is hardly
the case, themed places present themselves as if representation were
a straightforward relation. A theme exists in the gap and the connection between a themed place and its unifying prior meaning, even if the
meaning was established along with the themed place. A theme makes
an appearance of representation even when that relation is fictionalized.
Whether self-establishing or already established, themes are not simple
entities.

In some cases the prior unity of a themed place appeals to an established commercial brand, such as Hello Kitty or Star Wars. Or the
unity may be a historical locale or character that has effectively become
a brand, such as Paris. Not all themes become brands; most historical
themed reconstructions and tourist destinations do not achieve that

status. But perhaps all themes are brand wannabes. Themed places are meant to attract, and brands are successful attractors. Becoming a brand is one of those cases in which a change in quantity can bring a change in quality and relationship. As the prominence or the velocity of the theme rises above some threshold, it becomes a brand. It begins to be compared with other prominent theme-brands, and it may become a term used to characterize other experiences than its own—this is a Disneyesque place, that is a Star Wars sort of film.[8]

Brands pull other distinctions into the field of brand comparisons. Themes add meaning, but brands add velocity and celebrity. There is a Gresham's law at work. Brands push against you, urging you to take them into your identity. They can push against older unities too, as when tourist branding threatens to simplify a tourist destination. Themed places seem to epitomize our commercialized culture, but once again we should be wary of confusing legitimate issues about oversimplification with questionable criticisms that spread the accusation of theming or commodification so widely that the terms lose their critical bite.

ALL PLACES ARE OPEN TO BEING THEMED

Critics often treat themes as if they were some perverse addition laid over authentic places. But openness to being themed is inherent in the very conditions that make an area into a place. Any place must have some social norms, and the possibility of being themed is inherent in the unity of a set of norms. The conditions for the existence of places are such that theming is always an intrinsic possibility for a place, but it does not follow that all places are themed.

First, the social norms for a place distinguish aspects of the area and define local expectations. Some places have more detailed norms than others; a courthouse or a legislature might specify where you can walk, what you do in the room, what clothes are appropriate, how the room must be decorated, and so on. Themed places have very explicit normative meanings controlling many aspects of the place's appearance, atmosphere, and activities. But any place might have its norms extended in a similar way for other purposes, for architectural effects, security, to preserve uniqueness, and so on.

Second, no one lives in a pure state of un-self-presentation. Merchants in Boston's North End no doubt play up their Italianness when this facilitates business with outsiders. Is that much different from a medieval peddler appearing exotic for his customers, or a Turkish merchant emphasizing his identity in order to sell rugs to travelers? Chicago ethnic neighborhoods have been encouraged to erect markers at their entry points; these combine communal affirmation and touristic identification. They do not instantly make the neighborhoods into themed places, but the self-consciousness they provoke and celebrate can lead to the doubled self-presentation of a themed place.

Third, all places present their own unity. A place presents itself as a field for actions. Actions have to be identifiable in order to be intended, and actions stretch over time and space. So an identifiable field with temporal and spatial unity must be presented by the place. That unity might be unclassical and strange, but it has to be there. Action and place cannot be a totally disjointed multiplicity, as Kant showed by his arguments that some temporal and spatial structure beyond pure sequence is necessary for there to be experience at all. The presented unity of a place can be very minimal or quite baroque, and there are new kinds of discontinuous unities. In all cases there has to be some presented unity to the place, and themes present such unity in their own particular ways.

Fourth, no place has an identity that is purely internal. Describing a themed place as relying on an identity established elsewhere may seem to imply that nonthemed places have identities that are established wholly without external reference. That is not the case, for both the here and the elsewhere are what they are because of their relations and contrasts rather than as a result of immediately given identities. Many ordinary places have identities that include prominent references to other meanings and places. The norms of courtroom activities refer explicitly to earlier English and U.S. practices. Places of worship and shrines depend on distant references. There can be many kinds and degrees of reference, often leveled down, as with the commonly accepted American house styles. But there is no zero degree of relation, no place whose identity has no references at all elsewhere. Places involve meanings and norms, and meaning comes from contrast and relation to absent others. It is theoretically possible that there are networks of places that have no connections of meaning to our own, but there are no places that are purely single and self-referential. So a themed place's reference to meaning elsewhere is a modulation of something that happens in all places.

Since any place has a meaning that includes some reference to elsewhere, and any place may have its norms extended to cover more details of its character and actions, and since all places present their unity in at least minimally self-conscious ways, it follows that far from being a foreign addition to places, theming happens through a particular extension of what is already going on in all places.

However, we cannot conclude that all places are at least a little themed, for doing so would confuse unity in general with a specific kind of unity. All places have mediated unities, but theming consists in a particular kind of mediated unity and a particular kind of self-conscious unity. Those particular effects that themes create generally narrow the ways in which a place expresses the basic conditions that make it a place.

APPRAISING THEMED PLACES

Once we see how theming is always a possibility, we can also see why theming and simplification usually go together. Theming foregrounds a place and avoids complex intersecting roles and norms that would take a long time to understand and so decrease the place's immediate attraction. Theming's regimented design and action norms narrow the possibilities for places. A themed place may have an explicit and detailed character, but in order for it to be readily available the theme has to simplify the texture of any lived identity it refers to. Themed places suppress the way in which unities like Irishness are always under reconstruction and contentious reinterpretation. Themes discipline places. Theming restricts a place's natural connectivity down to one channel, and a themed place's explicit and foregrounded doubling of self-consciousness subordinates the many modes of self-reference to one dominant self-presentation. So what is needed to get beyond the theme is an awareness of the complexity and process beyond what is immediately presented.

What criteria can we employ to appraise themed places? Although there is no single master scale, we have a variety of measures. There are general criteria of architectural and aesthetic quality, and then there are criteria about theming in particular. Themes come in degrees of intensity and reach. Places can vary in the force with which the theme asserts itself, and in how far the theme norms reach down into details of decor and action. Themes also come with different spatial densities. For instance, at Disney's Epcot the Canadian section juxtaposes a few large buildings that are representative of Canada, whereas the English and

Italian sections mix many smaller references together. Themes vary in the degree to which they are established and familiar, and in how often they are referred to by other places. Finally, themes vary in the role they play. A theme can merely add titillation, or it can provide deliberate incongruity, or selling and consuming the theme can absorb the whole being of the place.

None of the variations just mentioned settle issues of quality, but they lead to more directly evaluative measures. One is the completeness and accuracy of the place's theme (especially relevant in educational themed places).[9] Another is the appropriateness of the theme for its intended audience, and another the moral and political rightness of the place's purpose.

Then there is the degree of complexity within the theme. At Epcot, the boat ride in the Mexican section runs the viewer by a series of tableaux and animatronic figures that enact the most clichéd stereotypes of Mexican tourism, whereas in the Chinese area a 360-degree film attempts to get beyond standard images of China.[10] At times it may be appropriate to have simplified themed places, but the judgment when that is appropriate already locates the simplified place within a more complex context. Complexity is also in the degree of explicit self-awareness the themed place encourages.

Another criterion often cited when discussing themed places is authenticity. This turns out not to be a useful criterion, however: it is not easy to decide just what authenticity is, nor how to apply it to concrete places.[11] For instance, tourists at Taos and other Southwest pueblos have been disturbed by the inauthenticity of Native Americans doing their ritual dances while wearing Nike shoes. However, since the dances are contemporary religious celebrations and not just staged performances, the Nikes are actually the more authentic footwear (Lippard 1999, 67). Also, inauthenticity may be quite acceptable when experienced in a sufficiently aware situation. "[Tourists] are not dupes, and they realize that the native performances on their tour itinerary are constructions for a foreign audience. Tourists are willing to accept a reproduction as long as it is a good one, or as one tourist brochure put it, as long as it is an 'authentic reproduction'" (McCrone 1995, 47).[12]

Whereas the cry against theming on behalf of authenticity is too vague to be helpful, the anxiety behind the cry is legitimate. Although theming can bring novelty and variety to places, themes narrow the range of references and the kinds of self-awareness in places. The content the theme offers is usually an oversimplified version of some way of life or social identity. So themed places can lead into that series of simplified intensities that is the bane of today's places.[13]

Such narrowing can be resisted. The complexity of a themed place is found in its borders, which are everywhere within it. The attraction of the themed place depends on the border, where it contrasts with the everyday. Themed places disconnect people from ordinary living while reconnecting them over the discontinuity. If that contrast is not active enough, the themed place will seem thin and stagy, as do many roadside themed attractions. Within its professional glitz, Disney must offer more points of contrast and borders with the everyday, delineating the theme from other unities of meaning. Those borders overdraw the unity and consistency of the theme, and its separateness from other meanings. Also, the norms for a themed place demand references to what is outside, though those references may be put out of explicit sight.

So it should be possible to increase the complexity of our inhabitation of the place by seeing the presented unity in the theme for what it is, and emphasizing references to the outside, and the place's insertion into larger contexts and processes. This does not mean we must deny all themes, but it does imply that we should refuse them total control. The thematic self-presentation is always already surrounded by richer context, so what is needed is for people attending themed places to amplify the modes of self-awareness and self-reference already operative until that awareness exceeds what is offered by the official self-definition of the place.[14]

DOUBLE DISNEY, DOUBLE THRILLS

This resistance to or supplementing of themed places requires a kind of doubled inhabitation. But that is already active at a themed place as users actively cooperate with the theme. If we look closer at the experience of a Disney theme park we can learn more about how to be more conscious in a themed place. Disney provides the master referent for so many discussions. Is it really a total fascination, the excessive Baudrillardian simulacrum, the pinnacle of the society of spectacle, and so on?[15]

The experience of a theme park is not a simple immersion in fantasy and spectacle. Inhabitation is doubled. Walt Disney is reported to have said that he wanted the public to feel they had entered another world, with no sight of the real world. (Over the entrance to Disneyland, a sign reads "Here you leave today and enter the world of yesterday, tomorrow and fantasy.")[16] However, the Walt Disney corporation would not want us to become totally immersed in its fantasies. If we were totally to *become* Mississippi steamboat passengers or Star Wars characters, immersed in their concerns and goals and fears and anxieties, we would not have the concomitant awareness that the experience was "fun" and "different." Would we *really* want to *fully* believe that Darth Vader was pursuing us? A theme park is an attraction, not a conversion to a new identity. For the themed place to exercise its attraction, we need a doubled inhabitation, one that plays at being in the theme, but is also aware of the theme's difference from everyday life, and enjoys that difference and the ways in which the themed effect is brought about.[17]

Riding the riverboat in Disney's Magic Kingdom, you can admire the pains Disney designers have taken to use a functioning steam engine on the boat. But closer examination and the feel of the boat as it turns will reveal that the big chuffing steam engine does not propel the boat. The boat is being towed along an underwater track, so that no steersman is needed and so that the animatronic events on the shore can be automatically triggered at the right times. It is not hard to discover that the boat is not propelled by the engine. There is enough realism for a surface effect, but it is quite acceptable to see the trick. Part of the experience is the wondering "how do they do this?" One enters into the fantasy world but also admires its staging.

Attacking Baudrillard's claim that Disney aims to create "an infantile world" (Baudrillard 1983, 26), Michael Pinsky points out that

> The willingness to participate implicitly in the simulations—that is, buying a ticket and entering the front gate—does not necessarily lead to a total acceptance of the originary structures which ground those simulations. As J. Derek Harrison states, "Most children are not fooled by electronic fantasies; on the contrary, they are curious to know how it works." What Baudrillard refers to as infantile is in fact an acknowledgment of a self-conscious position from which the simulation is both observed and critiqued. Few

> people are taken in by the illusions at Disney parks. . . . The simu-
> lated structures are both supported and undermined by the very
> act of complicity which allows the observer access to them. (Pinsky
> 1992, 101–2)

This is no simple absorption. Participating in the fantasies is like seeing a play or a movie, sweating and fearing with a character, while also admiring how the actress performs the role, and the way the background is altered in the special effects. The audience is involved in both the story and in its staging, and enjoys that interplay.[18]

Double inhabitation is inevitable and necessary for the attraction of themed places. Aviad Raz, however, argues in his study of Tokyo Disneyland that theme parks try to discourage explicit reflection on one's performance as audience or cast member.

> In Disneyland guests are never an active part of the show. . . .
> [The] absence [of fun house mirrors] from Disneyland is no ac-
> cident. Mirrors encourage reflexivity . . . they may very well destroy
> the performative illusion of Disneyland. . . . Seeing his or her re-
> flection in a mirror might also disturb a Disney costumed charac-
> ter. . . . acting as a cast member . . . involves maintaining . . . a split
> between bodily displays (such as a smile) and awareness of inter-
> nal, psycho-physical sensations (such as boredom or annoyance).
> Reflexivity . . . is, therefore, a burden in Disneyland for both visi-
> tors and employees. (Raz 1999, 188)

Raz does go on to say there are many kinds of consumers, not all of whom are so infantilized. "[Tokyo Disneyland's] Japanese visitors are also rational consumers, making their own choices, working Disney into their own everyday life. This, I would dare to suggest, applies just as well to many of Disney's American consumers" (Raz 1999, 198). Raz and I are speaking about different kinds of self-awareness. I am stressing the concomitant duality of immersion and staging, where both awarenesses are focused on the object, but in different modes. Raz is concerned about dualities where one awareness is on the object and another on the self, an act plus a reflection on that act. The unavoidability of my duality means that Raz's can never be fully blocked, but the first can exist without the second.

In his essay, "You Have to Pay for the Public Life," Charles Moore argues that Disneyland provides amid its fantasies a place that "re-creates all the chances to respond to a public environment which Los Angeles particularly no longer has. It allows play-acting, both to be watched and to be participated in, in a public sphere. . . . Disney has created a place, indeed a whole public world, full of sequential occurrences, of big and little drama, full of hierarchies of importance and excitement. . . . And all this diversity, with unerring sensitivity, is keyed to the kind of participation without embarrassment which apparently at this point in our history we crave" (Moore 2001, 126–27). Moore is describing a mode of double inhabitation where people enjoy real experiences of public participation that are created by the theme of Main Street. He admits that public life in Disneyland is incomplete since it lacks "the political experience," but he insists that more is going on than immersion in fantasy; indeed he judges the Fantasyland segment less successful because its full fantasy mode weakens the connection between its public spaces and our everyday desires for public life.

Sometimes Disney explicitly acknowledges this double inhabitation. In Disney's Animal Kingdom park in Florida, the zones of the park (Africa, Asia, Dinoland, etc.) are each themed with details drawn from familiar cinematic images. The zones are separated by belts of trees so that their themes seldom interact. However, there is an official backstage area that caters to our desire to see how the fantasies are maintained. On the train to this Conservation Station the narration points out the barns where the "wild" African animals come in the evening when they are called in to be fed, and in the station you can find out about how the animals are trained, the invisible ways in which they are kept apart from one another on what appears to be open savannah, their embedded identifying microchips, and their annual physical checkups. You can watch veterinarians caring for them, mixing their food, and so on. You presume there is a more distant backstage where the vets do gruesome operations out of the limelight. Some people wonder if the whole backstage is a put-on—a staffer said that she gets asked if the vets seen working behind the windows are merely actors. Such skepticism hardly reveals a total immersion in fantasy. While the official message of Disney's Animal Kingdom is conservation and protection of wildlife—you get instruction about improving the habitat for wildlife around your home, and other messages about care for the environment—the theme of the park is the myth of an unspoiled peaceful nature threatened by human evil. Ironically, in order to create the story line of an untouched nature, the African animals have to be extracted from their native environment, manipulated, and controlled, and the grounds have to be patrolled in order to keep innocent Florida wildlife from making an appearance. But this is not kept a secret, and at the Conservation Station you can learn how park staff round up trespassing raccoons, give them rabies shots, and release them outside the walls. A guide said regretfully that they had still found no way to keep local birds from appearing on the African scene.

People may fantasize a total immersion with no double of participating and staging, yearning for an impossible childhood. However, children too can live doubly. Once a three-year-old child and I were playing Scare Me!, making faces and popping out from behind cushions; the child seemed completely terrified—screams, frenzied face, trembling arms—then suddenly he became quite calm, suggested changes in my mode of scaring him, then became all fright again. We project simplicity onto children, as onto our ancestors.[19]

This doubled inhabitation does not occur between a social role and a neutral observer, but between two roles. The duality is not a division between a role being played and a Weberian or economic maximizer behind all the roles. The stage manager is not maximizing personal utilities from a position outside all rituals. There is no naked self behind it; the complex process is all. Such doubling can itself have many modes, and one goal of education is to create more subtle and critical modes of doubled inhabitation.[20]

Double inhabitation even occurs in what are called in Disney parlance screamers rather than dreamers. Although many of the thrill rides are themselves themed, what people remember most is the vertigo. Thrill rides do not need themes because their basic impact comes from context-free biological effects.

> Star Tours and Splash Mountain . . . are indeed the most popular
> in the park. . . . This is the play element described as illinx by . . .
> Roger Callois: "The pursuit of vertigo . . . consists of an attempt to
> destroy the stability of perception and inflict a kind of voluptuous
> panic upon an otherwise lucid mind." . . . The desire for disorder
> . . . normally repressed, is here given leeway to erupt—and then

repressed again, proving that everything is in fact under control.
(Raz 1999, 181)

Thrills can be desirable as a suspension of complexity by way of a thrust into immediate presence. Bodily disorientation and real or perceived danger pull us out of textual loops and confront us with our fragile existence. The advertisement for one Universal Studios park reads, "Are you ready to feel more alive?" and says that at the park "hearts pound, imaginations soar." (Does this say something about the routinization that makes daily life possible? A steady diet of extreme situations might level off into serial simplified intensities.)

Nonetheless, thrill experiences have their own doubled inhabitation. People talk enthusiastically about a roller coaster to those considering riding it. Usually the rides are in plain view, to attract riders but also to prestage their experiences. Then the ride itself is taken in a group. Afterward, people relive effects and thrills with one another. The talk surrounding thrill rides stages the thrill by preparing a space for enjoying it without real panic. In this way the roller coaster ride, too, is a staged ritual.

The most self-conscious staging for thrill rides that I have yet seen is found in virtual reality installations where you first design a roller coaster and then ride it. Individually or in groups of two or three you stand at a screen, choose a scenic environment, and assemble track segments from a menu; then you enter a capsule that spins and rotates so that while the screen inside shows the environment and track you planned, you experience the forces of its twists and loops and drops. This principle could be carried beyond vertigo thrills. Imagine specifying the plot of the virtual adventure your group is about to begin, perhaps choosing from among high-level constraints that will still surprise you by the details you encounter. You might select percentages of possible outcomes, or generic types of villains and obstacles. Imagine the social interaction among people who had to agree in advance upon the parameters of the adventure in which they were about to "immerse" themselves. Such negotiations happen among participants in multiperson online games.

Themed places, like religious and political rituals, and like education, involve the consensual engineering of experiences. Our economy makes business out of engineering what are supposed to be peak experiences, so it is tempting to downgrade all such experiences as artificial. But is there any peak experience that is not somewhat engineered? Think of sexual relating, think of religious meditation, a political rally, a class lecture, an oral examination, a mountain climb. In all these, we are both immersed in and staging the experience, and aware of its contrast with the outside. All involve shared artifice, without being artificial in the sense of replacing some natural experience of the same type. The most direct encounter is still staged. Even the spontaneous interactions of Zen pupils and masters come after long practice in spontaneity. Though we seek it, there is no pure ecstasy outside of the double—or if there is, then, as Plotinus says, there is no separate self when it happens, so it is not "an experience" except retrospectively, and thus doubled in a different way.[21]

Teachers engineer what they hope will be intense educational experiences, and people are supposed to learn from them, not just flow with them. This demands cooperative staging from people who have learned how to be students. Both teacher and student live the participant-staging duality, and their cooperative work may in the future become more like the joint staging of virtual adventures mentioned above. As for off-peak educational experiences, those straight transfers of information or completely prestaged spectacles that are not especially responsive to the present interaction of teacher and student, those experiences will likely be automated out of the teacher's hands.

We should not describe education—or the criticism of places—as if there were a completely new critical attitude to be added onto a naive immersion. Educators aim to strengthen the self-critical, "why are we doing this?" and "stage it more intensely!" attitudes that are already at work. Educators hope to enlarge students' scale of awareness so that students come to realize that they are already inside more and larger actions, games, rituals, ongoing projects, and histories than they think they are. They are already making moves in wider games, and they need to be self-consciously critical all the way up and down. This does not demand that they occupy some position outside the plays and rituals.

All of this holds as well for the experience of themed places. The real threat is not immersion but oversimplification. All themed places simplify, and most ask nothing more than cash and attention and some familiarity with cultural icons.[22] No change in attitude or behavior is needed. The representation stays within the familiar, for the greatest attractive power. There are carefully rationed doses of otherness; we may be informed, but we attain no new form.[23] The solution is not to occupy some position outside the place's plays and rituals, but to mobilize the native double inhabitation that is always already active.

DEALING WITH THE DANGERS OF THEMES

Self-aware complexity is a mode of critical living in places, and it provides one way around some problematic aspects of themed places. Architectural and urban writers enjoy attacking theme parks. Disney's success and its self-promotion as a land of innocence and true American values make it an especially appealing target.[24] Writers opposed to theming worry that seductive immersion in themes produces unrealistic dreams of a simpler life and reinforces ideological constructions that hide oppressions.

I have argued, however, that there can be no total immersion in themes because themes depend on doubled inhabitation and comparisons with everyday life. The attraction of themed places requires borders setting off their unity. The border is the place of seduction and encounter created by the place's disconnection from the everyday, a disconnection that must function all throughout the place. Besides, theme parks are only one type of themed place, and most themed places use themes as an attractive background for everyday activities: eating a meal, shopping, living in a neighborhood.

Critics also fear that themed places may form or educate people in dangerous ways, for instance through simplifications and passive receptivity.

> "What Disneyland proposes is a technique of abbreviated short-hand culture for the masses, a mindless thrill. . . . In a forthcoming time of highly governed masses in an overpopulated world, this technique may be extremely useful both as a substitute for education, and, eventually, as a substitute for experience. Disney's symbols, in other words, determine the limits of consumers' imagination" [quotation by E. L. Doctorow]. The troubling conclusion is that the space for imaginative play in the modern theme park has become so preconceived, textually sated, and institutionally self-referential (many of the areas of Disney World are recapitulations of Disney movies), that the experience has become strangely

passive despite the apparent imaginative exuberance that attends
it. (Harwood 2002, 66)

Simplification is inevitable in themed places, as I argued earlier in this
chapter. Themed identities become simplified for easy consumption,
and theming itself restricts a place's links and relations. However, simplicity and passive consumption are hardly unique to theme parks. The
system pressures for commodified simplicity are discussed in the previous chapter. In themed places such simplification may actually be less
worrisome, since themed places need to contrast what they present with
what is outside the boundaries, so their simplifications cannot go unnoticed. Still, insofar as a themed place offers what amounts to bad education, the solution will be better education that includes more complexity
and linkage. Themed places offer chances for such expansion because
their double inhabitation provides an opening for possibilities that go
beyond the discipline imposed by the theme. Passivity with regard to imposed meanings and values can be countered by an awareness of active
reception, for all places are maintained by active interpretation, even
though a place's norms and structures may try to hide that from its users.
Themed places demand more explicit acts of reception and contrast, or
else the theme sinks into a neutral background and loses its influence, as
do the historical styles in American housing.[25]

In multithemed places such as Disney's Magic Kingdom, the collisions
and comparisons among the themed areas emphasize the act of moving
from one to another and can increase awareness, reminding visitors that
their presence in the place is more complex than any single theme. In
a monothemed place designed to sweep visitors up into an intense flow,
there is still dispersal and unity, though now in the temporal dimension.
The theme's unity ties the flow together across time, keeping it from being an unrelated sequence of intense thrills. This provides opportunities
for emphasizing the flow as such, aware of its transitions as carried by the
visitor's active construction.

Then there are the references outside. All themed places are framed,
but once we are inside, the frame plays a double game of presence
through absence. Themed places cannot keep that game totally invisible or they lose their attraction. What seems like a suspension of the
larger context is a way of keeping it always present in the background.
The theme butts up against the everyday world, fostering awareness of

borders and limits and of links across time and out of the fantasy. Then at times the larger context is forced onto people, for instance when they have to deal with biological needs. Disney does not provide medieval bathrooms or period food service, so the ordinary world reaches into the theme. Theme parks may try to make standing in lines part of the themed experience, but the fact of crowds and waiting cannot be ignored. Disney tries to make trash removal unobtrusive, but the staff involved are not invisible, even if the machinery below the podium is. Then there is the penetration of the fantasy by the world around it. Cell phones ring. If to stop that interruption the cell phones were banned or turned off at the entry, the contemporary world would remain present as a lack.

One could imagine creating a theme park that deliberately exaggerated these discontinuities: space-age bathrooms inside a medieval hut, period food, or requiring visitors to change clothing or walk streets that harbored the filth and smells of old. Such tactics resemble Stan Allen's suggestion, cited in chapter 4, about making the simulacrum function as a reality. Such tactics might be useful for designing a theme park, but what can visitors do? Visitors are not passive; they help stage their experiences, and they could work at emphasizing contrasts and discontinuities.

Themed places are not received passively; they exist through cooperative staging. Critics of themed places would argue that themed places nevertheless manipulate people in dangerous ways. In cooperating with the theme visitors are practicing attitudes and behaviors that might not be socially beneficial. This fear seems odd if applied to the vast majority of themed places. Is there great social danger from Santa Claus Villages and Chinese restaurants? The real targets of the criticism are special places designed to foster particular nationalistic or religious behaviors and ideologies. These are not Santa Claus Village but historical reconstructions such as Virginia's Williamsburg and Sweden's Skansen, or homeland fantasies such as (parts of) Disneyland, and twenty-first-century religious theme parks.[26] Such places put the visitor into idealized settings that are meant to contrast with the present and show how life might be again if certain values and patterns could be restored.

> At Williamsburg, as at Disneyland, moreover, there is an implicit
> and carefully nurtured assumption that we live in a postlapsar-

ian America and are, as a result, consumed by a nostalgic long-
ing to regain an authentic national culture from which we have
grown increasingly distant. This lost but intensely desired culture
was grounded in a life of simple patterns in which no labor was
alienated and all social relationships were face-to-face. (Harwood
2002, 61)

More generally,

The ubiquity of the image in photographs, printing, and electronic
media has fostered a culture in which the look far outweighs the
substance. We can call it exotic; we can call it phony; we can call it
escapist; we can call it bizarre. But we cannot dismiss the power of
the image and the power of a themed environment to provide a
comforting barrier between everything we think is wrong with the
world right now, and everything we think was right with the world
back then—wherever in the world that "then" might happen to
have been. (Treib 2002, 234)

My definition of themed experience is one in which an element—often lifted from past or present reality—is projected out
of proportion. The theme is borrowed from a different time or
place and is promiscuously spread across new settings with minimal concern given to its role in the historical context or as a component in a larger social or political setting. Three disparate examples come to mind. European open-air museums commonly
show visitors a fantasized folk world in which each peasant house
is brightly colored and filled with delightful objects. Cupboards
groan under the weight of polychrome earthenware, and em-
broidered fabrics reach to the primly finished roof. Even in east-
ern Europe, where such museums once taught lessons about the
poverty of life in the presocialist dark ages, it's as though every
house and yard were tended by some Romanian Martha Stewart.
(Chappell 2002, 122)

However, themed places will not in fact make us forget the problems
of the everyday world, because that "comforting barrier" exists precisely
because we continue to be aware of what is on both sides. The fear is
rather that, since they gloss over the difficulties and oppressions of the
idealized past, such themed places will stimulate emotions and inculcate

values and ideals that will be brought back to the everyday and produce bad effects: manipulable citizens, backing for oversimplified or suspect policies, support for hidden injustices and oppressions.

Such ideological places function more like samples of utopia than like themed places in the commercial sense. They are like visiting another country and admiring its citizens' lives. In another way they are like summer camp or other separated and simplified environments meant to inculcate values and practices. Williamsburg presents itself as an educational shrine to the past, not a commercial operation, and the Holy Land Experience theme park was awarded tax-exempt status by the courts.[27]

Such propaganda places are exceptional among the growing crowd of commercial themed places. Yet it may be that we can learn from the ordinary themed places tactics that might blunt the impact of the propaganda places. All three dimensions of place complexity are relevant in themed places.

Themed places typically offer very explicit spatial structures, often episodic, combined with social norms that restrict people's reactions so that they do not break the theme. It is inappropriate to offer a cell phone to the person in eighteenth-century garb at Williamsburg, to discuss current politics with Goofy at Disneyworld, to offer biblical criticism at the Holy Land Experience. But temptations to such behaviors continually occur, as can be seen when parents have to discipline their children in the themed place. There are also the structural contrasts involved in the maintenance of the theme and the physical fabric of the place. The garbage and food service and financial details are taken for granted, looked away from, but are there to be seen, showing more complex interactions.

Themed places exist through continual cooperative interpretation. Because it is so explicit, that process of staging is always available for a heightened awareness that makes the experience of the place more complex and less passive. There are ways of getting self-consciously into a theme, enjoying and exploring it while testing its limits and simplifications. This requires alertness to the various symbols and decors and how they ask us to cooperate with them, then questioning their togetherness, and feeling for unintended resonances and connections that go beyond or complicate the official unities.

The easiest self-consciousness at a themed place is ironic distance. This can be helpful, but it may also be a subject position already in-

cluded by the theme. "The stories of Epcot's rides are usually didac-
tic, self-righteously validating, narrated from on high, and portentous;
the stories of Universal Studios' rides are theatrical, engulfing, and self-
parodying, poking fun at their illusions even as they glory in them"
(Brown 2002, 253–54). In this case, stepping back to the ironic position
still keeps the visitor within simplified dualities prescribed by the theme.
Awareness of complexity needs to go beyond simple irony.[28]

Ordinary themed places are blatantly commercial; the larger forces
behind their genesis are obvious, and this puts limits on their potential for education and propaganda. Williamsburg and other propaganda
places can and should be seen with the same jaundiced eye, even if the
details of their history and the more complex maneuverings behind, say,
Disney's Florida land deals are not readily accessible.[29] Since such places
set out to comment on the larger society, there is already a two-way street
established for such awareness.

Fear of the effect of themed places relies in part on the idea that places
enclose us and define us completely. But the inhabitation of places is not
all or nothing. Places are porous and linked, and we are not passive but
cooperating in their ongoing social validity. Themed places try to be enclosures, but their effect depends on continual contrast with the outside
everyday.

Visitors come to themed places with varying agendas. At a themed restaurant it may be only to have a pleasant evening in nostalgic surroundings. At Disney it may be to give their children special experiences, to
relive old memories, to feel an ambience that seems more harmonious
and peaceful than their daily life, to substitute for travel to exotic locales,
to check out the latest technology or ride, and so on. At Williamsburg or
other educational themed places people want to expand their acquaintance with their own roots or with foreign cultures and histories. These
goals require the doubled inhabitation that contrasts the themed experience with ordinary life, so the structural possibility is there for becoming
aware of oversimplifications. Ordinary life can appear thicker and more
real even if the themed place might illuminate aspects where it could be
improved.

Themed places have many virtues, not the least of which is to offer
locales for festival and "a non-quotidian encounter with architecture"
(Gottdiener 1997, 113). Some themed places are not worth visiting,
judged by the criteria suggested earlier in this chapter. Some try to in-

culcate questionable values and behaviors. Whatever their value, themed places can be inhabited more complexly. We should not hope to replace all themes by some naked living without fantasy. What should happen is not that we disown themes and fantasy, but that themes and fantasies do not own us. When they are placed in a fuller context than the theme alone, themed places can give us clues about how to inhabit today's strange places. Our aim should not be to eliminate themes from our society but to enjoy them for what they are, which is to refuse them dominance and to see them within more complex processes than what they want to define. This strategy applies as well to our dealings with other contemporary places.[30]

CHAPTER SIX

Suburban Promises and Problems

*In colonial New England the church authorities forbade anyone
to live more than a mile from the meeting house. Yet people
continued to move out, and Captain John Smith complained
that the very first colonists in Virginia wanted to abandon
Jamestown and settle far from neighbors.*
(John Brinckerhoff Jackson quoted in Lippard 1997, 236)

*Despite the much advertised charms of the densely built
metropolis, whatever policy the planners and politicians
have pursued, the inescapable background to the evolution
of the city in the last twenty years has been accelerating
decentralisation. The population of the central core of every
major city in Europe, America and Japan has fallen while
that of the constantly spreading outermost ring around them
has continued to grow.*
(Sudjic 1992, 25)

AS WITH THEMED PLACES, it is common to cite sprawling suburbs as
emblematic of what is wrong with places today. Yet the suburbs remain
the destination of choice for most Americans. Can the criterion of complexity suggest ways suburbs could take fuller advantage of the positive
qualities of contemporary places?

This and the remaining chapters discuss suburban sprawl in a manner
roughly parallel to the discussion in chapter 5 of themed places. I look
at definitions of sprawl, along with older and newer forms of suburbs.
Then I discuss positive and negative aspects of the current patterns of
suburban living and address the criticisms of those who favor dense cities over suburbia. The current shape of suburbia and the default modes
of development have good features as well as serious problems. As with
themed places, however, suburbs contain more complexity than is first
apparent, and their linkages and networks might be leveraged to lessen

some of their negative qualities. In chapter 7 I assemble some proposals for increasing the three dimensions of complexity of suburban life.

An individual suburban development can seem very controlled, yet suburban sprawl as a whole seems out of control, an irresistible mediocrity always managing to outflank efforts at larger civic order. Sprawl stands opposed by two ideals: the spatially dense bustle of a city that has more going on than we will ever know, and the bounded small town that frames a close and all-too-familiar life. In our time both large cities and small towns have been pervaded by wider activities and flows whose connections are more energetic and more intrusive. Suburban forms of inhabitation are neither deviant cities nor faux villages. The suburbs have appropriated many urban functions, so the urban centers become just another node in the network, perhaps specialized in providing density for special experiences such as sports events and expositions.

Suburbanites enjoy more space, greater privacy and mobility, contact with some nature, and often better schools and civic services than many city dwellers. They have more choices than the poor in cities, if not as many as the well-off. People move to the suburbs looking for a life that retains many urban features, rather than a dream of small town or rural life. As Lucy Lippard says, "Sentimentality about small-town living rapidly gives way to urban demands for convenience and comfort; urban escapees want solitude, authenticity, a good cappuccino, and a nearby health club" (Lippard 1997, 152).

SPRAWL

Suburbs in a general sense are an inevitable accompaniment of cities once a certain level of safety is assured so that people do not have to live behind city walls and can move away from the extreme densities characteristic of cities before the twentieth century.[1] But American suburbanization could have taken many shapes: new towns separated by green belts, the low-density spread of housing and workplaces envisioned by Frank Lloyd Wright, communities set along mass-transit lines, and other forms. Instead there is sprawl, a term that can describe the patchwork of large tracts with separated uses, and also the process of unplanned overall development. A typical definition of sprawl is "a low-density pattern of land development in which residential units are spread out over a large area. . . . Sprawl also encompasses the separation of residential from commercial land uses, the absence of clustered development or commercial centers, and widespread use of the automobile" (Dreier, Mollenkopf, and Swanstrom 2001, 63).

We may think we know sprawl when we see it, but it can be assessed in many ways that do not all lead to the same ratings. For example:

> The Galster study defined the six sprawl dimensions that could be measured as follows: (a) Density: the average number of residential units per square mile of developable land in an urbanized area, (b) Concentration: the degree to which development is located disproportionately in relatively few square miles of the total urbanized area, (c) Compactness: the degree to which development has been "clustered" to minimize the amount of land in each square mile of developable land occupied by residential or nonresidential space, (d) Centrality: the degree to which residential or nonresidential development is located close to the CBD [central business district] of an urbanized area, (e) Nuclearity: the extent to which an urbanized area is characterized by a mononuclear in contrast to a polynuclear pattern of development, (f) Proximity: the degree to which observations of a single land use or different land uses are close to each other in an urbanized area. (Lang 2003, 102–3)

Areas that score high on one measure may score low on others. Miami is among the most dense urban areas, but it ranks high on other measures of sprawl. Depending on which group of measures you use, the Los Angeles region either is or is not as sprawling as its reputation suggests. Its land use patterns resemble many suburban areas, with large tracts devoted to single uses. On the other hand "its density is twenty-five percent higher than that of New York, twice that of Washington and four times that of Atlanta, as measured by residents per square mile of urban land" (Harden 2005). Southeastern American cities such as Atlanta and Nashville sprawl much more than Los Angeles when measured by the area consumed by lower-density populations (see Jaret 2002).[2]

There is no firmly established definition of sprawl, though it is easy to point to examples that all would agree on. No matter how it is measured or defined, suburban development consumes open land, and the U.S. population is projected to increase by as much as a third in the next half century. The question is not whether there will be more suburbs, but what form that growth will take.

OLDER AND NEWER SUBURBAN FORMS

There were residential districts of single-family houses outside major American cities in the late 1700s. However, "the suburb, as a lifestyle separating and distancing the workplace from the residence and involving a daily commute to jobs in the center, can be dated to around 1815" (Gandelsonas 1999, 31). The late nineteenth and early twentieth centuries brought planned residential districts. Hayden 2003 discusses the varied patterns of development in that period, many with town centers and transit connections on streetcar or railroad lines. Today some of these suburbs have been incorporated into their central cities (as were the villages in the New York borough of Queens); others stayed independent (as did the towns along the Main Line outside Philadelphia or in New York's Nassau and Westchester counties).

After World War II there was a huge increase in suburban areas and populations.[3]

> Between 1950 and 1990, metropolitan areas expanded from 208,000 square miles housing 84 million people to 585,000 square miles housing 193 million. Population in these communities grew by 128 percent while the land area on which they resided grew 181 percent. Population density declined from 407 to 330 persons per square mile. Urban communities have been consuming land at a rate that is approximately 50 percent greater than the population growth. (Squires 2002b, 5–6)

> The suburbs' share of the U.S. population rose from 46.2 percent in 1990 to 50 percent in 2000, for the central-city share of the U.S. population actually fell, from 31.3 percent to 30.3 percent. As a share of the metropolitan population, the central cities declined even faster, from 40.4 percent in 1990 to 37.7 percent in 2000. (Jargowsky 2002, 42)

Postwar suburbs were built on a different pattern than the earlier suburbs. Hayden 2003 discusses the differences; in addition she points out that before the war two thirds of homes were built by individuals or small companies, but after the war two thirds were built by large corporations.[4] Whereas the older layer of railroad and streetcar suburbs often had their own downtown centers, civic services, and access to public transportation, beyond them arose an unordered expansion of residential, business, and commercial areas. Commercial areas came to be concentrated on strips and in malls. Civic services were left to counties or to new jurisdictions. Later the radial pattern of commuting to the center city for jobs weakened as retail and industry moved outward and service jobs multiplied in the suburbs. Suburbs now contained many of the economic and cultural functions that the city had previously provided. A multiuse and dispersed pattern developed, dependent on the automobile, and "not organized anymore in oppositional terms such as center versus periphery . . . but as a nonhierarchical fragmented urbanized territory" (Gandelsonas 1999, 37).

Recall the suburban areas described briefly in the first chapter: Garden City, New York, an early-twentieth-century railroad suburb adjacent to newer decentered developments, the expanding suburbs around Austin and around Washington, D.C., linear sprawl in Maine, and concentrated but suburban land use in Portland, Oregon.[5] Visible from the air around so many cities, today's sprawling suburbs show familiar patterns of large residential tracts with their own street patterns opening onto collector streets leading to freeways, commercial strips and malls, scattered office parks and workplaces, highway interchanges, and so on.[6] In the early twentieth century, suburban development could have been seen as heading toward a landscape of smaller centered developments linked by transit. Why then did the suburbs later develop into a decentered auto-dependent sprawl?

The larger and more remote forces and decisions shaping suburban growth have their own complex history. Policy decisions and "facts on the ground" (usually the results of earlier policy decisions) influenced each other to shape the options available to developers and home buyers.[7]

Increasing home ownership had been a goal during the decades preceding World War II, and key policies were already in place before the war ended and resources could be turned to meeting demand for housing. The idea was to discourage middle-class rental in city neighborhoods in favor of home ownership on greenfield developments. This pattern had been foreshadowed by decisions made during the war to locate defense plants and their associated housing outside of cities, where it was cheaper to build and labor unions were less influential. Banks, the real estate and construction industries, and local investors lobbied for policies that would encourage profitable large-scale construction on new land. The construction industry even persuaded the government to demolish clustered housing that had been built for defense workers, because such housing threatened the desired pattern. In Greenbelt, Maryland, built with apartments grouped around a center and protected by the greenbelt, construction of further centers was stopped and some agitated for the demolition of the prewar town. In senate hearings, Senator Joe McCarthy condemned clustered housing as un-American and a breeding ground for Communists.

New construction on vacant land offered economies of scale and freedom from restrictions. Allowing developers to concentrate on large tracts of houses without providing civic facilities and infrastructure shifted many costs to the public sector. Financial institutions wanted the low risk inherent in repeating standard patterns. The interstate and other highway programs discouraged public transit, sliced and segregated cities, and provided easy access to developable land. The automobile helped create the sprawling suburbs and became necessary to living there.[8]

Policies encouraging construction outside of cities went hand in hand with policies encouraging families to buy suburban homes. The federal tax subsidy for interest on home mortgages favors owning over renting. There were also preferential treatments for suburban mortgages. As Robert Fishman noted, "A white home buyer who wished to stay in his old neighborhood had to seek old-style conventional mortgages with high rates and short terms. The same purchaser who opted for a new suburban house could get an FHA-insured [Federal Housing Administration] mortgage with lower interest rates, longer terms, a lower down payment, and a lower monthly payment" (quoted in Dreier, Mollenkopf, and Swanstrom 2001, 111). "The government-backed mortgages were only good in 'low-risk' areas, which meant newly built, low-density, white areas—in other words, the suburbs" (Flint 2006, 33).

In the cities, bank loan policies redlining neighborhoods along racial and economic lines encouraged not reconstruction but what became known as "flight." In the newer suburbs, as town governments began to compete for tax base, school funding policies increased the effects of property values on the education of the next generation. Meanwhile, generous depreciation allowances encouraged the construction of disposable industrial and commercial strips. Tax breaks allowed the cost of a commercial building to be written off in only seven years, instead of the previous forty years. These accelerated depreciation allowances were available from 1954 until 1986. They encouraged owners to build cheaply with a short time horizon, to skimp on maintenance, and to sell the building after recouping the cost of construction in seven or eight years. Then the new owners could begin the cycle of tax allowances again on slightly less generous terms. (See Hayden 2003, 162–64.) High-value commercial and residential property tended to concentrate in quarters favored by environmental values and by the cumulative results of past decisions and policies.

These policies met with an enthusiastic response from people ready to move out of crowded cities and find more space, more privacy, more choices. People wanted less-congested surroundings that were well land-scaped and convenient. Home ownership gave them more control over their fate and an investment that might appreciate. Suburban life was seen as more convenient and more pleasant, away from the dirt and disorder of the cities that needed improvements in their infrastructure and housing stock.[9] "Generous suburbia is easy. It's roomy. It means low house prices and an air-conditioned drive to work and low prices and convenience at big-box stores. We accept the traffic jams as part of the territory" (Flint 2006, 5).

People choose suburbs through a combination of positive pulls and negative avoidances. Driving an extra fifteen miles may mean a less ex-pensive house. Yards can be bigger, schools and public services better; taxes may be lower. Street crime is reduced. Suburban development was also fueled by a desire to escape from the crowded immigrant neighbor-hoods many had grown up in, and by a wish to move away from the im-poverished, especially from the increasing number of African Americans migrating into the cities from rural areas. "Commentator Bill Shipp . . . asks who would want to live in a high crime, high-tax city with bad schools when one could move farther out and feast on all the amenities there? A collective inability or unwillingness to resolve serious social problems creates a strong motive to move far away to places people think will not have those problems" (Jaret 2002, 181). Residents seek a sense of secu-rity and developments are planned to offer that feeling.[10]

In the early days of Levittown on Long Island, residents were not al-lowed to hang laundry outside to dry, for fear that the visual impact and the habits encouraged would be too close to those of crowded inner-city neighborhoods. Although public housing was built to alleviate some inner-city problems, it was sited so as to keep poorer citizens out of the suburbs. When close-in suburbs began to house poorer residents, the dynamic of spread and flight was repeated farther out.

In recent decades a new exurban form is developing far from the original cities. A vaguely rural look remains, but the rural economy is gone. Commuting times are long and lead to destinations spread throughout the area rather than concentrated in the center city. Most exurban developments aim for the wealthy, segregating by class. Other outlying developments aim to attract less-affluent residents from cities and older suburbs, offering lower real-estate prices as a trade-off for the increased commuting time.

CRITICISMS OF SUBURBAN LIFE

Suburbia meets many needs and fulfills the desires of many residents. However, postwar suburban development in the United States has been attacked as too tame, too sterile, too uniform, and as embodying "American identity by subtraction" (Liggett 2003, 140). Suburban life has been described as representing stifling uniformity and fear of the Other. "The sameness, security, and comfort of what we might call the moral order of the suburbs exclude difference as difference beyond control" (Liggett 2003, xii). "Safe, sanitized spaces where people can experience the thrill of the different without taking any risks . . . where community can be synthesized in a manner that offers some of its benefits and none of its costs" (Barber 2001, 206).[11] "[Suburbs] replace reality with 'a more agreeable product,' a 'selective fantasy'" (Huxtable 1997, 15). "Generic spaces—the shopping mall, the food court, the hotel lobby—. . . bear the same relation to life, perhaps, that Muzak does to music" (Iyer 2000a, 43).

Such blanket criticisms of suburban life are neither accurate nor helpful. Many criticisms stem from urban intellectuals' "haughty repertoire of cosmo attitude in which the term 'suburban' is automatically derogatory" (Ross 1999, 321). "Sprawl has become the whipping boy for a variety of ills, including the destruction of nature, the decline of inner cities, the predominance of consumerism and the loss of civic consciousness. . . . Yet simply demonizing the suburbs—and idealizing the traditional city—will not do. For one thing, sprawl was hardly mindless; the industrial American city, with its tenements and downtown factories, was a nasty place. In a country as large as the U.S., a horizontal form of urbanism was probably inevitable" (Rybczynski 1999).[12]

Some critics seem to be claiming that the only solution to sprawl is to ban it completely: stop all development on farmland, stop building highways, revoke all tax policies that favor sprawl, and implement other all-or-nothing measures. Such critics have little use for attempts to ameliorate sprawl, and nothing to say about already existing suburbs. They resemble those who opposed attempts to lessen the misery of nineteenth century industrial workers in the hope that increased suffering would push the workers towards total revolution.

Indeed, "everyone loves to hate the suburbs, except for the people who live there, people who, sometime in the last few years, became a majority of all Americans. . . . Academic revisionists are reporting that suburbia, far from crushing lives, has had a liberating effect on residents, particularly many women. They have found that the sense of community can be as strong on a suburban block as it is in a small town. And they record how homeownership produced a significant increase in the standards of living and personal wealth for generations of former urban renters. . . . There are people who are beginning to think of the suburbs as a place, as opposed to no place" (Peterson 1999, 46).

While we cannot underrate the positive accomplishments of suburban living, we should not ignore its problems. In terms of my criteria from chapter 3, suburban communities are thin and historically diluted as well as weak in place complexity. In the next chapter I argue that they do possess more complexity than first appears, and that this could be further increased.

Kelbaugh 2002b and Flint 2006 provide useful summaries of many problems with contemporary suburban forms of growth. In the terms developed in chapter 4, many of these problems are system effects. Suburbs bring "near-total dependence on the automobile, a pervasive privatization and loss of public space; and . . . endless sprawl that endangers the very union with nature it was intended to promote" (Fishman 1997, 15). They promise open space that they busily devour. Suburbs subdue the variety of rural land uses into a uniformity; destroy wetlands, forests, and animal habitat; waste and pollute water; and add to air pollution. The social costs of lower density living are not fairly distributed, and segregation by income is increased.[13] Suburban isolation demands long commuting and daily trips for errands, school, children's activities. Despite the open space, people do less walking (Ewing 2003). Scattershot developments are sited without concern for future use or overall plans. Distinctive architectural character is often reduced to marketing glitz.

> Although this deeply embedded system may seem rational to suburban residents and public officials, it has produced dysfunctional consequences for the larger society. Metropolitan political fragmentation has encouraged unplanned, costly sprawl on the urban fringe. It has imposed longer journeys to work on commuters, allowing them less time for family life. It has undermined the quality of life in older suburbs, hardened conflicts between suburbs and their central cities, hampered financing for regional public facilities such as mass transit, and encouraged disinvestment from central cities. (Dreier, Mollenkopf, and Swanstrom 2001, 176)

As a result of current practices, norms, and system effects, jurisdictions are forced to compete to attract higher-income residents and exclude the less well-off. Home prices, zoning, civic amenities, exclusionary practices, schools, land use regulations, and tax breaks all become weapons by which towns try to maintain their rank in the regional pecking order. This makes it difficult for jurisdictions to cooperate on matters for which the larger region is the natural unit of concern.

Although financial arrangements are largely determined by municipal boundaries, these boundaries are constantly transgressed as travel, work, and environmental influences knit the area together into a region that is not well expressed in its governance, planning, or finances. Jurisdictions are at the mercy of inhabitants and businesses whose "fear of falling" will result in their eventual exit if they are not reassured and given incentives to stay.[14]

The current configuration of the suburbs increases segregation by income and concentrates poverty in less favored areas. Land values both confirm and are influenced by the racial and economic status of the inhabitants.[15] The results reinforce economic disparities and hand them on to later generations growing up with inadequate schools and civic facilities. The result is that "only those with significant means can choose to have all the benefits of a metropolitan association, and [they are able to] externalize many of the social and economic costs on the other, less fiscally strong communities" (Orfield 2002, 238). So, many social costs are shifted to those least able to support them.[16]

THE MARKET DEFENSE

Although it is tempting to argue that the postwar suburban and the newer exurban patterns are the inevitable result of market forces working to meet consumer demand, that explanation is as inadequate as is any abstract appeal to "the market" that does not examine concrete policy details and limitations on choices.

For example, Charles Tiebout and many libertarian writers defend the economic inequities of suburban development by appealing to the free market. Economic diversity across city and suburbs is supposed to have resulted from people choosing to work and live with their own groups. The differentiation among suburbs improves the market when different jurisdictions offer different "amenity packages" to be chosen. According to Charles Tiebout, "The consumer-voter may be viewed as picking that community which best satisfies his preference pattern for public goods. . . . The greater the number of communities and the greater the variance among them, the closer the consumer will come to fully realizing his preference position" (quoted in Dreier, Mollenkopf, and Swanstrom 2001, 97).[17] This market defense sounds plausible, but is there really a free market here? Both the offerings in the market and the buyers attending it are questionable.

The options available in the current American real estate system may seem natural, but they are the result of government influence and design. Choices are made among options that have long been controlled and limited; many paths ruled out earlier by influences favoring specific industries might be premier choices today if they were still available.

Also, many people are precluded from entering the market. The rules of the game do not give all people and places equal chances. Middle- and upper-class homeowners are the privileged players, whereas "people with fewer means (or the wrong skin color) have a highly constricted range of choice. The market not only fails people who live in poverty; it punishes them through the negative effects of concentrated poverty" (Dreier, Mollenkopf, and Swanstrom 2001, 99). Market choices and arrangements favor those with the ability to enter and exit the housing market at will. But if so, it is difficult to claim that the facts, including economic segregation, result from free-market choices by everyone concerned.

It is one thing to say that suburban living may be preferable to many city conditions; it is another to say that the ways such choices are precluded for poorer people is itself a rational market result. The nineteenth-century argument that those unable to enter the market are unworthy of entering—perhaps because they are supposed to lack the work ethic imagined as typical of suburbanites—is as unconvincing today as it was then.[18] Furthermore, it "ignores all the other features of society that constrain or empower people's ability to choose" (Dreier, Mollenkopf, and Swanstrom 2001, 99). The system favors those who can shift costs onto others: "the costs of sprawl are gradual and dispersed across a huge land mass, while the profits are immediate and substantial" (Savitch 2002, 152).[19]

If different policies had been adopted for postwar development, for instance if all the prewar patterns had remained in the mix, the suburban choices available would be quite different today. If there had been more efforts at mixed-income housing and regional financial arrangements, today's landscape could have produced more equitable choices and a more diversified local labor market in suburbia. More people would have had access to better schools and services, and suburbanization would not have caused such concentration of poverty.

Appeals to the market also overlook system effects that no one in the corporate sector can see any way to profit from. According to Lars Lerup, "If suburbia is a microcosm of who we are, it is because we make all these things without paying attention to each other. That produces what I call a toxic ecology whose consequences inevitably flow downstream. Nobody wants to deal with the downstream consequences because you cannot expect market forces to take care of them. The private sector wants to make money, and thinks the public sector is there to help the private sector make money. We need a public domain that is now missing" (Lars Lerup, in Fishman 2005, 43).[20]

Using the market to justify the existing default patterns of development also downplays the entrenched power of the financial, real estate, road, and construction industries who have seen little profit in changing the default pattern of development. The entrenched power of a constellation of industries and government regulations has helped the growth machine resist change (see Flint 2006, 59).

Although the operation of the market has not been as free as defenders of the status quo claim, it is nonetheless true that one of the keys to improving suburbia will be to find ways to make the market freer, to al-

low more people to enter and to allow experiments that go against standard patterns, and then see what people do with the new options. For
instance, new family patterns may put pressure on the default patterns.

> I work with people who spend billions of dollars on those ques-
> tions. They come to me now and they say, 'We got it wrong, it's no
> longer a single family world. . . . Our market is no longer the young
> family with kids. Our market is an urban market of young single
> people and older empty nester people. They want townhouses.
> They want walkable environments, they want urbanism. Can you
> give it to us?' These are the people who do the market analysis and
> do the surveys. It's a huge hangover myth that suburbia is what
> people want. People no longer want just the car. The want the car
> and also want walking and transit. They want all of the above. . . . If
> the American dream is transformed, what do we do, and what are
> the appropriate urban design forms? (Peter Calthorpe in Fishman
> 2005, 58)[21]

SUBURB VERSUS CITY

So far this discussion of suburbia has concentrated on general historical
and critical issues. I have argued against blanket condemnations and
have pointed to suburbia's real advantages as well as its admitted problems, especially economic and ecological problems. Now I want to look
at those criticisms of suburbia that relate more closely to my discussion
of place complexity. These criticisms usually compare suburbs negatively
with the dense complexity of city life. My strategy is to look for ways in
which suburbia already does have, and could have more of, the positive
features traditionally associated with life in the city. Most critiques of suburbia share the presupposition that spatial proximity remains our most
important mode of connection, so only the spatial density of the city will
bring a richer life. But spatial proximity is becoming just one mode of
connection and community affiliation; there are more modes of contact
available, and these can bring complex encounters and self-redefining
innovations.[22]

The dense and spatially concentrated urbanity of classic cities has become only one form of life within wider flows that the city no longer
wholly dominates. Before, it was only in the city that one touched di-

rectly on larger flows of resources and lived within wider horizons. Now, resources and culture come together in new ways and places, often in temporary relations that connect more widely than to a few major centers. New arrangements can be less spatially dense because networks of all kinds bring flows to bear from many directions into many places. They no longer converge only in cities. Communication does not always require face-to-face encounters, economic resources flow in new paths, and productive groupings can be widely spread.

Arguing that cities have become elements in wider networks, Robert Fishman concludes that

> Cities . . . have come to the end of a master narrative . . . the story of the opposition of town and country. . . . Cities brought change and communication to agricultural regions, but only by concentrating people and resources at a few uniquely favored points. Crowding worked because it enabled cities to create within their teeming streets those multiple possibilities for face-to-face exchange and communication necessary for commerce and culture. . . . [In the twentieth century, decentralizing forces provided] giant grids that enabled one to "plug into" systems of power and communication from any point in the region. These grids supplanted the characteristic hub-and-spoke technology of the 19th century that had privileged the metropolitan hub over the regional spokes. The automobile grid, supplanting the railroads, was perhaps the most powerful technology; but one should acknowledge the influence of the giant grid spreading electrical power over a region, as well as the effects of telephone, radio, and television, and of new systems of production and distribution that bypassed the city. (Fishman 1997, 14–15)

Frank Lloyd Wright, who was no friend of large cities, saw central hierarchies fighting a losing battle against modern mobility. "Centralization, whether expressed as the city, the factory, the school or the farm, now has the enormous power of the machine-age setting dead against it. It is in the nature of universal or ubiquitous mobilization that the city spreads out far away and thin. It is in the nature of flying that the city disappears. It is in the nature of universal electrification that the city is nowhere or it is everywhere" (Wright 1932, 8).

Mobility, decentralization, and networks have undermined older hierarchical arrangements. What surrounds cities takes on new functions and achieves new kinds of density across links rather than through immediate spatial proximity. This changes cities, which no longer monopolize innovation and production, and it changes suburbs, which are no longer so tightly bound to nearby cities for jobs and finance. In the following sections I examine arguments that exalt the city against the suburb, and I show that the defenses of the city appeal to just that kind of linking and connection that is also happening in the suburbs.

CONTROL CENTERS AND DISTANT CONNECTIONS

Historically, dense cities concentrated resources where social and economic energies and elites converged. So the cities were the privileged locations of cultural and economic creativity and control. Defenders argue that cities continue to be privileged locations for control and creativity even as production and communication are widely dispersed. However, cities now control far-flung networks rather than their own geographical regions.

Manuel Castells agrees that we live in a network connecting scattered locations in a way that ignores spatial proximity, in what he calls "a space of flows." He points out that in a networked world the link between cooperative action and spatial proximity has been broken. "It is fundamental that we separate the basic concept of material support of simultaneous practices from the notion of contiguity, in order to account for the possible existence of material supports of simultaneity that do not rely on physical contiguity, since this is precisely the case of the dominant social practices of the information age" (Castells 1996, 411).

Castells insists, though, that the networks still require controlling nodes that will be huge megacities. Their control is exerted on faraway regions, not necessarily on their own geographical regions. What they control is dispersed and linked rather than spatially continuous.

Castells's megacities are centers of economic, technological, and social dynamism in cultural and political innovation. "Megacities articulate the global economy, link up the informational networks, and concentrate the world's power. . . . they are connected externally to global networks and to segments of their own countries, while internally disconnecting local populations that are either functionally unnecessary or socially disruptive. . . . It is this distinctive feature of being *globally connected and lo-*

cally disconnected, physically and socially, that makes megacities a new urban form" (Castells 1996, 404, my emphasis; see also 384–86, 409–10).

The pattern that Castells traces, citing the researches of Saskia Sassen and others, involves concentrations of corporate control in a few large centers linked to dispersed regional nodes specialized for production and other functions. Sassen argues that major cities maintain strategic roles as command posts because they offer spatially dense sources of services that corporations need (finance, lawyers, accountants, communication and media, advertising, etc.). They also provide places where less regulated interactions can occur, and markets for new products and innovations (Sassen 1991). Castells adds that major cities also provide special opportunities for elite personal enhancement, status, self-gratification, and preservation of the value of corporate fixed assets. So their central role depends on spatial proximity for their auxiliary services, combined with far-flung spatial discontinuity of the corporate functions they control. In both cases the networks themselves are important; some require spatial proximity, some do not. Even within a city, a corporation will develop its own network of connections spread over the urban area.

Castells's megacities do not all resemble New York or London. Newer cities may include discontinuous constellations of spatial fragments, along with different functional pieces and social segments (Castells 1996, 407). Large areas within the megacity may be exiled from the major networks. There may be rural areas mixed in the city area, as in the growing south China megacity that Castells discusses. So the megacity could itself be a kind of sprawl with large nodes, rather than a traditional dense city center.

Castells and Sassen analyze megacontrol cities, but what about the other cities? Castells argues that the arrangement of command centers linked to spatially dispersed functional units replicates itself at different scales. What remains constant at any scale is that dynamic sectors and regional nodes are linked to one another across distances much more tightly than they are linked to whatever happens to be spatially nearby. So although medium-sized cities may persist and grow, they too are nodes in a network rather than central representatives of their local regions, which may be cut adrift outside the network. Castells insists that "the importance of the city as a center of gravity for economic transactions will not vanish" (Castells 1996, 381–82), yet the mass for which the city acts as center of gravity may not be its geographical region.

Castells argues that average-sized cities will retain their attractions even though their original functions might be absorbed by the mega-cities or dispersed into the networks. This is because cities continue to provide the "workplaces, schools, medical complexes, consumer services outlets, recreational areas, commercial streets, shopping centers, sports stadiums, and parks" that people will use (Castells 1996, 398). But this list does not differentiate a city from an area of suburban sprawl that includes all those items.[23]

What Castells contributes to my inquiry is that neither the classic image of the hierarchical city nor Wright's image of a totally decentralized suburbia is adequate to the scene in the twenty-first century. Network links transform an area by connecting it to distant locales. Those connections are not external to the function of local places; they are part of their being. The local architectural form of cities and suburbs no longer expresses their whole reality. In the past a great hierarchical cathedral or monument or civic building could try to sum up the reality of a city or region; that is no longer possible. But note that this also means that the banal architecture of suburbia cannot tell suburbia's whole story.

INNOVATION AND PROXIMITY

Kevin Lynch claims that "rapid communication and processing of information is the hallmark of a city—perhaps its major reason for being today—and is an important gauge of its quality" (Lynch 1981, 353). That rapidity is happening on the networks, even in cities. The classical city has thousands of years of history to testify to how economic and cultural creativity grow from spatial propinquity. Yet today's new modes of relationship ask whether it is possible "to accommodate the social and political advantages of spatial agglomeration within a far-reaching decentralization of urban settlement patterns" (Grabow 1977, 123).

Castells also defends the importance of cities by arguing that sources of novelty in ideas and products ("milieux of innovation" such as Silicon Valley and its rivals) need to be relatively large, dense, and spatially coherent. "At least in this [twentieth] century, spatial proximity is a necessary material condition for the existence of such milieux, because of the nature of the interaction in the innovation process. What defines the specificity of a milieu of innovation is its capacity to generate synergy"

(Castells 1996, 390). He does concede that twenty-first-century technology might allow more dispersed innovative milieux.

Mario Gandelsonas goes further in praising the unplanned dynamism of large cities. "The city as a process, as an economic dynamo, a place of both physical and non-physical exchange, has always resisted the suppression of time, of difference, of the contingent, of its reduction to the status of a building; that is, to the spatiality and totalizing nature of the object implied by the architectural urban practice. . . . The city presents to architecture an open play of differences within a potentially infinite field of shapes. Since this field resists closure, the city stands as an obstacle to the architectural effort to domesticating that play, to impose a totalizing order" (Gandelsonas 1999, 60–61).[24]

Gandelsonas tries too hard to make the creative city become the poststructuralist play of difference, for that play can never be made to appear as such. He is right that cities provide a spatially dense mix of differences and forces that mutate and reindividuate and recombine and cannot be overseen and controlled. Such density and interaction leaps beyond the accepted, with "the contingent, the violent emergence of something that defies the limits of the established field, the limits of what one holds for possible" (Gandelsonas 1999, 38). He offers as examples of such unexpected changes both our current "unexpected massive entrance into the virtual city" and the way in which the entry of women into the workforce "shattered the stability of the suburban order." Yet the examples Gandelsonas cites are changes and recombinations that are happening in the sprawling suburbs, not just in cities. Spatial proximity is not a necessary condition for the openness and changes he describes. Convergences and creative combinations that take new patterns are occurring out in linked suburbia. There may not be enough yet, but the possibilities are open.

Jane Jacobs offers a related argument for cities as centers of innovation. "Some of my friends think cities are obsolete now because modern communications make it easy to link into webs of customers and suppliers no matter how small the settlement you're in. . . . a village doesn't include a wide enough range of skills, experience, and equipment to produce a wide range of the various kinds of goods and services it imports. Being small, it's just not that versatile economically" (J. Jacobs 2000b, 73–74).

Sometimes, she says, scattered networks do manage to "add value to each other's products with their own goods and services, as happens ordinarily within city economies," but Jacobs thinks this seldom happens in small communities (J. Jacobs 2000b, 162). Besides their small markets and lack of variety, villages cannot match the cross-fertilization and creativity of a metropolitan economy that "teems with thousands of enterprises, most of them supplying goods or services, or both, to one another and to the local population" (J. Jacobs 2000b, 59). Should a village manage to begin this process, it will grow and become a city; villages cannot be so productive and remain what they are.

However, Jacobs begs the question by presupposing that effective markets and interacting skill bases have to be local to one geographical area: either a village or a city. This is just the issue in contention. She does not sufficiently consider the possibility—beginning to be realized—of a vigorous exchange of goods and services across scattered settlements linked electronically and by rapid and inexpensive transport of goods and services.

In all her books Jane Jacobs targets theories that demand localities specialize, whether those localities be zones of a single city, or metropolitan regions, or nations. She urges, at all scales, complex mixings and interweavings of functions that can feed off one another culturally and economically. But as the transaction costs for mutual interaction and delivery decrease, new kinds of linked combinations become possible. This is most obvious currently in the case of software, music, and other products that can be produced and delivered digitally, but it is beginning to happen with products that require physical transport.

From Jane Jacobs and Castells we see the importance of connection and availability for innovation and creativity. But there are many kinds of connection, and as they mutate spatial proximity becomes only one mode of availability. The growing importance of digital connections (instant messaging, mobile phones and their text messages, broadband portable internet, podcasting, and so on) suggests that nonspatial connections are beginning to provide the dense linkage that enables innovation and creativity. There is no doubt that spatial proximity has its advantages: spatial connections are always "on" and cannot be controlled as easily, and proximity facilitates informal arrangements and collaborations.[25] On the other hand, digital connections to distant places are altering the way business is done in cities. Consider groups of teens or college students linked by cell phone and text messaging, or groups of businessmen linked by their Blackberry e-mail, or the global community of workers in the financial markets. These groups function in new ways that do not depend on dense spatial connection, though they will take advantage of that when it is appropriate. My argument is not that cities can be fully replaced, but that growing linkage is changing both cities and suburbs into new kinds of places. It is the changes in suburbia that need to be emphasized.

ENCOUNTER AND DEBATE ACROSS LINKS

Richard Sennett argues that urban close face-to-face confrontation with people who have different values is required if citizens are to learn how to conduct civilized debate with people unlike themselves. "Aristotle thought the awareness of difference occurs primarily in cities, since every city is . . . a drawing together of different families and tribes, of competing economic interests, and of natives with foreigners. . . . He also included the experience of doing disparate, even incongruous things—such as praying and banking—in the same space. . . . Aristotle's hope was that, becoming accustomed to a diverse, complex milieu, citizens would be less likely to react violently when challenged by something strange or contrary. Instead, this diverse environment should encourage and support the discussion of differing views or conflicting interests" (Sennett 1999, 68–72).

Like Jane Jacobs, Sennett begs the question by presupposing that the alternatives are a spatially dense and diverse city population or a homogeneous small town. Suburbia is neither of these forms. Also, there is the danger of romanticizing face-to-face encounters on city streets. Most city encounters are superficial. A tourist sitting in a café in Paris watching the French is having a superficial experience, we are told, but is the same person, sitting in a café in New York, deeply encountering the Other? What is the difference between visiting Beijing as a tourist and going to Chinatown in New York for dinner? I am not claiming that they are the same, only that they are more similar than they might seem at first. Urbanism can be tourism, but also tourism may be more like urbanism than those who attack the first and defend the second want to admit.

Urban direct spatial confrontation is not the only way to a complex and self-aware life. Chinese poets spent time in the forest as hermits, yet remained interactive within a complex social world through their writing and visiting. Urbane critics such as M. Christine Boyer who idealize Greenwich Village as the best environment for human life employ overly simple oppositions (see Boyer 1994 and 1996). Boyer and those who agree with her oppose dense urbanity against monoculture, thinness, bigotry, boredom, and so on. But our links and connections can be of many types and rhythms, and they don't all demand spatial proximity.

Sennett urges that what matters is not casual encounters, but having to debate issues of mutual concern with people of different values and priorities. "The urgent necessity for democratic deliberation today is that people concentrate upon, rather than 'surf' over, social reality. . . . The polity further requires a place for discipline, focus, and duration. Decentralized polities especially need such places" (Sennett 1999, 71–72).

With the rise of blogs and similar Internet sites, there is more focus and discussion on the Net, but much of it does not meet Sennett's criterion for encountering the Other. Net discussion is largely conducted within groups that already agree with each other rather than across large differences. Still, the mechanisms of connection are there, and common concerns can bring people together. Much of the discussion in blog circles is unconnected to specific action goals, so it is easy to ignore or vilify the Other. When common issues demand focus on and debate over specific proposals, say about a school funding increase or a new sewer line, then a dispersed set of conflicting groups may bring its divisions into direct encounter, both in face-to-face meetings and in digital communications. Philip Nobel claims that "It's all so quaint now, this concern for reaching the people through physical contact, in physical spaces, when minds can be much better led with the right digitalia. There are fewer public places for protest today—granted—but protest has largely gone off the streets and has been empowered by the move" (Nobel 2007, 72). It is through the media that corporate and political authority increasingly tries to exercise control. Resistance to that control comes through the media as well, especially on digital networks where we have only seen the barest beginnings of using networks to create new voices and agents on the political scene.

In sprawling suburbia as ecological and shared resource issues press harder on people's lives people will come together. Despite their dispersion, suburbs and networked places need to come together to discuss how to live together. Even if there were nothing but divided and gated communities that resembled the vision offered in G. K. Chesterton's *The Napoleon of Notting Hill* (Chesterton 1994), none of them would be economically or ecologically self-sufficient.[26] Inside a gated community there may be a homogeneous population, but those people will still have to deal with more and more disparate others over more and more infrastructure and resource issues such as water, transportation, garbage, schools, taxes, energy, waste management, and other shared issues.

Systems penetrate places no matter what their social norms, making the places possible and also restricting them. Infrastructure problems demand democratic planning that should not be left to engineers alone, because the solutions involve priorities and values that direct the application of expertise. Systems and their causal sequences become topics for dialogue and interaction. Usually this happens because of scarcity: Who gets the water? Do we need to build more sewers? Don't put that power plant in my back yard. Going it alone is not a long-term option; suburbia is too tightly interdependent for that, despite its appearance of separation. Water supply and waste treatment are probably the current leading issues forcing dialogue, but there will be others.[27]

Current political and economic arrangements tend to forestall such debates; existing power imbalances foreclose the issues, forcing less influential locations to bear scarcity or pollution. There are signs, though, of growing awareness that these decisions need to happen through debate rather than power plays. Regional bodies, land trusts, and other nongovernmental agents introduce new voices and represent shared interests beyond the competition built into the fragmentation and competition of jurisdictions.[28] Further development of new social actors through network connections as well as geographical proximity should help this process.

Sennett denies that electronic communications can mediate deep encounters with other people. "It's sometimes said that the Internet might be a new space of democracy. But screen communications emphasize denotative statements and short messages; to exit from painful confrontation, you need only click a mouse. Easy, quick decisions are encouraged by such conditions, not the difficult sorting out that requires time and commitment" (Sennett 1999, 71–72).

Sennett here equates technology's promise with its current abilities.

Nonetheless he is right that "difficult sorting out" in dialogue requires habits of interaction and concentrated discussion that current media do not encourage. On the other hand, anyone who attends civic face-to-face meetings over controversial issues realizes that those habits of interaction are lacking there, too, even though a face-to-face meeting makes it easier to discover new dimensions in one's opponents and partners. Sennett's democratic conversations do not always proceed best face-to-face. A "place for discipline, focus, and duration" does not always require spatial proximity. Nor does every kind of interaction benefit from proximate contact. Some civic disputes may be better carried on in a slower medium that allows time to reflect, think up alternatives, and deal with emotions.

It is true, though, that spatial proximity offers a greater repertoire of convenient contacts, and face-to-face contact provides the widest channels of communication and observation. Novel and unexpected encounters happen more easily. Innovation can be nurtured because of the availability of resources, talent, and chance informal contacts. Power can be accumulated and demonstrated more quickly. On the other hand, given class divisions and isolations, a city may or may not offer such opportunities. And in business, as Boden and Molotch (1994) argue, while managers and leaders deal through face-to-face presence, many in the lower levels find their modes of communications increasingly restricted.[29] Informal contacts become regularized and diminish the creativity arising from unexpected face-to-face meetings.

Although density of interaction and opportunity is important for creativity and for fostering civic virtues, spatial proximity is not the only kind of density. There can be links through letters and books—a lone scholar in her library may be living in a dense social situation—as well as through the Internet and other media. The city is being augmented by the digital world. Wall Street lawyers sit at their face-to-face meetings tapping keys on their Blackberry devices. Silicon Valley technologists do e-mail on their laptops during committee meetings. In the city the possibilities for interaction are being supplemented by just those kinds of connections that are also active in the suburbs.[30]

Michael Benedikt worries that "If we are always reachable via the phone or the Net, we no longer need spatial habits—favorite cafes, park benches, clubs—and the city need not provide urban concentration points such as public buildings, parks, and squares" (Benedikt 1999b).

But what has in fact happened is that special meeting places have multiplied to include cafés and gyms as well as conference centers. Even in cities, sustained debate happens increasingly over networks or at times and places scheduled through the networks. If our debates with the Other begin to happen on the networks, or in meeting venues that are prescheduled using the networks, then even in cities democratic discussion will be more separated from the day-to-day unpredictability of city contacts.

In a city I can walk and encounter far more different people than I would walking in a suburb. But the relevant contrast is not with walking distances but with the larger range of travel suburban days include. Suburbia is less diverse over the spatial scale of a mile or so but is becoming more diverse as a whole. Both city and suburban geographies include a texture of relations and links that are more than spatial. It is important to pay attention to those links; they are processes rather than static references. As they become more dense some effects of physical proximity are attenuated while others are increased. Social power and innovation find new ways to grow.

Cities and suburbs feed on flows that are never totally controllable and which allow odd systems and cultures to flourish, linked in unexpected ways. There are always rival distributions, parasitic systems, subterranean connections, invisible relationships. Such complications need to be discussed and dealt with in suburbia too, as new linkages and connections provide new modes of contact and connection.

CENTER VERSUS NETWORK

Although Henri Lefebvre argues that new spatial forms are created with the development of new productive forces, he does not see new spatial forms developing out of the new linkages, new productive techniques and new social relations in cities and suburbs. For him suburbs are "illegitimate hybrids of country and city. . . . these bastard forms degrade both urban and rural space. So far from transcending the conflicts between the two, they thrust both into a confusion" (Lefebvre 1991, 387). He wants the traditional centralized city, though he realizes that it will be a node in a larger space of production.[31]

Lefebvre's fixation on urban centrality is typical of many critics. Norberg-Schulz condemns contemporary cities and suburbs because they lack centered and neatly divided classical unities. "Spatially the new settlements do not anymore possess enclosure and density. . . . Streets and squares in the traditional sense are no longer found, and the general result is a scattered assembly of units. This implies that a distinct figure ground relationship no more exists; the continuity of the landscape is interrupted and the buildings do not form clusters or groups. . . . As a consequence nodes, paths and districts lose their identity, and the town as a whole its imageability" (Norberg-Schulz 1984, 189).

But linkage provides new forms of unity, of which the list-with-links on the commercial strip is only one example. With Lefebvre's emphasis on economic spaces that extend beyond a given locality, one might have expected him to be more open to the network society. However, he believes that centralization is "the form of social space—i.e. the centre-periphery relationship" (Lefebvre 1991, 149). This he bases on a narrow contrast with natural spaces. "Natural space juxtaposes—and thus disperses; it puts places and that which occupies them side by side. It particularizes. By contrast, social space implies actual or potential assembly *at a single point or around that point*" (Lefebvre 1991, 101, my emphasis). However, both nature and society contain systems that interact in other ways than by juxtaposition, and assemble in other ways than around a single point. Every social space does not need a Paris.[32]

For Lefebvre the relation of center/periphery forms a spatial pattern that can be understood independently of any social content. "Centrality is . . . a form, empty in itself but calling for contents—for objects, natural or artificial beings, things, products and works, signs and symbols, people, acts, situations, practical relationships. This means that centrality closely resembles a logical form—and hence that there is a logic of centrality" (Lefebvre 1991, 332). But there are other patterns with their own differing logics. They are not so immediately perceptible because they involve other than spatial juxtaposition. Suburbia is not organized by immediate spatial patterns such as symmetry or centrality. Suburbia's interactive patterns are less like its blocky spatial layout and more like the entwined overlay of paths and nodes in a rain forest, where clearings and connections for different uses are mixed together, connected by twisting links, lacking any easily visible order. Density and interaction are already happening in suburbia. How can they be made more self-conscious and more active?

DISPERSED YET CONNECTED

The dream of suburban life combines stability and roots with mobility and freedom. In 1932 Frank Lloyd Wright proposed in his Broadacre City vision an endless low-density spread of individual residences amid decentralized production and commerce. This seems to resemble a nightmare vision of isolated sprawling suburbs. But Broadacre City was not to be a formless sprawl; it mixed its functions artfully in loose grid and linear combinations, and it was to be supervised and planned by regional architects. Wright imagined each family living on at least four acres of land, which provided some food and leisure activities. Workplaces could be individual and attached to the housing or group workplaces scattered in small specialized centers. Medical and cultural institutions would also be repeated frequently on a small scale. There would be no large conglomerations, but the small centers would not be isolated. Wright's individuals were to be highly mobile and tightly linked.[33] Though each house would have its own small garden or farm, people would be linked by telephone, radio, large highways, and those personal flying machines that appear so often in 1930s visions of the future. Wright wanted to lower density while increasing communication and linkage.

Others too have envisioned a scattered net of linked small industrial and research regions. For example, Kevin Lynch offered a utopian vision that has affinities with Wright's ideas. "Imagine an urban countryside, a highly varied but humanized landscape. It is neither urban nor rural in the old sense, since houses, workplaces, and places of assembly are set among trees, farms, and streams. Within that extensive countryside, there is a network of small, intensive urban centers. This countryside is *as functionally intricate and interdependent as any contemporary city*" (Lynch 1981, 294, my emphasis).

Suburbia has the potential to be a complex and urbane place with its own modes of connection and interplay. The question we turn to next is how that potential can be realized.

CHAPTER SEVEN

Toward More Complexity in Suburbia

To focus on the characteristics of sprawl as symptoms of
urban form run amok presupposes an absolute form for
urban life and prevents us from seeing a new urban order.
(Snyder 1999, B3)

THE PREVIOUS CHAPTER ARGUED that suburbs are more complex places than many critics admit. Are there ways that suburbs can become more self-aware about their own growing complexity and involvement in larger linkages and processes? This would not solve all their problems, but it would help open new possibilities and create pressure for changes toward greater equity and environmental health. This chapter considers the New Urbanism as an expression of place complexity, and a variety of other measures, organized according to the three dimensions of complexity outlined earlier. Describing the New Urbanism as an expression of place complexity might seem paradoxical, since New Urbanist developments are often attacked as nostalgic retreats from the complexities of the contemporary world.[1] But I argue that the New Urbanism is one way to produce more complex suburban places.

COMPLEXITY IN THE NEW URBANISM

The reform and planning movement known as the New Urbanism has been receiving increasing media coverage for its attempts to change the patterns of development. The movement tries to widen the set of options available within the present real estate system and its incentives. New Urbanist towns such as Kentlands (Maryland) and related neotraditional towns such as Celebration (Florida) have been the object of media scrutiny and debate. "Traditional neighborhood developments seek to create an entire, integrated neighborhood with homes, businesses, schools, parks and community centers—a dramatic departure from the suburban pattern of street after street, cul-de-sac after cul-de-sac, of garage-dominated homes" (Breyer 2000, G1–2). Making a livable place becomes a central goal of the planning process, not just a means to sell real estate, though of course more livable places do sell well.

Facing off against the simplified planning and regulation that have produced suburbs dominated by single-use zoning of huge tracts, the New Urbanism seeks to produce experiences of denser living amid varied uses and differently scaled spaces. The movement has elaborated a set of development proposals. Though more New Urbanist developments are urban infill than suburban greenfield developments, it is the suburban projects that attract media attention. They have already influenced other developments, though often in superficial ways that are not backed up with significant changes in spatial arrangements or social patterns.[2] Suburban New Urbanist developments are my focus here, though what I say is even more applicable to the urban infill developments.

New Urbanists have been criticized for building sugar-coated reproductions of American small towns, aimed at the descendants of people who fled such towns. It is true that many New Urbanist spatial ideas are taken from older towns and cities, and arguments for New Urbanism and sales propaganda for its projects often make use of traditional small-town imagery.[3] But both the attackers and the publicists are mistaken if they assume that the goal is to create bounded and self-enclosed places where people reside in isolated communitarian completeness.[4] That is not what happens, nor is it intended by the movement's theorists, who are equally concerned about how communities link into larger networks.

The New Urbanism is not primarily a stylistic movement.[5] It is concerned with spatial and social arrangements. Multiuse development should allow as much daily activity as possible to take place within walking distance of home or work, and, ideally, should provide access to effective public transit. Community units should include mixed-income housing in styles that do not sharply distinguish income levels. Parks and civic buildings should be incorporated into the street layout to give shape to a public realm. Public parking should be located in the interior of blocks, but there should also be on-street parking to slow down traffic and buffer the sidewalks.

Urban architectural codes for each community should provide guidelines for the proportions and sizes of streets and the location of houses on their lots, and for home design insofar as that impacts public spaces—matters of size, style, facade treatments, and the like. These regulations should aim for both variety and harmony. In general they suggest shorter residential blocks and a preference for tight grids over cul-de-sacs, with service alleys leading to garages behind houses that stand closer to the sidewalk than to the back of the property, with porches or other intermediate spaces addressing the street.

The New Urbanism offers detailed advice on practical matters ranging from the radius of a corner's curve to the layout of a metropolitan region. "Many misconceptions are caused by focusing on New Urbanism's neighborhood-scale prescriptions without seeing them embedded in regional structures. . . . Replacing cul-de-sacs and malls with traditional urban design, although desirable, is not sufficient to solve the problems of modern growth, either practically or ideologically. Without regional form-givers like habitat and agricultural preserves, urban growth boundaries, transit systems, and designated urban centers, even well-designed neighborhoods can contribute to sprawl. Infill and redevelopment, although a high priority for New Urbanism, cannot accommodate all the growth in many regions. A regional plan is a necessary armature for the placement of new growth" (Calthorpe 2000, 178–80).[6] So the New Urbanism urges metropolitan areas to build toward a denser polycentric form made up of many distinct mixed-use neighborhoods or towns rather than a spread of large single-use tracts. Concentrations of commercial and civic activity should be embedded in neighborhoods rather than strung out along strips.

Compared to familiar suburbs, New Urbanist developments are more concentrated, with smaller lot sizes and houses arranged to address streets whose layout and dimensions are planned to encourage interaction and neighborliness. Some projects plan for secondary pedestrian paths from the beginning. The architectural codes may give the impression that the developments spring from the ground full-grown, self-enclosed, and complete, but in fact they are usually slower to "build out" than standard subdivision developments or the nineteenth-century instant towns that sprang up along railroad lines.

The New Urbanists would reshape sprawl into a field with many nodes; no single node would be dominant, nor would it be isolated. Such polycentrism also appears in Christopher Alexander and his coauthors' related model for incremental urban design, which emphasizes a texture of overlapping but nonconcentric wholes (see Alexander, Ishikawa, and

Silverstein 1977 and Alexander et al. 1987). Alexander and his coauthors, as do the New Urbanists, aim for continuous spatial wholes. Their ideas could be supplemented by more recognition of the discontinuities and links that weave separated spatial areas into new kinds of complex unity.

Neat and centered New Urbanist villages look like they reject everything characteristic of contemporary places. But we should not confuse a place's architectural style with its social patterns and norms. New Urbanist developments combine spatial features of older towns with economic and cultural characteristics of today's linked and mixed places. The lists and the nonconcentric and the virtual penetrate the pretty villages, which cannot close on themselves. The strips wait just outside. Though the neighborhoods have local centers, they remain nodes in the networks. They exist through links for jobs, for shopping, for communication and self-definition beyond the local community. They live in a condition defined by forces in multiple economic and cultural networks that reinforce multiple place norms. For instance, in Celebration, attempts to create a new type of school brought into conflict innovative educational reformers, conservative and meritocratic parents, and an impecunious county school board, all struggling to adapt to changes of the kind Gandelsonas mentioned that were altering the field of available options.

New Urbanist plans try to keep services and commercial development within walking distance of homes. However, unlike the relatively complete commercial centers of small towns, walkable New Urbanist commercial centers meet only limited needs. Celebration's commercial center offers basic groceries, boutique clothing, home decorations, books, real estate, legal services, but there is no supermarket, no hardware stores or home repair shops, no gas station or car maintenance facility, no pharmacy. The strip just outside the town is more efficient at these services. As the town grows, retail Darwinism may produce walkable services more aimed at residents' daily needs, but the efficiencies of the mall and the big box and the Internet will not go away. At Kentlands the New Urbanist planners argued for a shopping area on the edge of the development to include big-box stores that offer more daily items, so that the inhabitants would not have to leave the town area so often for shopping.[7] Nonetheless, these developments still have centers of economic gravity outside themselves.

New Urbanist developments put school, playground, day care, and some basic stores within walking distance, so that stay-at-home parents are less imprisoned in an isolated subdivision, not forced to be chauffeurs (Ross 1999, 301–2). But the communities still embody an expectation that most wage earners and entrepreneurs will leave the community to work elsewhere. A traditional town might have small-scale production and a few larger productive sites scattered throughout rather than absent or banished to outlying areas. New Urbanist communities emphasize, by the absence of such local productive sites, their insertion into the extended system of economic linkages and processes.

There is much easy disdain in attacks on the New Urbanism, as there was in the attacks on Wright's Broadacre City and other proposals that accepted the inevitability of suburban development.[8] Compare, for instance, the attacks on New Urbanism with the attacks on earlier attempts elsewhere. For instance, the 1950s Stockholm suburb of Årsta was one of the first Swedish attempts to plan a suburban housing development that included a town center with commercial and leisure facilities and municipal services. "Critics attacked the very idea of neighborhood planning and community centres as such, seeing it as a romantic dream [of a design] that could create a sense of community and transform people in the mass into active democrats. An art historian, Göran Lindahl, considered that these 'collectivistic villages' could just as well create isolation, stagnation and finger-wagging supervision; he recommended instead 'the living big town.' He saw Årsta Centrum as a warning example. 'Perhaps this sort of thing would suit little children and pensioners, and maybe even an exceptionally meek victim of asthenia'" (Rudberg 1998, 120–21). The macho tone of this 1950s criticism can be heard in attacks on New Urbanism as soft living for those not tough enough to live in a Real City.

In the standard press coverage, New Urbanist developments are all alike. Although they do share common spatial strategies, at least six different types are already discernible, with more likely to appear. They differ in their expectations for employment and in their relations to their surroundings. Kentlands in Maryland is a suburban bedroom community in the midst of other subdivisions but has its own attached shopping area. Celebration in Florida and King Farm in Maryland are a different type, bedroom communities that have more economic weight of their own. Celebration includes a regional hospital, a large office complex, and room for some manufacturing; King Farm includes a large office complex near a transit stop.[9] A third type is exemplified by Seaside in Florida, the first New Urbanist community, which serves as a vacation resort or "horizontal hotel." A fourth type includes New Urbanist town centers being built in already existing suburban subdivisions.[10] A fifth type is urban infill redevelopment such as new developments in Orlando and Austin that apply the movement's principles to urban redevelopment. The redevelopment of Denver's Stapleton airport is a growing example of this type.[11] A sixth type is the Transit Oriented Developments championed by Peter Calthorpe and currently in progress around several cities on the West Coast.

A common criticism of the New Urbanism is that it builds theme-park replicas of an unreachable past. But New Urbanist developments are not themed places in the sense I discussed earlier. It can seem that they are standard suburban developments masquerading as traditional towns. Actually they are new kinds of places whose norms and patterns of living differ from both older towns and standard subdivisions. The emphases on community and the denser spatial arrangements are not being themed as different from residents' everyday life; they *are* that everyday life.

It is hard to think beyond the image of cheerful families on old-fashioned front porches on a New Urbanist street.[12] However, "you go to Stapleton [the redeveloped former Denver airport], and as a designer you'll hate it because it's very nice, it looks so pretty with white picket fences, the ad nauseam New Urbanism. But if you walk around and talk to people there, because of that income disparity that is already embedded in that community, and because they walk and you have a neighborhood school they can walk to and they have parks they can get to on foot, they actually encounter each other and they have more unexpected experiences than in the traditional suburban world. I consider that the foundation of freedom, to have those unexpected events in one's daily life. That's urbanism. And it can happen with picket fences" (Peter Calthorpe, in Fishman 2005, 65).

The conflicts that shadowed Celebration's first years show that not all is poster-uniform even in a fairly homogeneous population. When there were disputes over the school's policies and its relations with the larger school district, when shoddy building practices were revealed, and when the development corporation changed its policies, the residents of

Celebration came together in formal and informal ways for debate about communal values and priorities.

> Rudely dispossessed of any lingering illusions that they had moved to an instant utopia, Celebrationites encountered obstacles to happiness that compelled them to forge community bonds for which there was no planning blueprint. The strong community its creators had hoped for would come into being as much in response to adversity as to the conveniences and advantages built in the town's design. The sense of community that was most authentic and resourceful emerged in response to perceived threats, challenges, and barriers to people's well-being, and, above all, to their property values. . . . Interests beyond their control, whether commercial (the developer), philosophical (the school), or cultural (media and outside opinion), had imperiled Celebrationites' sense of security. It had taken the bitter taste of jeopardy to arouse the appetite for strong society. (Ross 1999, 318)[13]

The result was a skein of interacting social roles and differing values that showed and increased the complexities of the place's norms. People were recognized as citizens and recognized others as partners and opponents in dialogue.[14] All suburbs need such politicizing institutions and self-reflective practices to supplement social clubs and block parties. When such practices work, a community can become aware of its complex mix of norms and social roles. Both despite and because of interior tensions, the community can help fill the void left by the way current politics and markets weaken intermediate-scale associations.

Such connection can be oppressive as well as liberating. Although civic arrangements to bring people together can encourage liberating kinds of interaction, they can also become instruments of social control.[15] Speaking of New Urbanist developments in connection with the movie *The Truman Show*, Reed Kroloff worries that "we wonder just how much identity, freedom, or variety we're willing to sacrifice in order to purchase the stability these places seem to offer in an increasingly unstable world" (Kroloff 1998, 11). *The Truman Show* exteriors were filmed in Seaside, the first New Urbanist icon. Herbert Gans and Robert Bruegmann have argued, though, that complaints about suburban conformity are marked by stereotyping and class bias.[16] Investigating the conflicts in Celebration, Ross concluded that while individuals in Celebration do have plenty of personal "identity, freedom, and variety,"[17] the residents were being pressured to conform by the need to be consistent with their choice to come to a town with such a public emphasis on community. It was also important to keep up the image of the town in order to protect the property value of their homes. What is significant is that these pressures arose not from a supposed closure of the community but from how the town was inserted into the wider flows of capital and images.

Some New Urbanist communities encourage their residents to feel self-consciously different and engaged in the project of recovering community life. This is most extreme in a highly publicized place such as Celebration, where dealing with inquisitive media becomes part of the local way of life. The effect of this self-consciousness and media attention is to keep the "outside" present at all times as part of the identity of the citizens. Residents quickly discover that they have not escaped, although they may have altered, their insertion into today's global network processes. They are not defined by a single civic or economic center.

The key suggestions of New Urbanism are about land use, street layout, how buildings should address civic areas, transit, and other spatial issues. These principles do not demand the traditional house styles that have dominated the built form and the visual images of existing New Urbanist developments. There is nothing that could not be accomplished with houses and apartments in more modernist styles, and steps along these lines have been taken with a development in Miami and others on the West Coast. New Urbanists argue that the traditional look of current developments results from consumer preference and market forces. For the most part, suburban home buyers do not negotiate with architects; they purchase ready-made products. In America traditional house styles fit buyers' preconceptions, while other styles are taken to signal either eccentricity or poverty. As a consequence, traditional styles can facilitate the goal of mixing income levels, since when all the buildings share these styles, lower-income houses lack the stigma that was attached to modernist styles and public housing.[18]

New Urbanist planning insists on architectural codes that discourage context-ignoring monuments while avoiding cookie-cutter sameness.[19] The result may be greater stylistic uniformity than in a traditional town that has grown up over time, but less sameness than in standard subdivisions. The challenge is "how to deliver an urbanism that is more open to change and flexibility. Its immediate problem is how to embrace contemporary architectural languages and tectonics . . . [There is also] the related problem of integrating contemporary building materials and practices into neo-traditional architecture" (Kelbaugh 2002, 178).

The issue of style will eventually be forced when residents begin to remodel their homes. In the late 1940s, in Levittown, "covenants forbade the construction of fences and specified permissible renovations— including colors and materials—and other conditions of residence" (Kelly 1993, 51). Despite the prohibitions, "by the end of the first decade, the visual landscape of Levittown—both interior and exterior—had been almost totally redesigned, not by the builder, but by the homeowners. It became apparent that the domestic space of the Levittown houses would not stand still . . . The redesigned environment was far more 'vernacular' than the original subdivision had been, and the residents more autonomous" (Kelly 1993, 6). Such pressures for change will surely develop in New Urbanist neighborhoods.

The New Urbanism, even aside from its regional recommendations, does not simplify suburban life but adds to its complexity by providing new spatial arrangements and social incentives that can increase the thickness of suburban places and lead to greater awareness of the place's internal complexity and external connections. The spatial arrangements open more possibilities for contact and interaction. Local retail and services can be meeting places. Local political and economic issues can become more prominent, as in the disputes at Celebration. All this is overlaid on the network of external economic and cultural connections existing in any suburb but foregrounded in a New Urbanist development because of the explicit contrast between the chaotic outside and the centered spatial order within.

Community in the sprawling suburbs is based less on local enclosure and centering than on linkage and communication. The automobile, transit, telephone, and the Net all connect and link. If these were combined with the kinds of spatial arrangements and locally available services that the New Urbanism tries to foster, what might develop could be what William Mitchell looked forward to in both cities and suburbs: "new-style live/work dwelling in twenty-four-hour neighborhoods that effectively combine local attractions with global connections" (Mitchell 1999, 78). Such locally livable, walkable communities would link together in ways that will be neither centered cities nor traditional towns nor isolated suburbs.

TOWARD LINKED COMPLEXITY IN SUBURBIA

Spatial patterns such as those suggested by the New Urbanists can be important as growth continues, but they are not the only alternative. Other patterns for new development are possible, for instance cohousing groups, clustered housing around community greens, and even traditional cul-de-sacs, if designed to open onto greenbelts or other shared community spaces.[20] Experimentation with new forms is needed, and this requires battles against the default patterns and regulations. Then there are the electronic links and additions of virtual spaces through the internet and its creation of dispersed but linked communities.

However, besides seeking out more livable spatial patterns for new construction, it is important to ask what might be done to increase lived complexity in already existing suburbs. Except for scattered infill, no large architectural changes are likely there. A majority of Americans live in suburbs with houses and schools and strips and roads and utilities already built and subject to myriad legal and financial restrictions. Wholesale rebuilding of existing suburban housing is not an option. Banking practices, mortgage patterns, homeowners associations vigilantly guarding property values, zoning restrictions, cumbersome approval processes—many factors make it all but impossible to rebuild existing suburbs. Small interventions are possible, but large-scale retrofitting of housing and spatial patterns seems unlikely except through infill that might gradually change the rhythms of the whole. If massive rebuilding of housing and streets is not going to happen, then it is important to reveal and encourage the new kinds of places that existing suburbs are becoming even without being rebuilt.

Commercial strips in suburbia, however, can change thoroughly and quickly, since the strip buildings are constructed to have short life spans. Strips have gone from small shops to strip malls to big malls to big boxes to lifestyle malls, with each wave leaving behind remnants. Attempts to alter patterns in existing suburbs are likely to be most successful when building on disused or outmoded commercial space. For example, some dead malls have been redone with housing in the parking lots and the mall buildings converted to a neighborhood center or school. Dead malls have been remade as urban villages with housing, shopping, and office space in St. Paul (Minn.), Orange County (Calif.), and Lakewood (Colo.). Malls have become urban shopping villages in Winter Park

(Fla.) and Tucson (Ariz.). "'It's the Joni Mitchell song in reverse,' says Chuck Repke, head of the local neighborhood planning council [in St. Paul]. 'We took the parking lot and turned it back to paradise'" (El Nasser 2003; see Barber 2001, 210–13 for other examples).

Are there architectural and nonarchitectural ways to make life in already built suburbs thicker, more complex, and more self-aware? Today's suburbs are not so isolated and simple as they may seem; their complexity can be revealed and increased. In his lament for the lost harmony of Michigan Avenue, Paul Goldberger pointed out that "the truly special quality of North Michigan Avenue came not from buildings that were extraordinary things in themselves, but from good buildings that [came] together to create an extraordinary ensemble" (Goldberger 1996). Goldberger's traditional mode of wholeness fits less well in the age of the list, but we might take his words as a suggestion. Do buildings that are not extraordinary in themselves come together to create a new kind of suburban whole when their coming together happens not through spatial proximity but through other kinds of links and connections?

Suburbia presents the design challenge of dealing with large tracts of simplified local order making up a larger-scale clutter. Are there ways to turn this into more complex local order and larger-scale interrelation? Just as a themed place can try to enforce a single resonance and meaning, so developments in suburbia aim at marketable homogeneity. As with themed places, though, there are complexities in the borders and the unities of suburban areas. Unlike themed places, suburbia has another register of complexities when the architecture recedes into a formative background and people get on with their relations to one another and to the wider world.

The spatial form of suburbia is not equivalent to its social place form. To condemn suburban sprawl as isolated blotches thrown about the landscape misses its place structure. In its interconnections with other places and wider processes, in its larger built context, and in its changes over time, suburbia is already complex. Perceiving this complexity demands a sensitivity to contours and links that are more than spatial. We need to be alert to the complexity that is already there as well as that which will come through new kinds of connections and new social agents and patterns. Such complexity often hides in invisible links and in the intersection of different place norms; can these links and norms be made more visible, increasing the awareness of links and the thickness and historical density of suburban places? I am suggesting not that suburban architecture is secretly wonderful, but that debates about architectural quality can obscure the more complex place forms in suburbia's overlay of norms and networks.[21]

EMPHASIZING STRUCTURAL COMPLEXITY

In this and the following sections I suggest ways to increase complexity in suburbia and to make it more self-aware, retaining the earlier organization by the three dimensions of place complexity and their corresponding diagnostic questions. The suggestions start with small architectural and artistic interventions aimed at increasing the awareness of local complexity. Then they turn to encouraging more active reinterpretation of place norms, and finally to large-scale political and economic policy issues. Creating greater awareness of complexity within existing suburbs is partly a task for artists and educators, partly an issue for architects working on additions and infill, partly a need for planners and engineers to stop simplifying, partly a matter of transportation and wiring, partly a demand for new laws and policies that will change the incentives and open new possibilities.

The first dimension of complexity discussed in chapter 3 was the interacting multiplicities in the spatial structure and the interweaving of social norms for a place. Becoming more aware of this *structural* complexity involves living more consciously the intersecting roles and the interplay between spatial and social structures.

The first diagnostic question for structural complexity was: *Is the place totally foreground, or does it interweave foreground emphases and more banal, everyday stretches?* Suburbia can seem all background, with an occasional self-important civic or commercial monument thrusting itself forward from the repetitive housing and commercial buildings. The complexities of the place are hidden by the banality of the architecture. A true perception needs more awareness of the everyday links and intersections and rhythms that permeate and structure lives in the banal background.

Similar issues arise with the criteria mentioned earlier about complex routes of action. Suburban actions and roles may seem too linear, too loosely connected, lacking variety and interaction. Their complexities, again, need to be partly revealed, partly created. For this, the diagnostic questions I suggested were: *Can the place be lived as a unification of the multiple factors resulting from its social and spatial divisions and unities?* Are the place's normative routes and paths of action linear or not? Are these routes parallel or loosely connected, or are they interwoven and interacting with one another? Does the place embody a single straightforward social role, or multiple aspects and multiple interacting roles? If the social roles involved in the place are multiple (whether thick or thin), how does the place define them to be together? Do they intersect or run in parallel? If there are multiple competing social norms and spatial divisions for different inhabitants of the place, do they coexist in ways that make it more complex or do they make it into several overlapping simpler places?

Except in small, highly controlled suburban developments there is no purely homogeneous "our community." Even where the population appears homogeneous there are differences. Those 1950s and 1960s films and novels depicting lurid conflicts and unlikely intersections lurking beneath the placid streets of suburbia recognized divisions and differences but kept them safely referred to standard norms. Nowadays there are many different social and place norms for action, for gender roles and family life, for education, as more diverse populations move into suburbia. Sometimes this diversity creates excitement, sometimes conflict.[22] "Most places (even lookalike suburbs) are more layered and diverse from the inside, and understanding that local history, economics, and politics is a complex, fascinating, and contradictory business everywhere" (Lippard 1997, 292). Recall the discussion earlier of the conflicts in Celebration.

Artists and designers could take up the task of making suburbia more self-aware of its own complexities. To paraphrase Louis Kahn, the joint is the key. To counterpoise connected complexity to serial dispersal, we need to encourage self-awareness of multiple norms and routes of action by emphasizing their temporal and spatial edges, their connections and discontinuities. This means accentuating borders and links and rhythms. The goal is increased density of connection and encounter, together with greater self-awareness of the temporal processes of living in place.

One might imagine small-scale artistic interventions (perhaps architectural follies in pocket parks, or other artworks that gathered or twisted or connected) aimed to make people perceive anew their world and their own processes of place making. Outside Portland, Oregon, the suburb of Lake Oswego has installed a series of sidewalk sculptures that comment on the locality, the weather, and themes other than the standard civic topics of public art. There are many reasons, some rooted in class divisions, why public art and ornament in the suburbs too often restricts itself to simple identities and unities, whether to affirm or to criticize them. Neither facile celebrations nor easy irony helps suburbia to a more complex vision of itself.

Here is an example of an intervention that revealed and increased the lived complexity of a place.

> Tobias Armborst has redesigned a strip mall [on the edge of Cambridge, Massachusetts] according to the simultaneous presence of multiple temporalities. . . . Armborst began his project with an intensive 24-hour ethnographic investigation of this mall . . . an absolutely ordinary place, a collection of ordinary functions . . . Armborst designed a series of projects to produce what he called "public time" (as opposed to public space). Each of these times emphasizes different temporal activities and different groups of people. By extending and making visible all these multiple and co-existing interpretations of this place, he built up "thick" layers of meaning, transforming the experience of being there. He did not attempt to change the fragmented and incoherent quality of the mall, but to accentuate the pieces . . . . He did this by focusing not only on what is present in the banality of everyday life, but also on what is absent yet might be there. At the end of the day, what did he achieve? . . . The mall doesn't look that much more beautiful, it's not less fragmented or more coherent. It hasn't been transformed into a little town center in the New Urbanist mode or a modernist programmatic assemblage à la Rem Koolhaas. Intensifying what was already there produces a new type of urbanism that enhances daily experience, building in a kind of ordinary magic that was absent in [the] mall's previous everyday life. (Margaret Crawford, in Mehrotra 2005, 32)

Although it is true that in many ways "it is up to the architects to make the moves" (Wigley 1995, 94), it is also true that we need many small acts of "tinkering and modification" by ordinary people (Lerup 2000, 152).[23] The cumulative effects of such bricolage could change the sense of the whole.[24]

Spatial tactics could be adapted from the New Urbanism and older towns to increase the density of encounter and linkage in existing suburbs. Infill construction could pay attention to the ratio of street width to building height, the length of blocks, and other issues of proportion and placement. Streets could be narrowed, corners changed to slow down traffic. More "possibilities for attachment" (Hertzberger 1991, 177) could be created along the edges or borders of suburban open spaces, by adding niches or low walls or other in-between features that encourage sociality and the formation of temporary places where the unexpected might happen. Parks can be designed to encourage encounters. In Eugene, Oregon, a wide fenced-in field encourages dog owners to converse informally while their dogs romp.

Bike paths and footpaths and small parks could be fitted in, to increase the sense of being in a connected neighborhood. Zoning could be changed to allow more small local stores. New patterns can be invented. "If we want to respond to the multiplicity in which society manifests itself we must liberate form from the shackles of coagulated meanings. We must continuously search for archetypal forms which, because they can be associated with multiple meanings, can not only absorb a programme but can generate one" (Hertzberger 1991, 149).[25]

If it is not possible to break the monopoly the traditional palette of house styles has on the American imagination, there might be ways of adding on to or twisting those styles already built to make them acknowledge the complexity of their situation. Could one alter architectural details or add ornament to celebrate complexity and connection or to show multiple social norms and undercut perceived segregation by class and lifestyle? Ethnic migrations, increased choices in popular culture, and new household and family patterns are bringing more cultural diversity to similar-looking suburbs. What ways might be found to make visible these differing norms for household, family, children, work, or leisure? Some people are using lawn ornaments and banners as assertions of individuality or affiliation; should such decorations and symbols be multiplied?

To combat the image of suburbia as the land of behavioral conformity and cookie-cutter houses, could we find and emphasize local items that do not fit the standard categories? "It is the residual, the irreducible—whatever cannot be classified or codified according to categories devised subsequent to production—which is, here as always, the most

precious" (Lefebvre 1991, 220). There are more odd corners and ec-
centricities than are usually visible. Show off the local Watts Towers or
Katy China.[26] Some of this may happen if there is competition for tourism, but there will be other odd items that might not attract the outsider
but could increase the residents' sense of locality. "Seek the tiny spark of
accident, the here and now" (Liggett 2003, 126).

Another diagnostic question about structural complexity was: *Does the
place show explicit spatial or symbolic links or signs of its connection to other
places and processes?*

The centered and bounded architectural form of many suburban
developments does not encourage awareness of linkage, yet suburbia is
more connected than its visual image avows. Are there ways to acknowledge the links and the non-self-sufficiency of suburban places in the
sprawl? Could one do publicly for the suburb what Lefebvre wants to do
by analyzing a house? "A critical analysis would doubtless destroy the appearance of solidity of this house. . . . our house would emerge as permeated from every direction by streams of energy which run in and out of
it by every imaginable route: water, gas, electricity, telephone lines, radio
and television signals, and so on. Its range of immobility would then be
replaced by an image of a complex of mobilities, a nexus of in and out
conduits" (Lefebvre 1991, 93).

It is hard to acknowledge architecturally how links constitute places. It
is not just that my suburban castle has holes in its walls, but that my castle is what it is because of its linkages. Links do not connect self-sufficient
places; links permeate and help define local places. Nothing there is
simply there. Yet the look and spacing of existing suburbs asserts disconnection. Suburban homes pretend to be self-sufficient estates, office
buildings appear as isolated palaces, malls look like complete shopping
environments, yet all is interrelated and temporary. The task is to make
visible the links and systemic connections that tie together and flicker
across the solid-seeming suburban landscape, denying its isolation and
knitting it into much denser places than it appears to be.[27]

Medieval cathedrals used sculpture and imagery to show their links
to other sacred places, and to an overall vision of the cosmos. Should
we then find some modern equivalents of statues and stained glass?
Karsten Harries claims that architectural ornament makes community
ideals and values present (Harries 1997, 50–69). But today the ideals

and values are multiple and complex. There is a clue in Louis Kahn's remark that "the joint is the beginning of ornament" (Kahn 1987, 9). Although Kahn was speaking about the joints between different building materials, we can extend his remark to the joints between different sets of social and place norms, different functions, and the intersections of global and local, transit and home, inner and outer, on which suburban life depends.[28] There should be artistic and architectural ways of making those joinings salient, and so making the complexities of the whole more visible in the parts. The goal is to find ways to encourage people to see what is around them as more than simple given presences confined to one physical location.[29]

TAKING UP THE TASK OF INTERPRETATION

The second dimension of complexity is in the active processes by which place norms and structures are interpreted, reproduced, and passed on. Becoming aware of complexity in the ongoing processes of interpretation involves consciously taking up the interpretive task and its internal multiplicities, conscious of the different kinds of change and adaptation that it produces. The diagnostic questions were: *Does the place encourage inhabitants to be aware of their own processes of active interpretation and their resolution of multiple roles and demands? Are there opportunities to participate in reformation or reproduction of the place's spatial structures and social norms?*

The goal is greater participation in the definition of suburban places and their norms and practices. Given the inherent multiplicities, there is no reason to assume that this will be a peaceful process. As Doreen Massey points out, "all attempts to institute horizons, to establish boundaries, to secure the identity of places, can . . . be seen to be attempts to stabilize the meaning of particular envelopes of space-time. . . . Such attempts . . . are constantly the site of social contest, battles over the power to label space-time, to impose the meaning to be attributed to a space, for however long or short a span of time" (Massey 1994, 5).

The process of defining and imposing place norms and structures is continuous. Claiming that norms are stable and fixed is a defensive move in that struggle, not its resolution. Making the process more evident and encouraging more participation can increase the lived complexity of suburban life. This requires interventions that are themselves processes rather than the artistic and architectural interventions suggested in the previous section. What is important is the realization that place norms are not final and complete but are complexly interrelated and porous within larger flows, and always under reconstruction even when they appear fixed.

Some New Urbanist developments include a normative expectation for people to work intentionally to produce a sense of community. The processes that interpret and reproduce and perpetuate the place's norms are made explicitly self-aware and consciously taken up by explicit planned organizations, civic events, and attempts to create interaction. A well-financed example is the Celebration Foundation, which encourages volunteering and community projects. A resident of Celebration said to me, "We're the meetingest community."[30] Other suburban areas may not have such official efforts, but there are a multitude of familiar organizations that think of themselves as passing on and protecting the values and norms of their community. Homeowners associations, traditional service organizations such as Rotary, chambers of commerce, neighborhood associations, church groups, and the like all work to sustain and reproduce values and norms for a place. Such organizations may be inclusive in dealing with the complexities of the community, or they may be defensive of narrow visions and economic privileges. In either case they seldom realize how much they are reinterpreting and altering a place's norms to fit new circumstances.

There might be small interventions that could make communal processes of interpretation and reproduction more present in the suburban surroundings and encourage people to participate more actively. Imagine reports on local environmental processes, changes, and debates presented on screens outside of civic buildings, or on news tickers on the broadcast of a local cable TV station. Suburban houses and institutions are constantly being reworked; are there ways to point this out architecturally? Are there ways other than defensive zoning and planning hearings to give people a sense of participating in the process of change? Such processes are sometimes made explicit by staging intense design charrettes in which many local inhabitants of different status and expertise can participate. The occasions need not be about zoning or land use; they could be matters of school or recreation policy, utility regulation, disputes with neighboring areas, and so on. Such discussions make everyone involved more aware of the complexities of the place and the active effort needed to interpret and carry on its norms in new situations.

Because it facilitates the shaping of small, temporary discussions, the Internet can assist in making more explicit the processes of interpretation and reproduction of place norms. Community blogs and forums about community issues can provide contact that goes beyond what might be available in spatial proximity. Since the discussions are asynchronous, people can find more time to participate. In this way electronic links can help knit together suburban dispersal and create more interactive community processes for reinterpreting and reproducing multiple social norms.

DEALINGS WITH COMPLEX OUTSIDE FORCES

The third dimension of complexity is in the relations of a place to the multiple flows, systemic effects and political decisions that impact it. The place exists within environmental, economic, and political systems. The standard patterns of U.S. suburban development were set by government and corporate policies working in and with the real estate market. Most of the suggestions in this section deal with policy changes that might alter the default shape for new suburban growth and allow new kinds of infill construction in existing suburbs.

Suburban developments live on continual contrast and connection with the outside and its flows. Just as we need to live themed places more broadly than their themes define, so we need to live suburban communities in a more porous and connected way than standard images of suburbia suggest. The norms and expectations of a place should acknowledge its linkages and flows, so that these are not taken as intrusions on some whole that was supposed to be bounded and complete. It may seem paradoxical, but a sense of being in wider economic and political flows can strengthen a sense of unique locality, just as a better awareness of how it fits into the ecology of a wider region can both enlighten and strengthen one's loyalty to a particular valley. More complex inhabitation does not eliminate the sense of homeyness and safety that many seek in the suburbs, but that sense of center and periphery, home and community, gets located within larger nets of meaning and system flows. This does not erase local centers, but it keeps them plural and interacting.

PERCEIVING WIDER CONNECTIONS

In the complexity chapter, the first diagnostic question for the third dimension of complexity was: *Does the place show explicit spatial or symbolic links and signs of its belonging within larger systems, social contexts, and their genetic processes?* Participating in local processes that sustain and reinterpret place norms and structures (the second dimension of complexity) leads to an awareness of the larger forces impacting the local region. Are there means to accentuate this sense of larger systemic and political connections and the intersections of the local and global forces?

Environmental connections are the most obvious case. Environmental pressures come home through debate on issues related to water and air quality, as with efforts to deal with remote sources of pollution. Dealing with waste can bring a sense of connection that leads to new kinds of organization and activity. Perhaps those trash bins and loading docks that are usually hidden should be made more visible?[31] Efforts to increase the consumption of locally produced food add awareness of worldwide networks of commerce and their environmental effects. Labeling products with their provenance can alter the perception of everyday consumption. Perhaps the sense of insertion into environmental processes could be strengthened by resuming Louis Sullivan's search for decorative themes based on local plants and environmental features.

In a different kind of connection, cell-phone towers remind us that links work in nonconcentric, nonhierarchical ways in all directions. Could we find designs for those towers that a suburb could see not as an eyesore but as a celebration of connections and reach? In the Southwest there are phone towers shaped like saguaro cacti; a suburb in Texas has one in the shape of a cross. Some in Oregon are disguised as trees. Imagine that instead of these disguises there were locally significant shapes that celebrated the connections.

Could there be other ways of acknowledging far horizons by gestures toward them, such as public maps and signposts that show distant as well as local destinations, or the public equivalent of those walls of screens bearing images from all over the world so popular now as the background of TV news shows? The aim would be to remind people that they live in the networks and processes of change, and not just in the local enclave.

The Internet and its communities formed for discussion or games or commerce expand suburban space in discontinuous ways. My room is linked with places all over the globe. This provides a wider forum for awareness and action on issues that go beyond the local horizon.

ACTING IN WIDER CONNECTIONS

The remaining diagnostic questions for the third dimension of complexity were: *Do the place's norms and spatial articulation and architecture make it easier to become aware of the political and economic processes,* the systemic pressures and constraints, the varied interest groups within and outside the place, and their procedures of negotiation or imposition? Are there possibilities for intervening in or redirecting those larger processes? Or does the place enforce the illusion that its social and spatial structures are immediately given and natural?

Proposals for linkage and complexity need to beware the error that Doreen Massey finds in many recent discussions of sprawl and urbanism, namely, a "frequent abandonment of any progressive project other than multiplicity" (Massey 1994, 223). A strategy of increasing suburban complexity and the awareness of that complexity does not by itself solve the larger problems of suburbia, but the awareness it fosters can deny "go-it-alone" fantasies in an individual or a town. A sense of complexity can lessen the hold of simplified values and make it more difficult to restrict politics to polarized resentments and single issue identities.[32]

The complexity of people's actions and debates grows as their awareness of larger forces increases. "In truth there is no laissez-faire approach to growth. It's all regulated . . . it's all a series of political questions and major public investments" (Peter Calthorpe, in Fishman 2005, 19). The larger flows and decisions that both open and constrain possibilities for suburban development are not automatic machines; interventions are possible, if difficult. When new options are desired, they have to be created. The inertias built into the default processes and patterns of growth need to be pushed against if new patterns are to be possible.

One way of putting this is to say that while the market needs to be freer, certain barriers keep new products and processes off the market. Habitual perceptions, the way financial risks are defined, zoning regulations, corporate self-interest—all conspire to keep suburbs growing the way they have. The current processes of development subsidize one pattern of growth. The way roads get built and infrastructure paid for, the way school districts arrange busses, tax depreciation allowances, zoning regulations all support the default pattern (see Flint 2006, 78, 166). Put more abstractly, the system has settled at a local maximum that satisfies many interests and needs, and it resists the shocks and innovations that might move it to a higher maximum that would satisfy those and more needs.

I turn now to changes in policy and politics that might push suburban growth into new patterns. Most changes are aimed at increasing the density of spatial connection in new construction or in infill projects, ranging from those that work within the current arrangements to those that challenge their basic concepts. The changes are policy decisions that could be debated, but the inevitable shocks to the system—especially the rising price of oil and energy—that happen no matter what people say or do may make policy changes happen more quickly.

WITHIN THE CURRENT FRAMEWORK

There are many changes that would be relatively easy within the current framework for development and that would open new patterns and increase the lived complexity of suburban life. For instance, altering zoning regulations to allow multiple uses above commercial spaces could change the feel of a suburban downtown. Requirements for on-site parking for new commercial facilities could be relaxed to allow denser development. State requirements about school athletic fields and parking could be reduced, avoiding the pressures to build new schools on empty land outside of towns. Expanding the requirements for building affordable residential units could bring more economic diversity. Increasing tax credits for preservation and streamlining procedures would facilitate creative reuse of facilities such as old malls or outdated garden apartments and industrial parks. Subsidies and cost-shifting that encourage development out on the edges could be made more evident, so decisions could be made in view of the true costs for utilities, infrastructure, roads, school expansion, and the like.

One pattern not likely to change is suburbia's dependence on the automobile. It would be good to have the full costs of automobile use made evident. However, despite complaints about traffic, dwellers in already established suburbs firmly favor automobile transportation. It is not the gasoline-burning car as such that is crucial, but the ideal of being auto-mobile, self-moving. Some device that did this better and more ecologically than a gasoline car could win out in the end, as long as that ideal was sustained (see Lynch 1981, 419–36). Where there is effective mixed-use planning, at short distances walking can be the original auto-mobile.

In new construction greater density and complexity of contact can be obtained by combining public transit with automobile use. So-called transit-oriented developments integrate pedestrian-scale pockets of dense development near light rail, and a different pattern of roads (see Calthorpe 1989 and 1993, Calthorpe and Fulton 2001, and Kelbaugh 1997 and 2002). But even then people would have good reasons to want their cars.[33] For existing suburbs that cannot be rebuilt, one analogue of public transport might be better communications systems.

SMART GROWTH INITIATIVES

Some policy changes that have garnered attention in the last several decades aim at smart growth. This malleable term covers a multitude of land use and zoning policies, transit policies, regional cooperation, and market-based incentives aimed at guiding growth and encouraging infill. Smart growth has been supported by many different groups who saw it as helping their own interests, but they often disagree on what it means, demonstrating the multiplicity of norms and roles at play.

> Middle-class suburbanites noted the negative effects of decades of traditional land-use decisions on their lifestyle and seriously questioned the ideology of value-free development. Urban boosters, including businesses, sought to correct the balance of political power between suburbs and cities, by advocating region-wide interests. Land developers, responding to challenges to the growth machine, some sincerely concerned about the social costs of unchecked development and others motivated by the opportunity to take advantage of this new, palatable growth ideology to reframe themselves, shifted political grounds as development clout was challenged, increasingly successfully, by home owner groups, environmentalists, and community organizations. It is unsurprising,

then, that different constituencies promote different interpretations of smart growth. (Gearin 2004, 285)

Gearin lists eight primary goals for most smart-growth initiatives "direct-
ing growth, preserving land, reducing auto dependence, controlling
rate/amount of growth, redesigning communities, altering perception
of the environment, encouraging regional cooperation, and altering
the housing market" (Gearin 2004, 285). Other smart-growth measures
work toward historic preservation and farmland protection. Many measures parallel the New Urbanist encouragement of higher density and
small local commercial centers. Smart growth does not, however, address
issues of social and economic equity, and its tools can be used in exclusionary ways for maintaining privileged situations.

Except for the stronger measures introduced in some states (for instance in Oregon, New Jersey, and Maryland) smart-growth policies do
not challenge the default model too severely. While the policies have
had some successes, political reactions and property rights movements
have slowed or reversed their momentum; the policies were largely abandoned in New Jersey and Maryland and were weakened in Oregon. (See
Bruegmann 2005 for historical and libertarian criticisms of smart growth
policies, and Flint 2005 for the story of their successes and the growing
backlash against them.)

OUTSIDE THE DEFAULT FRAMEWORK

To bring about more lived complexity and linkage in suburban life, we
could imagine aiming directly at the ways in which oversimplification
is coded into the default patterns of development: zoning regulations,
infrastructure funding, and road patterns. Zoning mandates separation
of functions, a good tactic when cities were full of smoke-belching industries but now "an old, tired, and dysfunctional form of community planning and urban design" (Peter Calthorpe in Fishman 2005, 18).[34] "The
smartest of the smart growth governments are concentrating on changing zoning, the DNA of growth, on steering funding toward infrastructure
in built-up places, and on taking away the constraints that hobble good
growth. Consumers have to take it from there" (Flint 2006, 259; see 221,
254). So, "Throw it out. Start over. Conventional zoning is full of sense-

less loopholes and grandfather clauses. It's based on an outdated planning philosophy—the separation of uses—from the 1920s" (Flint 2006, 250). Wholesale reform of zoning sounds like a radical move, but it can be seen as conservative as well. "Clearing that underbrush is ultimately one of conservatism's primary acts: cutting regulation for business. The subsidies inherent in the country's post world war two framework for development are just the kind of exercise in government picking winners and losers that conservatives abhor" (Flint 2006, 248). New land-use policies such as the SmartCode proposed by New Urbanists (Duany, Wright, and Sorlien 2006) could change the default setting for suburban growth and allow more experimentation with more complex patterns.[35]

Another suburban planning tool that seems natural but enforces simplification is the hierarchy of roads, where a local area's streets have only a few connections to a larger road, which in turn leads to controlled access points onto larger roads and freeways. This pattern reinforces single-use zoning and creates choke points where congestion accumulates. If there were more ways that roads and areas connected to one another, there would be more paths for traffic to flow along and new connections would become possible among presently separated subdivisions.

An awareness of economic pressures and political forces combined with new modes of connection and communication can create more voices for dialogue about and with those larger forces and pressures. As I argued earlier, a community or a self does not contain a central fortress, a single point of creativity or of resistance that must be defended against outside forces. Selves and communities are flexible networks, so what is required to deal with outside forces is not dogged resistance at the walls of a central fortress but rather the ability to construct new networks and connections that can interact with and attempt to influence outside pressures.

Suburbs are not monolithic, and greater awareness of their internal and external linkages and complexities can lead to alignments that bring new agents onto the political and economic scene. This is happening as tentative regional collaborations, nongovernmental organizations, and other new and old civic groupings find ways to connect and make their voices heard. The new voices come both from ongoing institutions and from temporary bottom-up groups that arise in response to local situations. As suburbanites become more aware of their links and common interests across jurisdictional boundaries, new political coalitions can develop, as has happened with environmental issues and transportation policies.

Perhaps the clearest case in which new networks and new actors are needed is the regionalization of suburban tax bases and services. Whole metropolitan regions are increasingly acting like single competitive units in international commerce. The regions have common needs for educated workers, efficient transportation, reasonable tax policies, and other shared concerns. Taking initiatives across jurisdictions proves difficult where older regional elites have faded and newer leadership is fragmented along economic and racial lines. On the other hand, this provides opportunities for complex new associations to arise.[36]

In particular, declining older suburbs often find their political and economic interests paralleling those of city dwellers.[37] Even rich suburbs need their overall region to provide good educational opportunities and economic growth. But economic segregation pits jurisdictions against one another and ties the service capabilities of towns and cities to their demographic profile, so that providing services for the most needy is charged to those jurisdictions least able to pay. Regionalization of such expenses could benefit even the wealthy by increasing the economic health of the entire area. Regional financing of some services in Minneapolis and Portland, Oregon, has aided the areas' prosperity (see Orfield 2002).

Arguments for regionalization address problems of economic growth and equity as well as those environmental problems for which the federal government already mandates regional cooperation. There are many existing official regional bodies, but they have restricted scopes and their members are often appointed rather than elected. They may not have much political clout until their members are popularly chosen, since elections encourage regionwide discussion and can help people realize how much different jurisdictions have in common. This creates new forums for political deliberation over goals and priorities, even if the delivery of services continues to be through divided jurisdictions. A more controversial further step would be to give regional bodies formal authority to bring about coordinated action.

Regionalization of some functions would likely increase the complexity of neighborhood associations. "As the metropolis increasingly becomes the digit of national and international economic activity and growth, there will be increasing pressure for more regional governance, including regional planning, transportation, tax-revenue-sharing, even school systems. As municipal government slowly becomes less appropriate and begins to lose power to more regional forms of government, a vacuum opens up at the small scale. As a consequence, neighborhood and district planning, budgeting, schools, etc. will tend to become more important" (Kelbaugh 2002a).

Short of full regionalization, there are measures that could be taken to limit bidding wars between jurisdictions, for instance taxing local economic development subsidies and removing the tax exemption on local development bonds. Such measures would not be easy to implement but they would improve regional economic health. Beyond regionalization there is a need for national efforts to achieve full employment and offer some protection against health and economic disasters. Programs to raise wages, ensure health care coverage, provide affordable housing near job opportunities, and improve education could grow the economic health of a whole suburban region (see Dreier 2001, 205–8). In an age when the nation needs all the talent it can develop, geography should not determine the kind of education students receive.[38]

There are other ways in which the current framework for development could be challenged at a deep level. One would be to devise new revenue methods to replace the property tax that causes suburban jurisdictions to compete for tax base while avoiding new services.

Another more general shift would be to include civic responsibilities in the definition of private ownership. The framework of property rights has complex historical origins. A bundle of privileges and obligations that developed over time, the right of ownership could be assembled differently. It includes items such as the rights to be present, to restrict the access of others, to use and change, to build as one chooses, to appropriate the fruits of the land, and to dispose of the property by sale or inheritance. Kevin Lynch questions the notion of absolute land ownership (as does Wright in his Broadacre City vision). Lynch points out that other legal systems separate out and assign to different agents the various rights that are lumped together as individual ownership in the Anglo-American scheme (Lynch 1981, 205–6). The practice of selling conservation easements shows how one component of ownership might be separated out. It would be a deep change to redefine ownership to also include communal and environmental responsibilities. There are a few American examples where ownership rights are bundled differently: in Oregon and in certain cases in Maine the right of public access trumps attempts by private owners to close coastal beaches. Sweden provides a more sweeping right of access for anyone to any property in the countryside, as long as nothing is disturbed and a few restrictions are observed.[39] Property ownership is a more complex set of rights and duties than it first appears to be; it is imaginable, if not likely, that new combinations of responsibilities and rights could change the way suburban dwellers relate to places and to nature. This could change the ways people recognize one another as free and equal, which would modify their self-definitions and their vision of possible actions. The case of ownership rights shows how local norms are influenced by wider cultural and legal histories, and how a sense of the internal complexity of place norms might open new possibilities.

In this chapter I have tried to indicate ways in which we could come to recognize the complexity already present in suburbia's links and rhythms that go beyond its banal architectural form. Following the three dimensions of complexity I have suggested kinds of interventions that might help people to encounter the multiplicity of roles and norms in their everyday lives, to participate more fully in sustaining and redefining those norms, and to deal more consciously with the remote forces and the policies that shape the suburban environment. The last several sections have concentrated on policy issues that could lead to adding spatial density and regional connection to sprawling suburbs. This would help with suburbia's environmental issues and social inequities. But we should remember that spatial proximity is only one form of density. There are many kinds of connection and linkage already operative even in less dense areas. Today's places locate us in nonhierarchical and noncentered connections that open possibilities for both new freedoms and new responsibilities.

Afterword

> *The particularity of any place is . . . constructed not by*
> *placing boundaries around it and defining its identity*
> *through counterposition to the other which lies beyond,*
> *but precisely (in part) through the specificity of the mix*
> *of links and interconnections to that "beyond." Places*
> *viewed in this way are open and porous.*
> (Massey 1994, 5)

UNHAPPY WITH TODAY'S PLACES, Christian Norberg-Schulz denied that they could be real places where we could settle and dwell: "The essence of settlement consists of gathering, and gathering means that different meanings are brought together. . . . the modern world is 'open'; a statement which in a certain sense is anti-urban. Openness cannot be gathered. Openness means departure, gathering means return" (Norberg-Schulz 1984, 195). I have argued that contemporary places do just what Norberg-Schulz denied: they gather open relations of nets and links into new modes of noncentered, nonhierarchical unity.

The busy, flowing city is one symbol of our times, and city air brings freedom from the intimate oppressions of small-town life. Then both the city and the small town look disparagingly at the suburbs, and all three worry about other still more dispersed and networked places—and everyone worries about theme parks. Many critics reject today's places with a disdain that barely hides the critic's despair. In contrast, my approach may seem like pallid reformism. Yet many of the supposedly negative qualities of today's places do offer possibilities for new kinds of unity and complexity. (As software developers sometimes say about an unexpected behavior, "it's not a 'bug,' it's a 'feature.'") Today's places wield in new ways the conditions that make all places possible. There is no magic wand that will remove all their problems, but we can use some of the features of today's places (such as multiplicity and linkage) against others (such as simplification and commodification).

Discussing the differences between city form in Europe and in the Arab medinas, N. John Habraken points out that European form-making usually defines a public space within whose geometrical divisions individuals may do what they will. "Public space is predetermined. Within it, we make our spatial claim, such that we may leave one another alone." In the other pattern, form-making tends to start with negotiations among individuals whose mutual agreement about the relations of their private spaces leads to a redefinition of the public space. This is "a social contract without predetermined form. As long as consensus is obtained, most moves are possible." Streets get arched over or closed off, plazas encroached upon. The European model is "a form allowing play" while the Arab model is "a play that produces form" (Habraken 1998, 288–89). We need to become more involved in our own play that produces form, and understand the ways in which that process is and is not free.

A more complex suburbia will not please as a balanced whole. Its unity will be more linked and episodic, reread and remade without ever coming together hierarchically. As a shared story, its narrative form will not be a heroic epic, nor a well-focused nineteenth-century novel, nor a self-contained modernist work. It will be a joining of episodes where each has more than one focus as it moves and links in many directions at once.[1]

I have been arguing from a general ontological view that there is no final duality of structure and process. We should not take form for granted or as fixed, whether architectural form, city form, or place norms and social roles. Themed places provide an extreme example, with their double awareness of our immersion in the fantasy and of our complicity in its staging. But all places involve some doubled inhabitation. Our being spread out in time and space demands a level of reflective synthesis and space-time linkage, or we would not experience our places and selves in any kind of unity at all. The complexity of links and spacings in the time and space of places offers opportunities for more openness and awareness, including awareness of the aspects that are overlooked or made invisible.

Today's places are not solid structures threatened by corrosive processes. Social and architectural structures and norms exist within processes of social maintenance and reformation, and their inhabitants would be freer with a greater awareness of those processes and the linkages they work through.

Those activities and links can be made more self-aware in all three dimensions of place complexity: First, consciousness of the subtlety and multiplicities in place norms and structures, together with a willingness to increase that complexity and to engage their intersections. Second, being aware that places are maintained actively through contested processes of reinterpretation and reproduction that modify while sustaining place norms, together with a willingness to engage in those processes and those contests. Third, seeing the larger forces that shape a place, together with a willingness to create new social agents and dialogues to influence those processes. Find wider possibilities, create new networks and links, and make places and selves in ways beyond standardized purposes.

Many Americans change their place of residence often, and this weakens the sense of being rooted in one natural location. But all locations are now penetrated by wider flows and linkages. No place is fully self-enclosed. Even if they do not move often, today people do feel more self-consciously separated from natural-seeming rootedness. While there is no cure, there is a prescription: more complexity and more self-aware activity in the process of inhabitation, going forward into greater thickness. Place identity is not all or nothing; we do not have to choose between being rooted in the local soil or wandering in directionless space. Localities are moments in process, neither dissolved nor self-sufficient. That can feel like homelessness if we remain attached to solidity. We should grasp creatively the possibilities offered by contemporary places, without undue nostalgia or elation. Newer unities and connections will not eliminate dislocations and injustices, nor can they by themselves solve aesthetic and architectural problems. But richer inhabitation and more flexible identities can give society more room to deal with its injustices, and give imagination more openings to improve our planning and architectural forms.

Notes

CHAPTER ONE. PLACES TODAY

1. "It is ironic, at the end of a century characterized by the most dizzying urban transformation in human history, that academic readings . . . and projects of the city . . . remain haunted by the irrelevant ghost of the historically outdated European city center. . . .. The hegemony of the pedestrian, the plaza, the street, and the perimeter block must be challenged not because the values they embody are no longer valid, but because they are suffused with a set of fundamental misconceptions about the nature of contemporary civilization" (Lerup 2000, 180n7). Lerup's critique of this "positivity" moves in a different direction than my discussion, but we agree that the older archetypes mislead about the nature of today's places.

2. I wrote much of this book while associating with architects and planners, and it takes up issues from architectural and urban theory as well as from philosophical studies of place. I have written elsewhere about architecture—see the articles listed in the bibliography and my earlier book *Postmodern Sophistications* (Kolb 1990)—but this current book concerns places and not buildings. Even if designing a building is very much about articulating a place, the two are not identical. The unity of a building is not the unity of a place, and the function of a building is not the same as the social norms and expectations for a place. Also, this study concerns the place-nature of places rather than their aesthetic qualities. The two are not fully separable, but too much discussion of places today focuses on the ugliness or the bland boredom of many new places, without looking into their new kinds of connection and social norms.

3. At the time of writing, it appears that Measure 37, which mandates restitution for property value lost through regulation, could have profound effects on the Oregon system of land planning and regulation, and the state is struggling to decide whether or not to limit those effects.

4. Bureaucracy prefers concentric and hierarchical identities and places because these avoid jurisdictional disputes and keep things neatly accessible. It would be a mistake, however, to assert with some postmodern optimists that nonconcentric or nonhierarchical identities and places automatically offer resistance to those exercising control. A database does not need hierarchy. People and places can have many keywords associated with their designations; to keep tabs on them it is not necessary that they be located in one unique file

drawer. As long as a keyword is findable, that portion of my or a place's identity becomes available to the controller or the advertiser. Indeed, if my identity fragments into a list of keywords without central unity, I may be all the more open to manipulation.

5. In the Sprawling Places Web site I suggest that this travel-telecom assemblage may itself form a new kind of spatially discontinuous but socially unified place.

6. The weakening of hierarchy and center does not mean that all places are now on the same level or equally available. The new spatiality resembles the way Web sites relate to one another. Their links do not produce a flat collection of evenly empowered nodes. Instead of measuring centrality by degree of elevation in a hierarchy, the Web develops traffic patterns. The most frequently visited sites become centers, and as their rankings are published (by ranking agencies that are themselves ranked) the rich get richer as more links are made to them. Similarly, today's nonhierarchical spatiality does not mean that all places get leveled out into a bland availability. In the nonhierarchical, nonconcentric world, linkage differentiates and distances as well as connects. There is a danger in the resultant celebrity since substantively significant sites may be ignored in the process, but that is not much different from the way significant texts have been ignored by publishers, or significant places by transport systems. No topology of connection will by itself avoid the need for discernment and judgment.

7. In 1960, Kevin Lynch had said that "the hierarchical system, while congenial to some of our habits of abstract thinking, would seem to be a denial of the freedom and complexity of linkages in a metropolis" (Lynch 1960, 113).

8. In the Thinkbelt "there were to be three major 'transfer points,' where various types of mobile, prefabricated housing and classroom units could be transferred to and from the rail lines as needed. Some of these units included self-propelled seminar coaches, with scheduled service of class length between stops so that students could literally learn 'on the move.' Classroom and laboratory trains could be linked to form larger units. The largest lecture-demonstration units spanned three parallel rail lines and came equipped with foldout decking and inflatable walls" (Mathews 2000).

9. One of the striking characteristics of Price's architecture is the way he designed for unforeseen future changes in the use and shape of his buildings. Some of his projects included built-in machinery for moving walls and floors. Since the Thinkbelt project used rail lines and cars, it was inherently flexible. "The indeterminacy and capacity of the Potteries Thinkbelt to change over time is particularly significant given the instability of British culture at the time. As social instrument, Price's architecture is informed by his ethical and polemical perceptions of the fluidity of contemporary social, political and economic

contexts. . . . The Potteries Thinkbelt is an 'anti-monument' for a fragmented and chaotic Britain, far ahead of its time. Rather than lamenting lost 'order' and consensus or engaging in futuristic technological romance, Cedric Price perceived a coherency within the cultural 'chaos' of postwar Britain" (Mathews 2000).

10. While the contemporary flood of media and information threatens to overwhelm us, it also allows us to feel that data and information need not be personally hoarded, because it will remain available. "Like hunters and gatherers who take for granted the abundance of food 'out there' and therefore only hunt and gather enough to consume immediately, we are increasingly becoming a 'subsistence information society.' Rather than engage in long-term storage of knowledge in their memories or homes, many people are beginning to believe that information is available 'out there' and that individuals do not need to stockpile it. . . . The connections found are often consumed and digested immediately without being painstakingly linked to other knowledge and ideas" (Meyerowitz 1985, 317).

11. In recent years fast food chains have somewhat relaxed their looks, so that there are more styles of McDonald's than there used to be. The McDonald's in Freeport, Maine, occupies a remodeled colonial house; there is a half-timbered McDonald's in a suburb of Oxford, England. As people become accustomed to franchised identities, the corporations see profit in local variation as long as instant recognition can be maintained. Once the brand is established exact replication becomes redundant, and decor plus a logo may suffice.

12. See also my "Real Places in Virtual Spaces" (Kolb 2006b).

13. As Kevin Lynch notes, "making change and plurality comprehensible may well be the most challenging application of sensibility today" (Lynch 1981, 145).

14. Sometimes previously separated place norms combine into a mixed amalgam. Joshua Meyerowitz argues that the spatial isolations that allowed one set of social norms to "saturate" an area have been broken down by the intrusiveness of telecommunication media (Meyerowitz 1985, 124). As media alter the information flows and penetrate formerly separated physical and social locales, they create new mixed action situations that lack the sharp definition of the formerly separated situations for women, children, authority figures, and the like. Meyerowitz argues that this mingling has caused social changes such as a lessening of respect for authority figures, and redefinitions of childhood and masculinity. It may be, though, that Meyerowitz's conclusions depended on the state of the media in the 1980s when he did his study. Now mobile Net access, hundreds of TV channels, and innumerable Internet groups can resegregate social action situations. The annoyance felt when cell phone users discuss their

personal life in an airport lounge shows that while physical segregation of action situations has vanished, there is still a collision rather than an amalgam of social norms.

15. Reading Venturi over the years has reinforced both my reluctance to accept totalizing critiques of contemporary places, and my desire to look for what new possibilities they might offer. See Flanagan 2001 for a polemical defense of Venturi's and Scott Brown's importance as theorists and architects today.

16. In China and elsewhere in Asia, however, larger and larger enclosed malls are still being built.

17. Lifestyle malls put retail shops into separate buildings arranged to mimic town squares and city blocks. In this they hearken back to some of Victor Gruen's designs for the earliest post–World War II shopping centers. "Instead of all retail in one building, there are many buildings, some with one store—like Borders, others with a cluster of businesses. The Marble Slab ice cream parlor and Barnie's Coffee and Tea are just steps from the 20-screen Regal Cinema. The 10 restaurants are mostly chains, from the high-end Ruth's Chris to P. F. Chang and Taqueria Quetzalcoatl. World Publishing is strategically located next door to Blackfin, an expensive seafood restaurant and bar. An Albertson's, along with Pier One, Ann Taylor Loft, Metropolis and others, means you wouldn't have to leave the neighborhood for much. Each cluster has wide sidewalks, and many of the restaurants have outdoor tables. So it's kind of a hybrid of downtown and mall—walkable, yes, urban, no" (Thompson 2003). "Nationally, just three new regional malls were opened in 2003, four are slated to open this year and eight in 2005, says Patrice Duker, spokeswoman for the council. By contrast, 25 lifestyle malls opened in 2003, another 25 are expected in 2004 with 25 to 30 more due in 2005" (Mullins 2004).

18. Philip Nobel argues that with protest and community organizing moving onto the Internet, and with malls creating more mixed use spaces, "as malls get better, more like cities (even if toy cities), I'm beginning to appreciate them for what they are: rehearsal spaces for future urbanites" (Nobel 2007, 72). They provide "little training grounds for the experience of being with lots of other people on a street at the same time. That alone can build civic health. And subversion is only a wireless connection away" (74).

19. A driver navigating along a commercial strip lives in a different visual and tactile relation to the surroundings than does a walker along an urban street. "There is a driver (and passengers) in the car—a roving subjectivity whose body phantom apprehends the world in a vastly different manner, a manner that in turn will and must have consequences for the way the metropolis is designed" (Lerup 2000, 180n7).

20. The stores do have many "systemic" connections, in the sense I discuss later. Those connections are, however, seldom neatly hierarchical.

21. See Jane Jacobs 1961 and, for an insightful early discussion of urban community and spatial issues in the context of consumption, Goodman and Goodman 1947.

22. The overlaid patterns of activity and communication form a complex unity more like a multiply connected network than a linear list. It is true, though, that while a hypertext exists through its links, physical spatiality is both more easily hierarchical and more open to exteriorities that violate hierarchy. Buildings spread out in a physical space where what is naturally next to what, the weather, and steep hills to climb all put constraints on what linkages will function well. But these proximities are not as strong as they used to be. Our social spatiality is becoming more like that of Web hypertext, more influenced by the topology of its links than by the physical structure or background regions. For some this means a loss of place, but it creates a new kind of place.

CHAPTER TWO. WHAT IS A PLACE?

1. Simplified places such as parking lots and malls still fill important social roles. "Parking lots, alas, are often the only place where people interact—a type of public or semi-public space that we need to design better" (Kelbaugh 2002b, 151).

2. Moore's architecture is generally more flexible and less hierarchical than his notion of place.

3. Strictly speaking, hierarchical places have always been enfolded in nonhierarchical networks of trade and communication and environmental flows, but the relative strength of the centers and the slowness of communication and travel allowed places to seem completely centered.

4. A broader distinction could be made between space as an expansive array of qualities and features (textured or regioned space) and space as a collection of geometrical relations (geometric space). Edward Casey studies this distinction in the early chapters of *Getting Back into Place* (Casey 1993). What I call an *area* is a part of textured and regioned space (real or virtual), not just a geometrical expanse, though an area could be designated geometrically.

5. Though I have used the word *event* as if its meaning were clear, the word brings with it much-discussed philosophical issues concerning the relation of events to permanent things, what it means for an event to have a form, and the unity of objects and events through time. The examples in the text use *event* in a very broad sense that includes anything that happens to things or any change that can be designated by an action word and qualified with an adverb (the event happened slowly, inadvertently, and so on). This is the sense the word usually receives in Anglo-American philosophical discussions. This contrasts with another sense of the term, common in French theory, where *event* refers more to a special happening when systems of meaning or forms of life take on new

configurations or are interrupted by happenings unpredictable by their norms or unproducible by their algorithms.

6. Kant studied the combination of temporal dispersal and conceptual unity that makes experience possible. He argued that if there is to be experience at all, there must be conceptual norms and connections that link separate temporal and spatial moments together in more than a linear series of befores and afters. Experiencing a series of surfaces and colors as the perception of a house involves concepts and models through which I can interpret how this current visual impression and that one five minutes ago, though separated in time, are impressions of adjoining sides of the house. The temporal sequence becomes a unified experience because beyond the one-after-another sequence there are other categories and relations that allow a distinction between the structure of what appears and the order of its appearings. Kant argues that the ability to do this for concrete object demands general syntheses according to categories concerning causality, permanence in time, interrelations, and the like. For more arguments for the claim that meaning comes from contrast and relation to absent others, see Kant 1933, Hegel 1977, Husserl 1960, Heidegger 1996, Sellars 1963, Davidson 2001.

7. For Kant, every entity must be specifiable in quality and quantity and must be located within causal connections that link temporal stages and other objects. Place norms involve principles that designate appropriate qualities and quantities, as well as connecting principles that set up a network of cross-time relations, though these are not necessarily causal relations. Making further parallels with Kant, in particular to his Analogies of Experience, we could say that a place will require some constancy, to provide a relatively permanent background against which its distinctions and changes can be discerned. The place will need both repeatability and singularity, that is, types that can be duplicated and repeated, paths that can be retraced and actions that can be redone, and yet it will also need ways of marking this encounter at this time as unique. Synthesis rather than division may be the decisive move in place making.

8. Could there be places with no norms of action at all? No, since without social norms there is at most a locale, not a place. But there might be residual places where the norms for action reduce to very simple moves: cities in battle, predator-prey spaces. Adventure or chase movies may depict the reduction of highly structured places to that minimal condition.

9. Could there be places where the contrast with what is external was the only significant border? For instance, suppose that in a field there is a fenced-off area where a community goes to have leaderless egalitarian discussions of policy. Within the fence there are no differentiations of subareas from which to

speak, though there is a strong difference between how we behave and discuss inside versus outside that fence. But this isn't an exception to what was asserted, because the fence's bordering reaches all through the place and changes behavior everywhere inside it.

10. A purely geometrical conception of space is usually considered a modern invention, but Casey shows the surprisingly long history of the geometrization of space, starting as early as Greek philosophy shortly after Aristotle's time.

11. Casey uses the contrast between geometrical space and lived place to develop a critical concept of *site*, which is a constructed version of geometrical place and is opposed to truly embodied places. In *Getting Back into Place* (Casey 1993), he applied this concept too abruptly and uncritically in an attack on suburban sprawl. Casey has somewhat modified his views, beginning in *The Fate of Place* (Casey 1997). See the discussion of this issue in the Sprawling Places Web site.

12. The act of bodily orientation can be itself made explicit, and can be challenged to renew itself. The artists and architects Arakawa and Madeline Gins build experimental structures, and plan houses and towns, that attempt to slow down our perceptual unification of the environment. They want to force people to live slowly, with some effort, their act of siting of themselves and forming a unified world. Arakawa and Gins employ techniques such as the construction of multiple horizons that are equally valid, multilevel labyrinths, varying scales within the same building, disorientation of the ground plane, modular repetitions within a building or town, and other architectural maneuvers. "Arakawa and Gins see their job as forcing you to create new landing sites [for perception and movement] by systematically removing and reconfiguring your old ones. The body is redirected; the paths to old landing sites are blocked. New perceptual landing sites are installed, new paths to physical landing sites inserted. Straight paths are made curved, level paths are made to undulate. Contradictions—physical contradictions—are introduced. There is no longer a way to make unambiguous sense of the room" (Lakoff 1997). In some cases the dislocations are so extreme that constant attention would always be necessary, but in general their constructions have to deal with the issues created for awareness and complexity by habituation and distraction. In this case habituation could lead to new bodily attitudes and sensitivities. For a fuller discussion of Arakawa and Gins' proposals, see my review of their *Architectural Body* (Kolb 2002), and the essays collected in the 2003 special issue of *Interfaces* (no. 21/22) devoted to their work; the problem of habituation is treated there in Kolb 2003.

13. Places are social products, but a single individual can create a place, though in doing so the individual is not simply exercising a private psychological

reaction. An individual can create on her own the set of expectations that turns an area into a place, but the expectations cannot be purely private. Robinson Crusoe had no difficulty establishing places on his island, but he imported institutionalized distinctions from his earlier life. "I continu'd pensive, and sad, and kept close within my own Circle for almost two Years after this: When I say my own Circle, I mean by it, my three Plantations, viz. my Castle, my Country Seat, which I call'd my Bower, and my Enclosure in the Woods" (Defoe 1994, 120–21). It was not strictly necessary that he make these English parallels, but whatever he arranged for his island would remain social norms ready to be shared, as Crusoe's were when he was joined by Friday. His expectations and norms were describable in public language. If he could not name and discuss those norms and expectations, then there would be no way for him to know what he was trying to repeat. Although places can be established by individuals, their norms and expectations cannot be in principle private and incommunicable. This argument parallels one reading of Wittgenstein's famous "private language argument" (Wittgenstein 1953).

14. Individual and social cannot be separated, and both are spatial. "While it is surely correct to argue that space is socially constructed, the one-sidedness of that formulation implied that geographical forms and distributions were simply outcomes. . . . the social is spatially constructed too. . . . the spatial form of the social has causal efficacy" (Massey 1994, 254–55).

15. N. John Habraken makes an analogous point when he asserts that "territory is defined by acts of occupation. Form, as such, does not yet come into play. A corresponding space formed by physical parts is not required for territorial space to exist. All that is needed is an agent exercising spatial control" (Habraken 1998, 129). Though he insists that control of entry is the primary territorial act, perhaps this could be put in terms of defining of a place's social norms to regulate flows through the place.

16. See Norberg-Schulz 1984, 1985, 1996, and Heidegger 1971, especially the essays "The Thing" and "Building, Dwelling, Thinking."

17. There is an additional issue whether Norberg-Schulz's notion of place character demands an awareness that goes beyond immersion in a single region. Although a Swedish farmer can respond to the Nordic climate and light and land forms without needing any awareness of other ways of building, Norberg-Schulz himself encourages a *comparative* awareness of the Nordic *as such*, which requires more than immersion in the region; it requires contrasts with other regions (Norberg-Schulz 1996).

18. Kenneth Frampton's notion of "critical regionalism" uses an even stronger environmental component to define appropriate place characters for regions and cultures. See discussion of Frampton and Harries in Kolb 2007.

19. I have kept the discussion of place character on a fairly pragmatic level,

but there are deeper philosophical issues. The notion of place character that Norberg-Schulz uses relies on Heidegger's claim that the meaning of being in any area of experience is revealed in a fundamental mood (*Befindlichkeit*) or attunement (*Stimmung*) (see Heidegger 1996). It is necessary to look behind such claimed unity and immediacy for the social and other mediations that allow it to be. There is also a related issue, whether to accept Heidegger's claim that there is in any era only one fundamental meaning of being. I argue elsewhere (Kolb 1986) that we should reject this totalizing claim.

CHAPTER THREE. PLACE COMPLEXITY

1. Hannerz (1992) discusses cultural complexity in ways parallel to my discussion of place complexity. He argues against the ideal of closed uniform communities and against the image of larger societies as "mosaics" composed of relatively homogeneous subcultures, because interaction reduces the purity and homogeneity of such units.

2. It's not as if there are two rival social processes, one keeping social structures unchanged and another changing them. "We have exaggerated the distinctions between processes which sustain social organization and processes which change it" (Robertson 1994, 97). The very same processes maintain continuity and bring about change.

3. See Hecht 1994 for an exemplary study of the management of sacred space in Jerusalem that shows how explicit place norms that are believed to be constant over time are in fact managed in a historically changing field of contentious rivalries.

4. My treatment in this chapter and the next of the role of self-awareness and self-reflection in complexifying places has been influenced by Hegel's critique of distanced reflection and his ideas about self-consciousness as constitutive of social processes. In applying this to the reappropriation of so-called nonplaces, I have been aided by conversation with Gunnar Sandin and by reading Sandin 2004.

5. Julian Barnes imagines an entrepreneur buying the Isle of Wight and building there concentrated duplicates of British sites and archetypes, so that the inconveniences of actual travel in Britain could be avoided (Barnes 1999).

6. Recently the term *complexity* has become important for theories of self-adaptive and self-organizing systems. (For a general overview of theories of self-adaptive systems and their consequences, see Mark C. Taylor 2001.) Such "complexity theories" descend from earlier catastrophe and chaos theories. The systems they study involve many parts on many levels interacting in ways that produce self-organizing emergent properties. My use of the term *complex* does not have these implications, since complex places in my sense need not

develop emergent global properties. Whereas complex places could be items within larger self-adaptive systems, place complexity is not the same as system complexity.

7. For an example of architectural simplicity with growing place complexity, consider: "The other feature of a Ryokan [a traditional Japanese inn], which I have never experienced in a lifetime of staying in [other] hotels, is that, like the most alluring kind of partner, it reveals its secrets only gradually, one at a time; the longer you look, the more you are beguiled. When I first arrived in my room, I could hardly believe that I was paying hundreds of dollars a night for two largely empty tatami spaces; soon, I was thinking that I'd found a bargain as I settled into what felt like an ancient box full of hidden compartments" (Iyer 2000a, 159).

8. How much cultural memory is required to keep up a complex place? How many interlocking or contesting patterns of activity and learned behaviors are needed to maintain the place as it is? Places tend, if not kept up, to denature into interstitial areas without much social texture, or to fragment into areas gobbled up by other places.

9. I am adapting the term *contour* from hypertext theorist Michael Joyce (Joyce 1995). In reading a novel I anticipate events, and my anticipation changes as I read. Often an author provides deliberately misleading narrative contours so the reader will enjoy the experience of his or her abrupt change. Architects and landscape architects do the same with spatial projection and expectations. Part of the experience of a garden might be noting how the landscape architect has set up a promenade in which the experienced series of projections of the garden as a whole develops with its own rhythms and contrasts. Now I perceive the garden as small, now as large, now as small again. The series of such contours in a place could have its own second-level contour, at first appearing straightforward, then revealing modulations and complexity—and that second-level contour could be manipulated as well, perhaps by a sudden alternation of the rhythm at which the first-level contours change. It could even be that a place (or a building or a hypertext or a Pynchon novel) provides sets of social or spatial contours which refuse to integrate into a consistent landscape of narrative or possibility. Then the changing but never culminating series of contours might itself be the intended experience, though it might be difficult to avoid seeing the building or the novel as just a jumble.

10. This provides a justification along the lines of John Stuart Mill's arguments for poetry over pushpin.

11. Besides the practical consequences of living in complex places, there is a more general Kantian point that humans should be self-aware of their own activity of choosing and reinterpreting and legislating.

12. Experiencing such conflicts is different from the straightforward conflict of two simple intensities bumping against one another. A tragedy such as *Oedipus* differs from the thinner, repetitious intensity of an adventure movie. Compare the more melodramatic intensity of such a movie's straightforward characters with the baffling figure of Hamlet.

13. One consequence, Hegel argues, is that for modern people Greek tragedy no longer expresses today's tensions and contradictions, which must be expressed in other art forms.

14. Augé's *supermodernity* has many resemblances to Giddens's theory of modernity referred to in chapter 1.

15. Refugee camps develop their own new thicknesses of roles and complexity of interactions as time passes. That he takes such camps as nonplaces shows again how Augé's category of nonplace is linked to traditional anthropological notions of "native" spatial enclosures.

16. For instance, Clifford Geertz speaks about thick and thin "descriptions"; this is related to the discussion of thick and thin roles here, but is not quite the same since the modern abstract roles I am calling thin are not as avoidable as are Geertz's thin descriptions (Geertz 1973; see also Sack 1992, 112). It is also important to distinguish the thickness or thinness of roles from their degree of normalization in society. Thick identities can provide more resistance to pressures that try to simplify our lives, but roles of any kind can be normalized by social mechanisms. Complexity and thickness help resist such pressures but are no automatic salvation.

17. A full argument for the thesis that there can be no absolutely thin places involves the considerations raised in Hegel's discussion of the relation of the society of exchange to the community of politics. See Hegel 1967, and the discussion in Kolb 1986.

18. "A distinctive and legible environment not only offers security but also heightens the potential depth and intensity of human experience. Although life is far from impossible in the visual chaos of the modern city, the same daily action could take on new meaning if carried out in a more vivid setting. Potentially, the city is itself the powerful symbol of a complex society. If visually well set forth, it can also have strong expressive meaning" (Lynch 1960, 5).

19. See Kolb 2006a for a general comparison of the notion of authentic *content* with the notion of explicitly positing the *processes* by which particular social and individual determinations are realized.

CHAPTER FOUR. COMMODIFICATION, SYSTEMS, AND PLACES

1. Investors who build in city or suburb are called "developers," but they mainly repeat what has been profitable elsewhere. Despite their rhetoric they

seldom "develop" with a view to new kinds of possibilities within the city or suburb. "The truth is that while it is commercial development which shapes the city, it is in the hands of those who have no interest in using their powers for the long-term future. The commercial developers are in business to respond to opportunities. They are not interested in, or equipped for planning cities. Yet that is just what they are doing by default" (Sudjic 1992, 53).

2. A possible reply to such criticisms might be that for all its problems, the commodity economy is meeting people's needs. This is true in many ways, though inequities abound. In affluent areas needs themselves are manufactured, leading to what Baudrillard calls "a radical uncertainty as to our own desire, our own choice, our own opinion, our own will. This is the clearest result of the whole media environment" (Poster 1988, 209). Hence some argue that we have to simplify our lives and return to basic needs. Others, myself included, would argue that beyond survival needs there is no privileged set of natural needs to return to, yet we have to become more active in the definition of our needs rather than let the commodity culture set them for us.

3. Architects and urban planners unhappy with the dispersed results of today's development seek more fixed and centrally unified places and roles. Karsten Harries has argued that when places become tools rather than environing worlds, we find ourselves in a nihilistic vacuum in which all choices seem arbitrary. When we have to make our own meaning, none of it stands firm. "All meaning that presents itself to us as freely created must seem arbitrary, and whatever is experienced as arbitrary to that extent fails to convince. To carry authority [the form and meaning of places] must be experienced as creative responses to a more primordial and still inarticulate understanding of what it is to dwell" (Harries 1997, 291). Less conservative writers who are equally opposed to the commodification of places would argue that Harries is here nostalgically seeking an experiential plenitude to serve as a foundation for life. The deep issue dividing them from Harries is whether or not modern freedom is capable of giving itself norms and measures. Most responses to modernity, from Kant through Hegel and Marx and Nietzsche, have offered some version of self-creation as the appropriate ideal. Harries, following Heidegger, disputes the possibility of pure self-creation.

4. The Sprawling Places Web site lays out a general argument against theories that appeal to such strong totalizations.

5. For Heidegger's views, see the essays collected in Heidegger 1971 and 1977, as well as the interview in Heidegger 1981. For evaluations of his claims, see for instance Kolb 1986 and Harries 1997.

6. I am referring to Peter Mayle's *A Year in Provence* (1989) and Frances Mayes's *Under the Tuscan Sun* (1996).

7. See Hannerz's analysis of *partly* commodified personal identities (Hannerz 1992, 107) and his discussion of the local reception of commodified flows (65).

8. Computer games can provide almost pure commodified places, and virtual reality will provide even more, but the same expansion beyond the commodity form occurs as those become integrated into larger life rituals and narratives. So it seems unlikely that an absolutely commodified place could survive as such.

9. Just as virtual reality can provide almost pure commodified places with no staff or other users to make them more complex, virtual reality might also provide almost pure noncommodified places, the electronic equivalent of remote mountain villages. Such isolated virtual places that were almost impossible for anyone but the owners to access might then be sold as commodities to those wishing to escape from the usual commodified physical and virtual places.

10. In the larger flow it is not easy to find criteria for identifying systems unless they have feedback loops that preserve their identities. What are commonly called systems are often just conveniently designated causal sequences. Hegel's comment about animals individuating themselves with their claws and teeth points to a sort of system that strives to maintain its integrity against environmental pressures (Hegel 1977, par. 246). Organisms have to mediate conflicting feedback loops; determining what to do in relation to their internal goals is akin to normative interpretation.

11. My distinction of system from place derives in part from Wilfrid Sellars's distinction of intentional and causal, and in part from Jürgen Habermas's distinction of system from lifeworld. N. John Habraken offers a somewhat similar distinction between a system and a theme, and another between architectural form and territorial control, although his definition of a system includes normative elements as well as causal relations. (See Sellars 1963, Habermas 1987, Habraken 1998, and Kolb 1990.)

12. In economics as in politics and in sports, changes in "the rules" become something to be manipulated for strategic or tactical goals. Place norms and system patterns can both become means to larger goals.

13. Lefebvre talks about spaces (in his sense of the word) as enforcing "a body of constraints, stipulations and rules to be followed." He cites the way we might pause on the threshold of a building "while passively, and usually 'unconsciously' accepting a prohibition of some kind" (Lefebvre 1991, 319). His description of the overall space of work mixes causal and normative effects. "The space of work is thus the result, in the first place, of the (repetitive) gestures and (serial) actions of productive labour, but also—and increasingly—of the (technical and social) division of labour; the result therefore, too of the operation

of markets (local, national and worldwide) and, lastly, of property relationships (the ownership and management of the means of production)" (Lefebvre 1991, 191). It is important to distinguish the field of causal effects that economic and other actions have on each other from the normative field of approved moves that institutions might make toward one another, and from changes in that field. Lefebvre tends to reduce both place norms and system to the effects of pure power operating on habitual bodily movements. But normative and causal effects stand in complicated, often antagonistic, relations. He also does not distinguish systemic from political modes of centralization and interaction. This keeps him from any positive vision for suburban places.

14. Hannerz (1992) discusses the ways the older anthropological notion of a closed cultural totality does not fit current place and cultural mixtures.

15. Castells moves toward breaking down his dualities when he asserts that "The second and main agency [for cultural and social change today] is a networking, decentered form of organization and intervention, characteristic of the new social movements, mirroring, and counteracting, the networking logic of domination in the informational society. . . . It is this decentered, subtle character of networks of social change that makes it so difficult to perceive, and identify, new identity projects coming into being" (Castells 1997, 362).

16. Insisting on the power of space to impose ideology, Lefebvre says: "Practical space is the bearer of norms and constraints. It does not merely express power—it proceeds to repress in the name of power (and sometimes even in the name of nothing). As a body of constraints, stipulations and rules to be followed, social space acquires a normative and repressive efficacy—linked instrumentally to its objectality—that makes the efficacy of mere ideologies and representations pale in comparison. It is an essentially deceptive space, readily occupiable by pretences such as those of civic peace, consensus, or the reign of non-violence. Not that this space—dominating as well as dominated—is not inhabited as well by the agencies of the Law, of the Father, or of Genitality. Logic and linguistics conceal its latent violence, which to be effective does not even have to show its hand" (Lefebvre 1991, 358).

17. Lefebvre envisions participatory spaces that could heal the rifts caused by the simplified abstract roles and splits enforced in spaces dominated by capitalist instrumental rationality. "I shall call that new space 'differential space,' because, inasmuch as abstract space tends towards homogeneity, towards the elimination of existing differences or peculiarities, a new space cannot be born (produced) unless it accentuates differences. It will also restore unity to what abstract space breaks up—to the functions, elements and moments of social practice. It will put an end to those localizations which shatter the integrity of the individual body, the social body, the corpus of human needs, and the

corpus of knowledge. By contrast, it will distinguish what abstract space tends to identify—for example, social reproduction and genitality, gratification and biological fertility, social relationships and family relationships" (Lefebvre 1991, 52). This discussion of postrevolutionary spaces resembles Marx's early dream of freedom from the division of labor.

18. Talk about constructing identities, or about spatial areas receiving place norms, or about system effects being reinterpreted, may sound like yet another example of postulating an active subjectivity that bestows a form on passive data. This model has been attacked in its positivist guise by Wittgenstein, Sellars, Quine, Davidson, and Rorty, and it has been attacked in its Neokantian guise by Heidegger, Merleau-Ponty, Deleuze, and others. Lefebvre comments that "social space . . . is irreducible to a 'form' imposed upon phenomena" (Lefebvre 1991, 27). Spatial arrangements are not passive data waiting for an interpretation; they can shape us on their own and do not need to receive a form from some distanced individual or social subjectivity.

19. The more mutual interaction there is among different norms and patterns of action, the more there will be a single complex place rather than many overlapping simpler places. Could a place contain multiple social norms and patterns that have *no* relation to one another? The rabbits and the cows grazing in a meadow seem to pay little or no attention to one another's activities. Could people following different place norms so ignore one another? Probably not, for potential conflicts cannot be eliminated from awareness, and our self-conscious shared embodiment demands that we take the others into account.

20. A translation of the text based on the lecture can be found online at http://foucault.info/documents/heteroTopia/foucault.heteroTopia.en.html, accessed April 2007.

21. If we stand in the field marking out the streets for the new town, we create within the torsions and landmarks of a region of history and language. That region, in turn, lies within the ongoing process of making and remaking meaning, which is neither blank nor fully structured. Possibility and meaning are not just generated by rules of combination (as in structuralism or its counterparts in analytic philosophy). A texture of definite possibilities is itself an effect produced in a process not dominated by such definitions, though never without some prior definition that it overreaches. If there is in the sphere of meaning an equivalent to the surrounding richness of physical spatial regions, it is the expanse of meaning both made and traversed by this process. Like physical space it is not a smooth expanse, and like physical space it opens places out into uncontrollable externality. There is always more meaning available, always another signification, always another way of making signifiers or of reusing old ones.

22. Hannerz argues from a social anthropological point of view against totalizing views that see a hegemonic center or universal process completely erasing local autonomy and difference. See, for instance, Hannerz 1992, 80–83, 223–25, and his last chapter on "a creolizing world."

23. "Baudrillard's . . . theory of the 'simulacrum' can be seen as a theory of cultural imperialism; it certainly shares the latter's blind spot, namely, ignoring the audience" (Raz 1999, 10).

24. The reflexivity that Giddens talks about suggests the seductive idea of defining modern identities and places purely in terms of self-reflection and self-creation, with all history and geography as secondary content to be worked over by modern freedom. But the abstract or formally described processes of self-reflection exist only through and within the spacings and tensions of historical and geographical location. (See notes 18, 26, and 27.)

25. For more extensive discussion of the interrelations of subjectivity, norms, and history, see the Sprawling Places Web site.

26. Lefebvre highlights the relative independence of normative content when he insists that "of any actual historically generated space, however, it would be more accurate to say that it played a socializing role (by means of a multiplicity of networks) than that it was itself socialized" (Lefebvre 1991, 190–91). We are never in a position to dominate completely, or to create total rationality in the textures of action that define us, but we can come to be more critically aware of our participation in the process of their support and reinterpretation through time. Robert Pippin argues that automatic tensions are found between the structures of possibility within which we act and the self-active process by which those structures are created or accepted. As long as the textures of our world do not allow us to acknowledge the way in which those structures are developed and maintained, contradictions will push us in the direction of developing more modern political and economic structures and more direct self-awareness. There is no strict necessity to the process, but there is a kind of inevitability due to the constant tension caused by the inadequate autonomy allowed for by earlier social norms. I agree with Pippin's general strategy but differ with him about the role that history and purified self-consciousness play in the process. (See Pippin 1989, 1991, 1997 and the discussion in Kolb 1999a.)

27. There is no pure present time or place that can be detached from its past, and the past is always both threatening and enabling. "This position—of creating ourselves anew in the light of an inheritance that functions as a *pharmakon*, as both a nurturing opportunity and an overwhelming danger—is not just the situation of philosophy. It is at base what is distinctive about human existence—that we are not complete as natural beings and that it is only by acquiring culture that we become human. . . . [We need] a repetition that reworks [Heidegger's] account of . . . dwelling in terms of a response to a

structure of givenness, rather than the language of decision and decisiveness" (Wood 1999, 14–15).

28. Talking about architecture rather than places, Elizabeth Grosz asks a related question: "How move beyond the pervasive presumption that subjectivity and dwelling exist in a relation of complementarity, either a relation of containment (space or dwelling contains or houses subjects) or a relation of expression (space or dwelling as the aesthetic or pragmatic expression of subjectivity)?" (Grosz 2001, 59).

29. At the Sprawling Places Web site, see the discussion of Michael Benedikt (1987) and Anne Cline (1998) and their pleas for quiet and withdrawal from busyness in order to reconnect with fundamental materiality and mortality of our lives.

30. A strategy of complexity may lessen the risk of pessimistic withdrawal that has been a common reaction to the difficulties with strategies of unmasking.

31. For a discussion of different kinds of critical irony, see Kolb 1990, ch. 11.

32. Benjamin Barber suggests mobilizing the complexity of life in and around malls to make them function more as the spaces for public life that they present themselves as being (Barber 2001, 212–19).

CHAPTER FIVE. FULL THEME AHEAD

1. In addition to being found wanting in themselves, themed places are often said to highlight the basic problems with contemporary places. See the essays in Sorkin 1992 for numerous examples of this tendency. Compare, however, Young and Riley 2002 for nuanced analyses of the structure of and historical precedents for theme parks, and their long-term relation to political and cultural movements.

2. For a contemporary example where a way of life is exhibited to tourists but is still not a themed place, consider that there are official tours of Christiania that display its mode of life in this "free zone" in Copenhagen. (I owe this example to Cecilia Häggström.)

3. In comments on an earlier version of this chapter, Gunnar Sandin pointed out that my discussion of double self-consciousness resembles Schiller's notion of "sentimental" as distinguished from "naive" living. Sentimentality in Schiller's sense occurs when self-consciousness and awareness of the mediated situation is involved in the mediation of the situation.

4. A historical place, presented as historical, is not yet themed. That a tourist guide has been written for a town does not make the town a themed place, but because the guide asserts that a visitor's usual knowledge of daily life elsewhere will not suffice for encountering the place, the town then moves toward being

either a sample or a themed representation of some larger historical or ethnic unity. But what happens to the town or the church if there are no users for them other than tourists? Are they then themed places? Not necessarily, since a collection of samples is more a museum than a themed place. But the town's self-presentation could begin to move toward the doubled self-relation typical of themed places.

5. At the Sprawling Places Web site I consider some extreme situations that put pressure on the components of my definition of themed places, and I argue for these conclusions: (1) A whole city or nation could not be monothemed. (2) A whole city or nation could be multithemed, but the themes would not be stable. (3) It would be impossible to theme all places at once. (4) A city that has become deeply multicultural would not automatically theme all its places, and special themed places would still be possible. (5) Theming does not demand a single cultural hegemony to provide background contrast.

6. There are difficult intermediate cases, such as the festival architecture of Jon Jerde, which can seem now to be themed, now the product of an individual architect's code, and now the result of sophisticated calculations about the effects of various architectural gestures.

7. Not all writers about themed places condemn them as unreal. "Another example of the complex political valence of the three modes of assembly [discussed by Lefebvre] is the shop-worn critique that American culture is all Disneyland. This critique is the providence of social critics, who may assume they have the intellectual equipment not to be duped. On the other hand, Disneyland, in all its many guises, makes some people very happy. Lefebvre would see theme parks as wanting, because the experiences they encourage and maintain are limited to planned notions of predictable (and expensive) entertainments. The 'happiness' they produce is 'real,' but it does not contribute to participation in constructing the spaces that make us. Themed spaces are about consumption and also have symbolic dimensions, but these are repetitive. When and where the themes come first in contemporary spaces of experience, Lefebvre wants something beyond this—experience that is not completely preprogrammed and is free from the narrow demands on time and space that capitalist production and consumption make" (Liggett 2003, 86–87).

8. Themed places depending on corporate brands have less staying power. "In the old days, megacorporations sponsored pavilions at world's fairs and expos. Then they paid to build rides at Epcot. Now they want their own theme parks. The hope is that these so called brandlands will be more effective (and subtle) in bonding consumers to products" (Kirsner 2000, 192). But branded themes can be fragile. What happens if the corporation dies? Pocahontas and Snow White would survive as referents even if their current corporate remaking in films and books disappeared, but the Ronald McDonald theme for playgrounds

would vanish from consciousness and discourse if McDonald's were acquired by Burger King.

9. Themed places can be educational even though they are simplified. Themes offer an encounter with a normative identity that structures another world. Users can grow and learn new desires from a themed place. They can discover aspects of themselves that respond to the different world. They can also learn facts and some appreciation of history. Think of those historical villages with costumed tradespeople pretending to be living the olden times but eager to talk to you. Even the oversimplification can be helpful at first, though eventually it will interfere with learning.

10. The aim of the display is, of course, to promote a new stereotype of modern China, in this case as a tolerant multicultural nation.

11. Besides the sense of authenticity as direct connection with roots, there is another sense of authenticity as the lack of self-conscious design. "We often say of . . . undisguised places that they possess authenticity; they are the genuine article. After years of routine maintenance, they remain the very same places—with the same counters, stools, mirrors, and walls—we may recall from childhood, or imagine from a time past. But their appeal is not always nostalgic. Nostalgia arises from designs that date themselves. Places that evoke nostalgia were designed to be 'in style' once and have now gone out. Authentic places had little overt style in the first place. What appeals in authenticity is designer neglect: the absence of style intended to ingratiate, to excite, or to dazzle—to differentiate. Like old-growth forests, authentic places preserve the machinations of micro processes that are still occurring" (Cline 1998, 118). Cline's sense of authenticity connects with what Michael Benedikt calls "reality" (Benedikt 1987), and both contrast with themed (and other stylized) places. Cline's sense does not include some elaborately designed places that are also usually judged authentic, such as royal palaces with a long history, medieval cathedrals, or old fortifications.

12. Eric Cohen analyzes the complications in the staging of the Alarde, a public ritual in a Basque town. The ritual "became a major tourist attraction [that was so successful that] authorities declared that it should be performed twice on the same day to accommodate the large number of visitors." The performance then became staged, and because of that "the local participants lost interest." To restore interest "the municipal government was considering payment to people for their participation." Payment might destroy the meaning of the ritual, or perhaps it will enrich the ritual by bringing people back into it or by introducing new elements and meanings. (See Sack 1992, 159.)

13. Augé sees supermodernity as displaying neutered fragments of the past. "Supermodernity, though, makes the old (history) into a specific spectacle, as it does with all exoticism and all local particularity. History and exoticism

play the same role in it as the 'quotations' in a written text: a status superbly expressed in travel agency catalogues. In the non-places of supermodernity, there is always a specific position (in the window, on a poster . . .) for 'curiosities' presented as such. . . . They play no part in any synthesis, they are not integrated with anything; they simply bear witness, during a journey, to the coexistence of distinct individualities, perceived as equivalent and unconnected" (Augé 1995, 110).

14. Besides attempting to appraise themed places singly or as a group, we might ask whether there are some kinds of place unity that might be resistant to theming. What comes to mind is the list unity most obvious on the commercial strip. If you theme a whole commercial strip, perhaps through added architectural details and costumed salespeople, the themed unity may well appear extraneous and imposed because the disjoint unity of the strip asserts itself as a list rather than as the kind of organic whole that themes promote.

15. It is worth noting that theme parks share many features with older kinds of places that are not usually so condemned. "There is a certain attraction to people-watching and a certain eroticism in being watched. . . . Because most Americans live in suburbia, not the central city, and have limited opportunity to experience the anonymous crowd of public space, malls, theme parks, and large themed casinos supply this need. . . . Rural residents have for years enjoyed a kind of urban milieu—the crowds of the state fair. Unlike the city and very much like Disneyland, state fairs feature one attraction after another interspersed with places to eat. This form has entertained millions over the years. Theme parks replicate the urban ambiance and the state fair ambiance" (Gottdiener 1997, 148–49).

16. The contrast with the outside world is crucial, but Disney meant for the valences to be reversed. "Disappointed when, after a recent visit to Disneyland, [Billy] Graham merely noted that he had had 'a nice fantasy' there, [Walt] Disney is reported to have responded: 'You know the fantasy isn't here. This is very real. . . . The park is reality. The people are natural here; they're having a good time; they're communicating. This is what people really are. The fantasy is—out there, outside the gates of Disneyland, where people have hatreds and people have prejudices. It's not really real!'" (Harwood 2002, 61).

17. That themed experiences are not conversions to a new identity is most obvious in themes that would disrupt our lives with terror if we really believed them, but internal distance from the themed identity is also needed for themes that present idealized or utopian visions of one's own national or religious identity. Their power, too, depends on a continual contrast with the everyday. However, such positive themes raise other issues, discussed later in this chapter, about the function of themed places as propaganda and indoctrination.

18. In online worlds such as Second Life where people can help construct the environment, or in earlier MUDs and MOOs where players could attain wizard status and help set the rules, participants find themselves doubling their roles. They are both involved in the social adventures, and cooperatively planning and staging those experiences.

19. Lefebvre too easily speaks as if only moderns have doubled experience: "We must avoid attributing to an ancient Greek climbing up to the Parthenon the attitude of a tourist 'reading' or 'decoding' the prospect before him in terms of his feelings, knowledge, religion or nationality. Here, at the dawn of Western civilization, time contained the spatial code, and vice versa. There was as yet no possibility of displacement into aestheticism, of cooptation of emotions or of 'lived experience' by morality, or of any such 'decodings' imposed upon works which were still experienced and perceived in an unmediated fashion. The concepts of *intuitus* and *habitus* are used here in order to avoid an anachronistic application of categories of a later time, generated subsequently by the *intellectus*, and hence to obviate misunderstandings and misapprehensions. So long as time and space remain inseparable, the meaning of each was to be found in the other, and this immediately (i.e. without intellectual mediation)" (Lefebvre 1991, 241). Although Lefebvre is right to emphasize that the Greeks did not have a modern aesthetic or moralistic approach, he too quickly assumes that their experience was therefore "unmediated."

20. See Kolb 2002 for a discussion of techniques for criticizing immersive experiences by encouraging a committed double inhabitation.

21. See, for example, Plotinus, *Enneads*, VI.9.6.

22. The pressures for simplification in themed places are not all commercial. They can come from social developments that are praiseworthy in themselves. "As a result of the demand for active involvement, the traditional custodians of heritage are placed in a dilemma. They are forced to choose between defending their traditional activities and sites by letting stones speak for themselves, as it were, or becoming more interpretative of what they guard. So a controversy develops as to whether it is acceptable to build a replica of a Roman fort at Vindolanda on Hadrian's Wall — to give visitors a sense of 'what it must have been like to be a Roman soldier' — or to take refuge in the strictly scholarly and dry account, or to represent the past in some other way. Traditionalists may point out that this notion of heritage simply and quickly deteriorates into pastiche and 'Disneyfication.' They might argue that what is created is simply an archaeological zoo along with a theme park mentality which threatens the careful and scholarly attempts to build up knowledge from fragmentary evidence. . . . [On the other hand, these simplifications aid in] the rediscovery of 'people's history'. The new configurations of English economic

history at Beamish or Ironbridge may simply be collections of industrial pastiche owing little to the actual site itself (Beamish did not exist before the present reconstruction) . . . [but] they symbolize the common's past of labor, neighbour and netty, as distinct from the national past of Blenheim and the Tower of London" (McCrone, Morris, and Kiely 1995, 10–11).

23. Before we condemn such overly simplified themed places, we should remember that there could be a theme park analogue to the point Lucy Lippard makes about tourism: "Travel is the only context in which some people ever look around" (Lippard 1999, 13).

24. There are questions whether Disney parks are paradigmatic for all theme parks, especially those in other cultures. See Treib 2002 for a discussion of a park in Japan that presents a Dutch identity and a Dutch-themed residential quarter, Stanley 2002 for a discussion of theme parks in China, and Raz 1999 for studies of Tokyo Disneyland's role in Japanese life.

25. Most U.S. domestic residences show a historical style. Are they themed places? Modernist efficiency and universality never affected the look of U.S. residential architecture. Compared to European cities and suburbs, there is more variety of style and historical allusion on U.S. homes, with no attempt at historical or geographical consistency. U.S. real-estate advertisements almost always mention the style or period of the house, whereas house advertisements in Europe seldom do. Yet U.S. domestic styles are not lived as historical themes. No themed commercial district could set up the variety of historical allusions that are found on a single block in many residential areas. Americans would not feel at ease in a mall that changed its period decoration every twenty yards, but they accept this in residential neighborhoods. My guess is the styles are lived as just that, styles. They are how homes come, just as cars come as Hondas and Chevrolets. The names of the styles indicate historical regions and times, but the houses themselves are not perceived as historical, nor do their styles define life within them. So by my definition these styled houses are not themed places.

26. Marianland (http://www.marianland.com/marianland.html) and the Holy Land Experience (http://www.theholylandexperience.com/) are examples of religious theme parks. See also Norfolk 2005.

27. See "Christian Theme Park Wins Lawsuit Over Tax-Exempt Status," *USA Today*, 11 July 2005 (http://www.usatoday.com/travel/news/2005-07-11-christian-theme-park_x.htm). Themed parks are attacked for presenting themselves as places of entertainment and education that hide a financial goal. "One of the most impressive accomplishments of the Disney Worlds and Colonial Williamsburgs is the extent to which the fundamental goal of making money is successfully camouflaged by the corporation behind the articulated altruistic goal of catering to our imaginations, our need to escape, and our desire for

knowledge. I am by no means questioning whether this altruistic goal is genuine, but it is nonetheless important to register that leisure consumption is the engine that drives these undertakings. An important component of this articulated goal (most obviously, perhaps, with the Disney Corporation) has been the careful presentation of an image of a wise, virtually parental corporation that functions as the guarantor of an enduring but threatened set of national values. These values relate not only to entertainment but also to social relationships and work ideals, and they serve as a last bastion against a threatening and chaotic world" (Harwood 2002, 60). Considering the constant complaints about pressures to buy things inside Disney's parks, the commodification is not so hidden, and especially obvious in more routine themed places. The examples cited are atypical in that they take on the mantle of preserving American identity—recall Harwood's quotation from Walt Disney in note 16. No one doubts that a Santa Claus Village by the Interstate is a commercial enterprise.

28. Compare, for instance, the easy self-parodying irony provided in the Universal Studios park with the complex and unintended ironies Young 2002b finds surrounding the historical reconstruction Cades Cove in the Great Smoky Mountains National Park.

29. For Disney, see the account in Ross 1999; for Williamsburg, see Chappell 2002.

30. Heidegger condemned the contemporary art world as merely the provision of stimuli on demand. Whatever its validity about the art business, that charge applies to themed places. While writing this book I sometimes answered questions about it by saying that I was going to defend Disneyland against Heidegger. I imagined myself standing on the ramparts of the Disneyland Castle watching Heidegger roll up cumbersome Germanic conceptual machines to breach its walls. The actual machines brought against those walls have often been sleeker French models, but I enjoyed the image of Heidegger struggling to exist at all in California. My concern has been less about defending than about using Disney's theme parks to understand the other kinds of themed places that are appearing everywhere, and learning from dealing with themed places how we might improve other kinds of contemporary places such as those characterized by suburban sprawl.

CHAPTER SIX. SUBURBAN PROMISES AND PROBLEMS

1. See Bruegmann 2005 for a discussion of premodern city densities and their dispersal. He concentrates on the density gradient that flattens as cities mature, but he does not analyze the different forms that the dispersal has taken or other forms that might have resulted.

2. Far from being the poster child of sprawl, Los Angeles provides an

ambivalent example. "From 1982 to 1997, as part of a uniquely L.A. phenomenon called 'dense sprawl,' an average of nine people occupied every acre of newly urbanized land in metropolitan Los Angeles, the Brookings study found. That is nine times the average in Nashville during those years, four times that of Atlanta and three times that of New York. During these years, both the Washington and Los Angeles areas gained population at a brisk 30 percent clip. But Washington's growth gobbled up rural land at about twice the pace of Los Angeles', the Brookings study found. As a result, Washington had a 12 percent decline in overall density, compared with a 3 percent gain in Los Angeles" (Harden 2005). The city's density results from natural constraints on water and available land, coupled with developers' desire for profit and massive overcrowding of poor populations into existing housing stock. "In Los Angeles, the population grew by 11 percent between 1990 and 2002, but the number of households increased by just 5 percent" (Harden 2005).

3. American-style sprawl is not inevitable. "Compared with other countries, metropolitan areas in the United States are remarkably sprawled out. European cities are three to four times denser than American cities. The claim that American cities are sprawled out because we have so much land is countered by the example of Canada, which has more land per person than the United States but whose cities are still twice as dense. American cities have not always been this sprawled out. In the 1920s, they were twice as dense as they are now" (Dreier, Mollenkopf, and Swanstrom 2001, 51).

4. While there may be no overall plan for suburban expansion, individual developments are often very carefully planned and marketed. "Driven by irresistible economic forces and shaped by subtly shifting social patterns, they are being created, down to the tiniest detail, by a handful of major developers with a master plan for the new America. . . . [for instance] KB Home, one of the nation's biggest and most profitable builders with $7 billion in sales last year, which helped make it sixth among all Standard & Poor's 500 companies in total revenues. KB Home has 483 communities under development in 13 states and expects to complete more than 40,000 new homes this year. Yet it is just one of about two dozen such corporate giants fiercely competing for land and customers at the edge of America's suburban expanse. Poring over elaborate market research, these corporations divine what young families want, addressing things like carpet texture and kitchen placement and determining how many streetlights and cul-de-sacs will evoke a soothing sense of safety" (Lyman 2005).

5. For more examples and many images, see the Sprawling Places Web site.

6. Hayden 2004 provides an illustrated vocabulary and photo essay on types of sprawl as seen from the air.

7. Dreier, Mollenkopf, and Swanstrom 2001, Squires 2002a, Hayden 2000, and Wolch, Pastor, and Dreier 2004 discuss the political and economic forces controlling the shape of the postwar suburban boom. Bruegmann 2005 weights these forces differently, seeing a dominant role for individual choice. The other analysts emphasize more the policy decisions that controlled the options made available for individuals to choose among.

8. The current default process and pattern of suburban development favors certain entrenched interests. "Don't change the rules of development. . . . One doesn't have to look far to see who benefits from these views: conventional homebuilders, roadbuilders, big-box stores, chain and fast-food restaurants, and every other business interest, right down to the lawn care industry, that makes money being a part of existing suburban development patterns" (Flint 2006, 154).

9. Bruegmann 2005 emphasizes the positive choices being made in the move to suburbia, though he downplays the degree to which those choices could have been realized in other suburban forms, had the larger forces made other policy decisions. He also avoids balancing those positive values with some of their serious costs. "In his haste to discredit [antisprawl] crusaders, Bruegmann dismisses the merits of their complaints. Sprawl is destroying farmland and open space. It is producing an auto-dependent society. And it does facilitate community-sorting by income. These social costs may be worth bearing to obtain the private benefits of decentralized development forms, but Bruegmann does not make that argument, instead minimizing the importance of these costs" (Landis 2006).

10. Detailed market research determines what within the default patterns will be built. "In its most recent survey of Tampa home buyers, KB asked people what they valued the most in their home and community. They wanted more space and a greater sense of security. Safety always ranks second, even in communities where there is virtually no crime. Asked what they wanted in a home, 88 percent said a home security system, 93 percent said they preferred neighborhoods with 'more streetlights' and 96 percent insisted on deadbolt locks or security doors. So KB Home offers them all. 'It's up to us to figure out what people really want and to translate that into architecture,' said Erik Kough, KB's vice president for architecture. And the company designs its communities with winding streets with sidewalks and cul-de-sacs to keep traffic slow, to give a sense of containment and to give an appearance distinctly unlike the urban grid that the young, middle-class families instinctively associate with crime" (Lyman 2005).

11. Suburbs are not and never were as oppressive as popular images have portrayed. "The film [*American Beauty*] simply recycles a view of the

suburbs—that they are vortexes of tedium and alienation—which has been a staple of artistic contempt at least since John Cheever. This view has probably never been accurate. (Herbert Gans . . . shot it full of holes in *The Levittowners* more than 30 years ago.) But it is getting less accurate by the day, as the suburbs mutate in all sorts of interesting ways. . . . The most obvious change is that the suburbs are the smithies of almost everything that is new and innovative in the American economy. . . . Many of the most ethnically diverse places in the country are now suburbs. . . . Sprawl is now the home of almost everything that is most vital and daring, if not most beautiful, in America" ("When Life" 2000, 36).

12. By many measures—efficiency of government, retail success, condition of utilities and infrastructure, health and cleanliness, educational attainments, and so on—many suburbs are more successful at governance than are crowded and difficult cities. This has many causes: smaller population, clearer organization, newer construction and more recent capital investments, tax breaks and subsidies, avoidance of more diverse and difficult populations. (See Duany, Plater-Zyberk, and Speck 2000 for examples.)

13. There is debate about the balances of pushes and pulls leading people to move out of cities. "Suburbanization is common in all wealthy nations. As incomes rise, households want bigger houses and more green space around them. Suburbs clearly have attractions—the 'pull' factors in suburbanization. Scholars have debated over the years how much suburbanization can be attributed to pull factors as opposed to push factors, such as the desire to flee declining public services, rising crime, and concentrations of poor minorities. The free-market explanation holds that the well-to-do naturally prefer to accept longer commutes as the price for cheaper land and larger houses in the suburbs, while the poor prefer to live in crowded conditions close to their jobs. Both these assumptions are questionable. Most entry-level jobs are now located in the suburbs, where the vast majority of poor and working-class families would prefer to live. In other countries, the rich prefer to live near the center where they have easier access to high-paying jobs and elite culture. Something else seems to be going on in the American context to make the middle and upper classes flee to the urban fringe. That something else is the desire to escape the poor and minorities" (Dreier, Mollenkopf, and Swanstrom 2001, 51–52).

14. The "fear of falling" phrase is from Dreier, Mollenkopf, and Swanstrom: "Suburbanites have a 'fear of falling'—a fear that a sudden influx of poor people may cause the whole area to decline. They deal with this fear by banning apartments and requiring large lots for single-family homes. These regulations confine the poor to the urban core and foster leapfrog development that worsens sprawl. The fear of falling is not entirely unwarranted, at least in inner suburbs, because, as we have shown, poverty rates are rising in those areas.

Policies to limit sprawl and promote smart growth would push development back toward the urban core, increasing the access of those who live in concentrated poverty areas to jobs, taxable resources, and retail services" (Dreier, Mollenkopf, and Swanstrom 2001, 53). Current patterns, however, encourage flight to the periphery. "Sprawl is even more fundamentally self-propagating as a function of its consequences. When the problems of car-dependent, spread-out development start to reveal themselves, a common solution is to pick up and move to the next fresh suburb—a lot like those big-box stores that give up on a location and move a mile or two down the road to a better one. The dynamic is potentially without end, as long as conventional developers are around and the same old rules and automated protocols are all in place" (Flint 2006, 60).

   15. Racial motives and discriminations become built into the landscape. "A brief example will demonstrate how the concept of white privilege allows us to historicize environmental racism: a polluter locates near a black neighborhood because the land is relatively inexpensive and adjacent to an industrial zone. This is not a malicious, racially motivated discriminatory act. Instead, many would argue that it is economically rational. Yet it is racist in that it (1) is made possible by the existence of a racial hierarchy, (2) reproduces racial inequality, and (3) undermines the well-being of that community. Moreover, the value of black land cannot be understood outside of the relative value of white land, which is a historical product. White land is more valuable by virtue of its whiteness . . . and thus it is not as economically feasible for the polluter to purchase such land. Nor is it likely that the black community's proximity to the industrial zone is a chance occurrence. Given the federal government's role in creating suburbia, whites' opposition to integration, and the fact that black communities have been restricted to areas that whites deem undesirable, can current patterns of environmental racism be understood outside of a racist urban history? The final issue of white privilege is, At whose expense?" (Pulido 2002, 73).

   16. The economic savings realized by greenfield developers shift costs to other sectors. "When the annual costs and benefits to all groups are summed, Persky and Wiewel find that they almost cancel each other out: $2.6 million in benefits and $2.7 million in costs. In other words, they find no overall efficiency gained by developing on the greenfield as opposed to in the city, or vice versa. While the private sector captures considerable benefits, these are fully offset by costs paid by governments or imposed as externalities on the public at large. The bulk of this burden (about 70 percent) falls on low- and middle-income households, and especially on those who are city residents. The same low- and middle-income households take home less than 10 percent of the private gains, while the other 90 percent is won by high-income households with income from stocks and business ownership." (Wiewel, Persky, and Schaffer 2002, 261)

17. Another justification offered for fragmentation in suburbia is that multiplying small jurisdictions leads to more efficient services. See Musso 2004 for a study that shows how increases in efficiency are accompanied by increased inequities.

18. Here is a typical contemporary example of the "unworthiness" claim: "Moving to better neighborhoods is a mark of one's status, which, Husock argues, should be earned by hard work. Economic segregation reflects the rightful ability of those who have good values, whose hard work and saving are rewarded by the market, to move into good neighborhoods. Those who lack good middle-class values, who are lazy and live only in the present, do not deserve to live in such neighborhoods. If left to the free market, they would not be able to afford to" (Dreier, Mollenkopf, and Swanstrom 2001, 95). For an effective rebuttal, see Elizabeth Anderson's argument against equating market results with a retrospective judgment of worthiness, in "How Not to Complain About Taxes (III): 'I Deserve My Pretax Income" (26 Jan. 2005), at Left2Right (http:// left2right.typepad.com/main/2005/01/how_not_to_comp_1.html#more1, accessed April 2007).

19. The way costs are divided makes corrective policies difficult to enact. "Put another way, policies designed to encourage sprawl are filled with the ability to produce wealth and animate production. These are particularly potent because they encompass jobs, and income and tax revenues, which everyone values. By contrast, policies used to cope with the effects of sprawl are intended to alleviate the pain of poverty and racial segregation. Poverty policies may be tolerated, but they are rarely valued. In a contest between growth and alleviation, growth will invariably win. Even environmental policies designed to deal with excessive waste, like brownfield clearance, often lose out to cheaper and faster development of new land" (Savitch 2002, 151).

20. The current default processes of development make community actions difficult. "The combination of ease of exit for advantaged interests and spatial concentration of difficult problems may be contributing to . . . a broad loss of confidence in the likelihood that collective action can solve people's problems. The result is a self-perpetuating downward cycle in which ready access to the exit option discourages collective action, in turn making personal exit relatively easy and more effective. . . . Calls for equity-responsive metropolitan reform ultimately depend upon a belief in governmental capacity. In an era of privatization, the prospects are grim" (Henig 2002, 339).

21. As the population changes, suburbia's benefits decrease. "Because of the car, the old city failed young families. The young families did not want to be in the traditional city and the traditional city did not provide the kind of space they needed. Suburbia worked for (and only for) the young families. But

when you get old and the kids have moved out—or if you are a teenager—it's a terrible place. So there are all kinds of drawbacks here that came with the price of mobility" (Lars Lerup in Fishman 2005, 42).

22. In the text, I stress more those criticisms of suburban sprawl that come from an ideal of dense urbanity. There are also criticisms coming from the small-town ideal of leisurely familiarity, such as the following: "I think of San Cristobal, a town in southern Mexico of some 30,000 residents, of the way that as the shutters begin to go up on the stores at day's end, folk begin to appear in the Zocalo, strolling, sitting on benches, while the lights come on, the sky turns red and darkness drops on the town like a baby's blanket. Down on the corner a woman selling roast corn on the cob is doing a brisk business. Little kids are out at the hands of their mothers, young kids are chasing each other, older ones are plying the shoe-shine and evening-paper trades or flirting. Men chat about politics while their fathers sit on the benches with their hands cupped over the heads of their canes. And only slowly does this beautiful moment dissolve, the young families leaving first, then the older folks, last of all the older students, the young adults, some of whom can still be found here in the city's center hours later arguing politics or sex or aesthetics over a beer or a cup of coffee in the kiosk in the center of the square. . . . What do these people gain, strolling around the square? Why do they linger? Because this is what one lives for, this participation in a human community, this sharing of gossip, news, opinion, with one's fellow citizens. This is what it is all about, this is the point, the end of it all. It is like this all day in Cristobal, just as all day in the U.S. the parks and pedestrian malls and sidewalks are mostly empty" (Wood 1991, 44–45). Is it significant that these days San Cristóbal, in the state of Chiapas, is a center of the Zapatista rebellion that has learned how to use world media and the Internet to its own purposes?

23. Castells's list also highlights the increasing role of cities as special event venues for suburbanites rather than as work centers for the inhabitants of their region.

24. Suburbia is not an ersatz city but something new. "I believe that much of metropolitan America has been misunderstood. Many dismiss the nation's built environment, especially the suburbs, as crass, corporate, and alienating. Whole careers have been built out of trashing what are admittedly easy targets. But despite my pro-urban bias, I see no reason to join the chorus. The suburbs need to be understood on their own terms. For better or worse, America is now a suburban nation" (Lang 2003, xi).

25. The argument for spatial proximity stresses informal contacts. "Businesses that rely on exchanging sophisticated information that cannot be encapsulated in a formula or summed up in an e-mail message benefit from dense face-to-face relations. To be on the cutting edge of fashion, you need

to be connected to New York (or Milan or Paris). Innovation has increasingly become the key to profitability, because the first stages of the product life cycle can convey monopoly-like advantages. . . . Innovation, in turn, often stems from informal collaboration between firms. In her study of Silicon Valley in California and Route 128 outside Boston, AnnaLee Saxenian showed how the superior dynamism of the former depended on face-to-face networks among employees of competing firms" (Dreier, Mollenkopf, and Swanstrom 2001, 44–45).

26. The growing prevalence of gated communities symbolizes for many enemies of suburbia the lack of suburban encounter with the other. "Gated communities, now the most popular form of American residential development, are an extreme expression of this fear of the agora—homogeneous communities guarded and sealed off like medieval fiefdoms" (Sennett 1999, 70). With or without gates, encounter with the other is not easily eliminated from suburbia. Differences are enabled by generational frictions, and by music and other media that bring foreign attitudes in under the door. Keeping pure requires a constant effort that constantly fails. There is no escape from the multiplicity of today's world. Even if people with resources (or violence) at their disposal can filter their physical proximity, the media and the Net can get around any physical gate. So those who want to enforce conformity must resort to gated media, but this enhances the savor of the forbidden fruit.

27. Waste collection and treatment can lead to regional cooperation and new forms of governance. "Southern Williamson County is a Risk game of nearly a dozen cities, counties and municipal utility districts. It's an archipelago of subdivisions. . . . The one thing these communities have in common—besides, of course, a love of the Cowboys and a connection to the local cable system—is the flushing of the toilet. And the foul river created in that methodical act has produced a new government, one that is part Austin, part Round Rock, part Cedar Park, part Brushy Creek MUD, part Lower Colorado River Authority and part Brazos River Authority—and may soon be part Hutto, Leander and Pflugerville too. It covers almost 90,000 acres and could serve half a million people. It goes by an innocuous name: the Brushy Creek Regional Wastewater System. It's sole function is to collect sewage. . . . Brushy Creek, however, is also a model of what we are becoming" (Bishop 2000).

28. Encounters over shared systemic infrastructure may encourage new social norms, because discussing such topics inevitably gets into priorities and values. Common cultural values could develop through such a dialogue, but they are more likely to come through common inflections of different cultural traditions. For example, movement toward environmental concern might be explained and placed differently in different local cultures. Consider the change in attitudes over the past decades toward garbage and recycling. On the other

hand, often people estimate success by the invisibility of infrastructural linkage. This can be an attraction in its own right: "Engineering an infrastructure that has enormous efficiency and complete invisibility is one of Disney's major feats. Paradoxically, this feat is an attraction in itself and even a subject of advertisement, but primarily for city planners and environmental engineers" (Sack 1992, 164).

29. Hierarchical levels may use different modes of communication. "While executives consult computers on an as-needed basis, and higher technicians gain job satisfaction from creative challenges of programming and diverse manipulations, lower-rung workers are more likely to be routinized. Rather than working in the home or in service jobs that are interpersonally based (food service, retail sales), they may now be facing a communication deskilling analogous to the mechanization of the human body accomplished by the assembly line" (Boden and Molotch 1994, 275).

30. See Hampton and Wellman 2000, Wellman 2001, and Wellman et al. 2003 for discussions of the mixture of face-to-face and digital communication.

31. Lefebvre does admit that the traditional city is changing, and he does not try to forecast what shape it will take. But he insists that it will involve spatial density and the center-periphery pattern. See the discussion in Liggett 2003, and Lefebvre's essay "The Right to the City," where he insists that the "polyvalent, polysensorial, urban man capable of complex and transparent relations with the world (the environment and himself)" demands a "reconstruction of centrality destroyed by a strategy of segregation and found again in the menacing form of centres of decision making" (Lefebvre 1996, 149, 154). He does not take the next step expanding that "centrality" to a polycentric network form, but that could fit with his hope for a space of differences.

32. The relation of center and periphery also influences Lefebvre's Manichaean approach to place norms: "On this side of things are ranged the forces that aspire to dominate and control space: business and the state, institutions, the family, the 'establishment,' the established order, corporate and constituted bodies of all kinds. In the opposite camp are the forces that seek to appropriate space: various forms of self-management or workers' control of territorial and industrial entities, communities and communes, elite groups striving to change life and to transcend political institutions and parties" (Lefebvre 1991, 392). This stark dualism relies on a narrow set of possible relationships among different kinds of powers and communities and systems. Lefebvre's emphasis on urban and centralized space also relies on the Nietzschean presupposition that "there is no 'reality' without a concentration of energy, without a focus or core" (Lefebvre 1991, 399). Lefebvre intends this to provide a new notion of wholeness: "The notion of centrality replaces the

notion of totality, repositioning it, relativizing it, and rendering it dialectical."
However, a useful and more flexible notion can be developed from the concepts
of link and node, network proximity and systemic interactions, into the mutual
constitution of complex systems.

33. For an extended discussion of Wright's Broadacre City, see the
Sprawling Places Web site.

CHAPTER SEVEN. TOWARD MORE COMPLEXITY IN SUBURBIA

1. One complaint about New Urbanists is that they put too much faith in
the discredited modernist idea that architecture and planning can shape social
values. The same complainers often worry that New Urbanist architecture and
planning will enforce simplified nostalgic and oppressive values.

2. The rhetoric of "tradition" and "community" is imposed on standard
suburbs. Traditional architectural vocabularies can be used for cheap knockoffs
of New Urbanism. Along the adjacent Florida coast there are many bad imitations
of Seaside's styles and colors—but not its spatial arrangements. (See the images
of Seaside and its neighbors at the Sprawling Places Web site.) There is a danger
that the look of Seaside or Celebration will be used to create not complex new
places but self-isolating privatopias for the well-to-do. Yet even such places are
forced into the circulation and linkage of today's world.

3. It is ironic that Seaside and Celebration are accused of being nostalgic
American small towns when many of their most successful spatial patterns, such
as the hippodrome and the crescent, are taken from English cities and are
seldom found in older U.S. towns.

4. Although it is true that many contemporary places need to become
thicker and more complex, complexity and linkage tend to undermine the goal
of an all-supportive community. It is also true that the reduction of all relations
to market instrumentality should be resisted, and that places should become
more compassionate and just, but this does not imply that we must foster local
spatial community as always one's primary identification.

5. New Urbanists do not all agree about their primary emphases. "New
Urbanism struggles between two identities, one a lofty set of principles that
many criticize as utopian and the other a style which is stereotyped as retro
and simplistic. . . . even within New Urbanism there is debate as to whether the
movement is guided by an open-ended set of principles or a design canon with
specific forms and norms. . . . This tension is healthy . . . but should not deflect
the need to always judge practice by principles rather than formulas" (Peter
Calthorpe in Fishman 2005, 16).

6. The New Urbanism is meant to include more than is seen in the usual
press coverage of the movement. "Too often, New Urbanism is not understood
as a complex system of policies and design principles that operate at multiple

scales. It is misinterpreted simply as a conservative movement to recapture the
past while ignoring the issues of our time. It is thought to be driven by nostalgia
and ordered by outdated tradition. To some, the New Urbanism simply means
tree-lined streets, houses with front porches, and Main Street retail—a reworking
of a Norman Rockwell fantasy of small-town America, primarily for the rich. . . .
But nostalgia is not what New Urbanism is proposing. Its goals and breadth are
much grander, more complete and challenging" (Calthorpe 2000, 178–80).

7. The Kentlands story has its twists, involving financing the original land
deal by selling part of the land to a mall developer, original plans for the mall
going awry, the mall developer abandoning the project, and the involvement of
a bank that changed the plans further. The big boxes were put in the plans fairly
early on with the intention of enabling residents to remain in Kentlands for all
their shopping. In recent years the town center's smaller retail has also been
developed, giving Kentlands an unusually complete retail mix.

8. Controversies about the relation of New Urbanist developments
to standard suburbs were aired in an extended debate between Harvard
University's Alex Krieger and New Urbanist pioneer Andres Duany. The Website
of the Congress of the New Urbanism (http://www.cnu.org) contains Duany's
polemical summary of that debate. See Burns 1997 for the text of another similar
debate with seven participants, including Duany, held at Harvard in 1996.

9. See the Sprawling Places Web site for a discussion of the New Urbanist
development at King Farm, a 430-acre development in suburban Maryland
not far from Kentlands, that is trying to become its own center that will attract
workers living elsewhere.

10. Thanks to Cheryl Troxel for supplying the term *horizontal hotel*.
Regarding existing suburban subdivisions, in Washington Township in New
Jersey, in connection with state smart-growth legislation, a municipality planned
a New Urbanist town center for itself rather than just laying out zones and
letting developers fill in the blanks (Steuteville 2000). Municipal planners
have an advantage over conventional developers, since officials can deal with
issues developers cannot touch, such as larger-scale planning, traffic beyond the
borders of the development, and surrounding land uses. Other examples of the
type have been built in Oregon and Missouri.

11. As a demonstration project, the Austin city government proposed
incentives for developing a neotraditional neighborhood with home prices from
$80,000 for a townhouse to the mid-$100,000s for a single-family home, in a
city where the median home price is $135,000. The development is to include
apartments, a commercial center, a school, and office space. The city will provide
down-payment assistance, and the developer will split with the city any profits
above a certain amount.

12. The attraction of the New Urbanism need not depend on nostalgia.

"It's not that they believe they have found a perfect re-creation of 19th century America's small-town community life. It's that mere hints of that life strike them as an appealing contrast to the neighborhoods they see around them, and worth taking a chance on. If striving for the New Urbanist ideal requires a touch of fantasy, well, that is a quality that American suburbanites have always possessed in abundance" (Ehrenhalt 2000).

13. See the discussion of neighborhood identity and outside threats in Lynch 1981, 400–403.

14. Such modes of mutually finding oneself recognized and valued also develop in standard suburbs. But not every suburban development has Celebration's unusual resources and explicit pressures toward creating the formal and informal institutions that give body to the vague notion of community. Two aspects make many New Urbanist developments different: these goals are more explicitly embraced so that inhabitants arrive with that intention, and the area offers a physical layout that helps rather than hinders efforts to build local dialogue.

15. For a brief but intense discussion of this danger, see Harvey 1997.

16. Herbert Gans remarked in an interview that "the urban upper middle class . . . said, 'Look at those dumb ones who have moved out to the suburbs where they are conformists and being homogeneous and being unfaithful to each other'. . . . But if you look at it, the attack was always against the [lower] middle class" (Herbert Gans, quoted in Peterson 1999, 46; see also Gans 1967, and Ross's list of positive and negative analyses of suburban life, in Ross 1999, 335, nn6–7). Somewhat along the lines of Gans, Michael Benedikt wondered aloud at a seminar whether some of the hostility to New Urbanism might spring from another class bias. New Urbanist developments typically have the kind of "high design temperature" found in resorts for the rich and in other aristocratic places. Could some attacks on the New Urbanism stem not just from a general disdain for middle-class suburbs, but also from the mix of envy and hostility that one can feel toward upper-class environs?

17. Ross discusses the ways in which cultural and economic differences reveal themselves in Celebration, but also the economic and other filters operating there, which are not unwelcome to many inhabitants. He also indicates how for some of America's diverse groups the atmosphere of the place has little attraction, because the style of community interaction and the range of acceptable self-definitions and subject positions are too narrow (Ross 1999, 266).

18. Traditional house styles can make more acceptable the other New Urbanist innovations. "It is hard enough convincing suburbanites to accept mixed uses, varied-income housing, and public transit without throwing in flat

roofs and corrugated metal siding into the equation. . . . There is absolutely no incompatibility between traditional urbanism and modernist architecture—far from it: modernist architecture looks and works its best when lining the sidewalks of traditional cities. Some truly great places—Miami's South Beach, Rome's EUR District, Tel Aviv—consist largely of modernist architecture laid out in a traditional street network" (Duany, Plater-Zyberk, and Speck 2000, 208–12). For the Aqua development in Miami, see http://www.aqua.net and http://www.dpz .com, and the discussion in Hay 2005.

19. The New Urbanist emphasis on codes and local governance refuses to leave everything to the market. Apropos of retail in a town center, the authors of *Suburban Nation* write: "All the above techniques depend to some degree upon managed retail, a concept that causes some to bristle. 'Whatever happened to a natural diversity?' they ask. 'Are there any real places left?' The surprising answer to that question is that a lack of management has proven to be the enemy of diversity. It is why Key West has become an emporium of T-shirt shops, and why the only lunch available on Rodeo Drive for under ten dollars consists of potato chips and a soda. When left alone, retailers tend to repeat easy successes and entire sectors become homogeneous. Variety is achieved not through natural selection but through careful programming" (Duany, Plater-Zyberk, and Speck 2000, 169). The authors argue that because calculating the cost of capital involves discounting income earned further than a few years out, the private sector cannot be trusted, on its own, to create an urbanism that has lasting value (Duany, Plater-Zyberk, and Speck 2000, 220n).

20. See, for instance, the treatment in Marcus and Sarkissian 1986, and http://www.communitygreens.org.

21. Mario Gandelsonas points out two erroneous fantasies about Edge City sprawl. "[In one fantasy] Edge City . . . is seen as a necessary stage in the process of urban growth, an economic inevitability. While the center city is seen as an impossible condition, the very picture of present disaster, Edge City is described as a green Edenic space. Urbanism, associated with tall buildings and 'too much asphalt,' is worst [*sic*] than parking lots. . . . [In the other] fantasy the center, seen as the repository of history, identity, diversity, and the realm of culture, stands in opposition to X-Urbia, which is determined solely by economics. . . . Both fantasies deny the contingent, the violent emergence of something that defies the limits of the established field, the limits of what one holds for 'possible,' where possible is, so to speak, a pacified contingency" (Gandelsonas 1999, 38). But large-scale governmental and financial practices work to limit the emergence of fundamentally new patterns for suburban development.

22. Paul Vitello cites an example of how such conflicts come about: "Since 2000, the number of immigrants living in suburbs, legally or illegally,

has surpassed the number in cities, 52 percent to 48 percent. . . . The illegal newcomers have attracted notice in the high-cost suburbs primarily by overcrowding single-family houses, which neighbors then complain become eyesores, and by assembling for day laborers' jobs in parking lots and on street corners. The local response has been somewhat like the suburbs themselves: decentralized; somewhat haphazard; self-contained; aimed at enforcing a set of 'quality of life' standards that are defined differently from place to place" (Vitello 2005).

23. Architects have seldom been offered opportunities for large-scale design of suburbs, and have not always handled well the opportunities that did come their way. The New Urbanism is the largest architect-led redesign movement in many years.

24. "Once the micropowers of design begin to throttle through our new highways, unorganized coincidence may occur and design will well up from the floor of the metropolis" (Lerup 2000, 122).

25. Sucher 1995 contains a sampler of particular tactics and architectural and planning strategies, many of which might be of use in retrofitting existing suburbs.

26. Over a period of thirty years, Simon Rodia built the steel and ceramic Watts Towers in his back yard in Los Angeles (for photos, see http://www.arts .ufl.edu/ART/RT_ROOM/watts/tower2.html). In Katy, Texas, outside Houston, a Hong Kong real estate magnate created a forty-acre park containing miniature reproductions of Chinese buildings and sites, including the terra-cotta warriors from Xian. (See Forbidden Gardens at RoadsideAmerica.com, http://www .roadsideamerica.com/attract/TXKATforbidden.html, accessed April 2007).

27. Kevin Lynch discusses the ideal of a closed organic community (Lynch 1981, 96, 246–49, 394–95, and 400–404), and concludes skeptically "Urban North Americans. . . . may have a casual nodding acquaintance with a handful of next-door neighbors, but their important social contacts are with old friends, workmates, and kin, who are widely scattered over the city. They shop in one community, use the school of another, go to church in a third. Their interests are no longer local. They no longer stay in one place very long" (401). Lynch claims that in cities today "The neighborhood may not be essential to [today's citizens'] social relations, but it is, along with the main routes, an essential piece of their mental structure. . . . It is no longer a space within which people know each other because they live next door, but a space which is commonly defined and given a name, and within which people find it relatively easy to band together when things get dangerous" (247–48). A town or a neighborhood has social, economic, and cultural connections reaching beyond its borders. However much intense mutual social interaction occurs within, the community

cannot close around itself in today's networked and linked world. The organic neighborhood is penetrated and porous—as are organisms.

28. Another quality worth cultivating is a sense of the temporariness of social and architectural arrangements. This doesn't mean that every place should be temporary; there are amazing stabilities that get overlooked by those who want to picture our world as completely in flux. Still, a hated mall store might be perceived more fully not just as another instance of a franchise operation, but as itself a passing event, likely to be replaced, with its social relations existing in tension with the drive for profit. Our perception becomes more complex as we perceive systemic and economic linkages.

29. Some interventions could be invisible additions of virtual real estate that create mixed spaces. See the Sprawling Places Web site for a discussion of mixed places composed from virtual and physical spaces.

30. It remains to be seen whether other developments with less financial resources will be able to develop community institutions and norms to match their advertising. "Other developers who took the town as an industry benchmark were likely to plan well below the expectations set by Celebration, reasoning that they could not afford the full menu of infrastructure and community software that had gone into the town's design" (Ross 1999, 315). Community building takes effort and careful planning. Citizens in many of the knockoff developments that incorporate some New Urbanist features will likely have to supplement and improve the community-building equivalent of shoddy construction and superficial decoration.

31. Speaking of modernist design's goal of revealing a building's functions, Charles Moore said, "What they showed was the structure and the system. They showed the front organs, the things they wanted to show as being important in the hierarchy. And what they didn't show was the stuff which didn't fit, the odd-ball stuff, the functional misfits, the things which were unsymmetrical. I am interested in the other sort of backdoor stuff that didn't fit in that earlier kind of formal statement of the truth" (Moore 2001, 199).

32. Linkage creates more self-awareness of our insertion into larger contexts and processes. David Harvey argues that we have to "understand urbanization as a group of fluid processes in a dialectical relation to the spatial forms to which they give rise and which in turn contain them. . . . . enlist in the struggle to advance a more socially just, politically emancipatory, and ecologically sane mix of spatio-temporal production processes. . . . Building something called community coupled with the politics of place can provide some sort of empowering basis for such a struggle" (Harvey 1997, 69).

33. As metropolitan areas expand outward, destinations unreachable by public transit increase in number faster than transit stations can keep up. Private

vehicles are often faster, and offer more flexibility and lower marginal costs for changing trips en route.

34. Douglas Kelbaugh argues that reformers who disagree about the ultimate suburban form to aim at still agree on the need for more density. "A fairer sharing and finer-grained mixing of diverse land uses, household types, building types, age groups, and socio-economic groups need to replace the single-use zoning that has sponsored the all too-ubiquitous housing subdivision, the shopping mall and the office park, as well as excessive dependence on the automobile. This is a major paradigm shift that everyone from Everyday Urbanists to New Urbanists to Post Urbanists all agree is needed. This is a welcome, unusual convergence. Let's seize it" (Kelbaugh 2004, 2).

35. To download the SmartCode and its manual, see PlaceMakers, SmartCode files (http://www.placemakers.com/info/SCdownloads.html, accessed April 2007).

36. Discussing the Los Angeles region, Wolch points out that "the general fragmentation within and across cities has brought one positive trend: with other sectors weakened, community-based organizations as well as labor unions have grown in numbers and influence. These sectors create the potential for a political force that could challenge the widening economic disparities within the region. But without a common agenda—and a broad constituency—even these progressive forces are unlikely to promote regional approaches to metropolis-wide problems in areas such as infrastructure, planning, and housing. A new Los Angeles will likely require that these grassroots voices rise up and articulate a crosscutting regional approach. Fortunately, this has begun to happen in arenas as diverse as economic policy, transportation development, and environmental inequities" (Wolch, Pastor, and Dreier 2004a, 19).

37. City and suburb remain politically and economically linked. "The evidence shows that where suburbs are experiencing decline, suburbanites are more likely to vote like urban dwellers, except where that decline is perceived to emanate from adjacent central-city neighborhoods. More generally, the immediate economic interest of many suburbanites remains tied to the central city because many earn their incomes there. Suburban residents will also support our proposed reforms when their towns have lost out in the beggar-thy-neighbor game of metropolitan development and thus would benefit directly from many of the measures proposed" (Dreier, Mollenkopf, and Swanstrom 2001, 132).

38. Arguments for regional and larger policies rely "on securing middle-class and suburban allies by noting that evidence suggests that metropolitan regions paying more attention to reducing central-city poverty, city/suburban differentials, and inequality actually grow faster" (see Wolch, Pastor, and Dreier 2004a, 37). But even with agreement on general regional goals, negotiations

about means would bring into play all the standard strategies of cost shifting and the assignment of burdens. They would also come up against local autonomy and its attempts to defend positions of privilege, the current fear and disbelief in social democratic proposals and Big Government, and the American pattern of labeling people as winners and losers, then ignoring the losers.

39. A popular introduction to Swedish culture describes *Allemänsrätten* (the right of all) as follows: "As long as you do not damage growing crops or seedlings, and do not trespass in . . . the land immediately surrounding a private house, you can walk or ski on other people's land without having to seek permission from the owner of the property. If the land is fenced in you can still go across, as long as you shut the gate properly behind you and do not damage the fencing. . . . Any signs forbidding entry can only be put up with the permission of the local authority. . . . You may put up a tent and camp for a night or so . . . and you don't need to ask the landowner's permission. . . . You may pick wild berries, flowers, and mushrooms, and pick up fallen branches and dry wood" (Svennson 1996, 68–70). A right to this level of access seems unthinkable in the American setting, but it is a good example for challenging what is taken as unitary and natural.

AFTERWORD

1. Multiplicity and complex linkage show up in the way today's world gets narrated. "We hear a lot about the crisis of the modern novel. What this involves, fundamentally, is a change in the mode of narration. It is scarcely any longer possible to tell a straight story sequentially unfolding in time. And this is because we are too aware of what is continually traversing the story-line laterally. That is to say, instead of being aware of a point as an infinitely small part of a straight line, we are aware of it as an infinitely small part of an infinite number of lines, as the centre of a star of lines. Such awareness is the result of our constantly having to take into account the simultaneity and extension of events and possibilities" (John Berger, quoted in Soja 1994, 137).

Bibliography

This list also includes works quoted or referenced in the Sprawling Places Web site.

Abbot, Edwin. 1884. *Flatland: A Romance of Many Dimensions.* London: Seeley.

Adam, Ian, and Helen Tiffin, eds. 1991. *Past the Last Post: Theorizing Post-Colonialism and Post-modernism.* New York: Harvester Wheatsheaf.

Adams, Eric. 1998. "Unrest in Reston." *Architecture* (May): 91.

Alexander, Christopher. 1975. *The Oregon Experiment.* New York: Oxford University Press.

————. 1979. *The Timeless Way of Building.* New York: Oxford University Press.

Alexander, Christopher, Sara Ishikawa, and Murray Silverstein. 1977. *A Pattern Language: Towns, Buildings, Construction.* New York: Oxford University Press.

Alexander, Christopher, Hajo Neis, Artemis Anninou, and Ingrid King. 1987. *A New Theory of Urban Design.* Oxford: Oxford University Press.

Algreen-Ussing, Gregers, et al., eds. 2000. *Urban Space and Urban Conservation as an Aesthetic Problem.* Rome: Accademica Danica, L'Erma di Bretschneider.

Allen, Stan. 1995. "Dazed and Confused." *Assemblage* 27 (fall): 47–54.

Anders, Peter. 2000. "Acadia '99." *Architecture* (Jan.): 49.

Anderson, Elizabeth. 2005. "How Not to Complain About Taxes (III): 'I Deserve My Pretax Income.'" Online at http://left2right.typepad.com /main/2005/01/, accessed April 2007.

Andersson, Magnus. 1998. *Stockholm's Annual Rings: A Glimpse into the Development of the City.* Stockholm: City Planning Administration.

Appadurai, Arjun. 1996. *Modernity at Large: Cultural Dimensions of Globalization.* Minneapolis: University of Minnesota Press.

Aquinas, Thomas. 1970. *On Being and Essence.* Translated by Joseph Bobik. Notre Dame: University of Notre Dame Press.

Arendt, Hannah, ed. 1968. *Illuminations.* New York: Harcourt, Brace.

Attridge, Derek, ed. 1992. *Acts of Literature.* New York: Routledge.

Augé, Marc. 1995. *Non-Places: Introduction to an Anthropology of Supermodernity.* London: Verso.

Barber, Benjamin R. 2001. "Malled, Mauled and Overhauled: Arresting Suburban Sprawl by Transforming Suburban Malls into Usable Civic Space." In Strong and Henaff 2001, 201–20.

Barnes, Julian. 1999. *England, England.* New York: Knopf.

Bartolucci, Marisa. 1997. "Reinventing Place." *Metropolis* (Sept.): 60–61.

Baudrillard, Jean. 1983. *Simulations.* New York: Semioitext(e).

———. 1994. *Simulacra and Simulation.* University of Michigan Press.

Benedikt, Michael. 1987. *For an Architecture of Reality.* New York: Lumen Books.

———, ed. 1988a. *Buildings and Reality: Architecture in the Age of Information.* Vol. 4 of *Center.* Austin: Center for American Architecture and Design.

———. 1988b. "Editor's Introduction." In Benedikt 1988a.

———, ed. 1992. *Cyberspace: First Steps.* Cambridge: MIT Press.

———. 1999a. "Less for Less Yet." *Harvard Design Magazine* (winter/spring): 10–14.

———. 1999b. "No Place Like e-topia." *Architecture* (Dec.): 45–47.

Benhabib, Seyla. 1986. *Critique, Norm, and Utopia.* Columbia University Press.

Benjamin, Walter. 1968. "The Work of Art in the Age of Mechanical Reproduction." In Arendt 1968.

Betsky, Aaron. 1997. "Machine Dreams." *Architecture* (June): 86ff.

Bishop, Bill. 2000. "To Create Government That Works, Just Add Sewage." *Austin-American Statesman*, Sunday, 12 March, A1, A17.

Bodei, Remo. 1987. *Scomposizioni: Forme dell'Individuo Moderno.* Milan: Einaudi.

Boden, Deirdre, and Harvey L. Molotch. 1994. "The Compulsion of Proximity." In Friedland and Boden 1994, 257–86.

Borgmann, Albert. 1987. *Technology and the Character of Contemporary Life.* Chicago: University of Chicago Press.

Bourdieu, Pierre. 1977. *Outline of a Theory of Practice.* Translated by Richard Nice. New York: Cambridge University Press.

Boyer, M. Christine. 1994. *The City of Collective Memory: Its Historical Imagery and Architectural Entertainments.* Cambridge: MIT Press.

———. 1996. *CyberCities: Visual Perception in the Age of Electronic Communication.* New York: Princeton Architectural Press.

Brannen, Noah, and William Elliott. 1969. *Festive Wine: Ancient Japanese Poems from the Kinkafu.* New York: Walker/Weatherhill.

Breyer, R. Michelle. 2000. "Sittin' on the Front Porch." *Austin American-Statesman*, 26 Feb., G1–2.

Brown, Brenda J. 2002. "Landscapes of Theme Park Rides: Media, Modes, Messages." In Young and Riley 2002, 235–68.

Brown, Jules, James Proctor, and Neil Roland. 1997. *Sweden, the Rough Guide.* London: Rough Guides.

Bruegmann, Robert. 2005. *Sprawl: A Compact History.* Chicago: University of Chicago Press.

Brydon, Diana. 1991. "The White Inuit Speaks: Contamination as Literary Strategy." In Adam and Tiffin 1991.

Burns, Carol, Robert Campbell, Andres Duany, Jerold Kayden, Alex Krieger, Nancy Levinson, and William Saunders. 1997. "Urban or Suburban?" *Harvard Design Magazine* (winter/spring): 47–63.

Caldenby, Claes, Jöran Lindvall, and Wilfried Wang, eds. 1998. *Sweden: 20th Century Architecture*. New York: Prestel.

Calthorpe, Peter. 1989. *The Pedestrian Pocket Book*. New York: Princeton Architectural Press.

———. 1993. *The Next American Metropolis: Ecology, Community, and the American Dream*. New York: Princeton Architectural Press.

———. 2000. "Afterword." In Leccese and McCormick 2000, 178ff.

Calthorpe, Peter, and William Fulton. 2001. *The Regional City: Planning for the End of Sprawl*. Washington: Island Press.

Cannell, Michael. 1999. "Brain Drain: Young Architects Are Fleeing the Studio to Build in the Virtual World." *Architecture* (Dec.): 125–27.

Casey, Edward S. 1993. *Getting Back into Place: Toward a Renewed Understanding of the Place-World*. Bloomington: Indiana University Press.

———. 1997. *The Fate of Place: A Philosophical History*. Berkeley: University of California Press.

Castells, Manuel. 1996. *The Rise of the Network Society*. Vol. 1 of *The Information Age: Economy, Society and Culture*. Oxford: Blackwell.

———. 1997. *The Power of Identity*. Vol. 2 of *The Information Age: Economy, Society and Culture*. Oxford: Blackwell.

———. 1998. *End of Millennium*. Vol. 3 of *The Information Age: Economy, Society and Culture*. Oxford: Blackwell.

———. 2004. "Afterword: Why Networks Matter." *Demos Collection* 20, 219–25.

Cavell, Stanley. 1989. *This New Yet Unapproachable America*. Albuquerque: University of New Mexico Press.

Chadderdon, Lisa. 1999. "Eighty-sixing the Nine-to-Five." *Architecture* (Dec.): 93–94.

Chaplin, Sarah. 1998. "Authenticity and Otherness: The New Japanese Theme Park." *Architectural Design* 68: 77–79.

Chappell, Edward A. 2002. "The Museum and the Joy Ride: Williamsburg Landscapes and the Specter of Theme Parks." In Young and Riley 2002, 119–56.

Cheek, Lawrence W. 2000. "New Urbanism Sees Green: Civano Mixes New Urbanism with Green Design." *Architecture* (March): 74–75, 144–45.

Chesterton, Gilbert Keith. 1994. *The Napoleon of Notting Hill*. Oxford: Oxford University Press.

Clarke, Arthur C. 1956. *The City and the Stars.* New York: Harcourt, Brace.

Clay, Grady. 1994. *Real Places: An Unconventional Guide to America's Generic Landscape.* Chicago: University of Chicago Press.

Cline, Ann. 1998. *A Hut of One's Own: Life Outside the Circle of Architecture.* Cambridge: MIT Press.

Comay, Rebecca, and John McCumber, eds. 1999. *Endings: Questions of Memory in Hegel and Heidegger.* Evanston: Northwestern University Press.

Conan, Michel. 2002. "The Fiddler's Indecorous Nostalgia." In Young and Riley 2002, 91–118.

Corbin, Carla I. 2002. "The Old/New Theme Park: The American Agricultural Fair." In Young and Riley 2002, 183–212.

Davidson, Donald. 1980. *Essays on Action and Events.* New York: Oxford University Press.

———. 2001. *Inquiries into Truth and Interpretation.* 2nd edition. New York: Oxford University Press.

Dear, Michael J., and Steven Flusty. 2002. *The Spaces of Postmodernity: Readings in Human Geography.* London: Blackwell.

Defoe, Daniel. 1994. *Robinson Crusoe.* New York: Norton.

Deleuze, Gilles. 1993. *The Fold: Leibniz and the Baroque.* Minneapolis: University of Minnesota Press.

———. 1994. *Difference and Repetition.* New York: Columbia University Press.

Denning, Peter. J., and Robert M. Metcalfe. 1997. *Beyond Calculation: The Next Fifty Years of Computing.* New York: Copernicus, Springer Verlag.

Derrida, Jacques. 1988. "*Limited Inc.* a b c." In *Limited Inc.* Evanston, Ill.: Northwestern University Press, 29–110.

———. 1992. "This Strange Institution Called Literature." In Attridge 1992, 33–75.

———. 1994. "The Deconstruction of Actuality: An Interview with Jacques Derrida." *Radical Philosophy* (autumn): 32.

———. 1998. "Afterword: Toward an Ethic of Discussion." In *Limited Inc.* Evanston, Ill.: Northwestern University Press, 111–60.

Dewdney, Arthur. 1984. *The Planiverse: Computer Contact with a Two-dimensional World.* New York: Poseidon Press.

Dimendberg, Edward. 1999. "Building a Space for the Imagination: Modern Architecture and Cinema." *Harvard Design Magazine* (winter/spring): 81–83.

Dreier, Peter, John Mollenkopf, and Todd Swanstrom. 2001. *Place Matters: Metropolitics for the Twenty-first Century.* Lawrence: University Press of Kansas.

Duany, Andres, Elizabeth Plater-Zyberk, and Jeff Speck. 2000. *Suburban Nation: The Rise of Sprawl and the Decline of the American Dream.* New York: North Point.

Duany, Andres, William Wright, and Sandy Sorlien. 2006. *SmartCode and Manual.* Available for download at http://www.placemakers.com, accessed April 2007.

Eco, Umberto. 1990. *Travels in Hyperreality.* San Diego: Harvest Books.

Egan, Greg. 1998. *Diaspora.* New York: Harper Collins.

Ehrenhalt, Alan. 2000. Op-ed. *New York Times,* Sunday, 9 July.

El Nasser, Haya. 2003. "Makeovers Bring New Life to Old Malls." *USA Today,* 23 April. Available online at http://www.growthmanagement-icsc.org/press/ PC_MallMakeover.asp, accessed April 2007.

Erben, David. 2001. *Technology and Art.* Minneapolis: University of Minnesota Press.

Ewing, Reid. 2004. "The Health Effects of Sprawl." Robert Wood Johnson Foundation, http://www.rwjf.org/newsroom/featureDetail.jsp?featureID= 154&type=3&pageNum=3&gsa=1, accessed April 2007.

Fishman, Robert. 1997. "Cities after the End of Cities." *Harvard Design Magazine* (winter/spring): 14–15.

———, ed. 2005. *New Urbanism: Peter Calthorpe vs. Lars Lerup.* Vol. 2 of Michigan Debates on Urbanism. New York: Distributed Arts Press.

Flanagan, Barbara. 2001. "Born to Be Bad." *Metropolis* 20 (Oct.): 81–87, 130–33.

Flay, Joseph. 1985. "Experience, Nature, and Place." *Monist* 68, no. 4: 467–80.

Flint, Anthony. 2006. *This Land: The Battle over Sprawl and the Future of America.* Baltimore: Johns Hopkins University Press.

Forster, Kurt. 1999. "Why Are Some Buildings More Interesting Than Others?" *Harvard Design Magazine* (winter/spring): 26–31.

Foster, Hal. 1983. *The Anti-Aesthetic.* Port Townsend: Bay Press.

———. 1996. *The Return of the Real.* Cambridge: MIT Press.

Foucault, Michel. 1979. *Discipline and Punish.* Translated by Alan Sheridan. New York: Random House.

Frampton, Kenneth. 1974. "On Reading Heidegger." *Oppositions* 4 (Oct.). Reprinted in Nesbitt 1996, 442.

———. 1983a. "Prospects for a Critical Regionalism." *Perspecta* 20: 147–62. Reprinted in Nesbitt 1996, 470–82.

———. 1983b. "*Towards a Critical Regionalism: Six Points for an Architecture of Resistance.*" In Foster 1983, 16–30.

———. 1990. "Rappel à ordre, the Case for the Tectonic." *Architectural Design* 60, nos 3–4: 19–25. Reprinted in Nesbitt 1996, 518–28.

———. 1995. *Studies in Tectonic Culture: The Poetics of Construction in Nineteenth and Twentieth Century Architecture.* Cambridge: MIT Press.

Frankston, Bob. 1997. "Beyond Limits." In Denning and Metcalfe 1997.

Friedland, Roger, and Deirdre Boden, eds. 1994. *NowHere: Space, Time and Modernity.* Foreword by Anthony Giddens. Berkeley: University of California Press.

Gandelsonas, Mario. 1999. *X-Urbanism: Architecture and the American City.* New York: Princeton Architectural Press.

Gans, Herbert. 1967. *The Levittowners: Ways of Life and Politics in a New Suburban Community.* New York: Pantheon.

Gearin, Elizabeth. 2004. "Smart Growth or Smart Growth Machine? The Smart Growth Movement and Its Implications." In Wolch, Pastor, and Dreier 2004, 279–307.

Geertz, Clifford. 1973. *The Interpretation of Culture.* New York: Basic Books.

Gibson, William. 1999. *All Tomorrow's Parties.* New York: Putnam.

Giddens, Anthony. 1990. *The Consequences of Modernity.* Stanford: Stanford University Press.

Giddens, Anthony, and Christopher Pierson. 1998. *Conversations with Anthony Giddens: Making Sense of Modernity.* Stanford: Stanford University Press.

Gins, Madeline, and [Shunjuku] Arakawa. 1997. *Reversible Destiny: We Have Decided Not to Die.* New York: Guggenheim Museum/Abrams.

———. 2002. *Architectural Body.* Tuscaloosa: University of Alabama Press.

Giovannini, Joseph. 1999. "Time on His Side." *Metropolis* (Oct.): 171–73.

———. 2000. "The New Primitive Hut: From an Absolute Past to an Uncertain Future." *Architecture* (Jan.): 112ff.

Goldberger, Paul. 1996. "Chicago, A Tale of Lost Magnificence." *New York Times,* Sunday, 16 June, 38H.

Goodman, Nelson. 1976. *Languages of Art.* Indianapolis: Hackett.

Goodman, Paul, and Percival Goodman. 1947. *Communitas.* New York: Random House.

Gordy, Peter. 1999. "The Subtle Shock of Seaside." *Seaside Times* (summer). Seaside, Fla.: Department of Public Works.

Gottdiener, Mark. 1997. *The Theming of America: Dreams, Visions, and Commercial Spaces.* New York: Harper Westview.

Grabow, Stephen. 1977. "Frank Lloyd Wright and the American City: The Broadacres Debate." *Journal of the American Institute of Planners* (April): 115–24.

Grosz, Elizabeth. 2001. *Architecture from the Outside: Essays on Virtual and Real Space.* Cambridge: MIT Press.

Gruen, Victor. 1955. "Cityscape and Landscape." In Ockman 1993, 193–99.

Guardini, Romano. 1994. *Letters from Lake Como.* Translated by Geoffrey W. Bromiley. Grand Rapids, Mich.: W. B. Eerdmans.

Haar, Michel. 1985. *Le chant de la terre*. Paris: L'Herne.

Habermas, Jürgen. 1987. *Lifeworld and System: A Critique of Functionalist Reason.* Vol. 2 of *The Theory of Communicative Action.* Translated by Thomas McCarthy. Boston: Beacon Press.

Habraken, N. John. 1998. *The Structure of the Ordinary: Form and Control in the Built Environment.* Edited by Jonathan Teicher. Cambridge: MIT Press.

Hafner, Katie. 1997. "Disney's Wizards." *Newsweek*, 11 Aug., 48–51.

Hall, Peter. 1988. *Cities of Tomorrow.* Oxford: Blackwell.

Hall, Ron. 2000. "Big." *Condé Nast Traveler* (March): 160–65, 206–13.

Hamilton, William. 1999. "How Suburban Design Is Failing Teen-Agers." *New York Times*, Thursday, 6 May, D1.

Hampton, Keith N., and Barry Wellman. 2000. "Examining Community in the Digital Neighborhood: Early Results from Canada's Wired Suburb." *Digital Cities*, 194–208.

Hannerz, Ulf. 1992. *Cultural Complexity: Studies in the Social Organization of Meaning.* New York: Columbia University Press.

Harden, Blaine. 2005. "Out West, a Paradox: Densely Packed Sprawl." *Washington Post*, 10 Aug.

Harries, Karsten. 1988. "The Voices of Space." In Benedikt 1988a, 34–49.

———. 1997. *The Ethical Function of Architecture.* Cambridge: MIT Press.

Harrison, Steve, and Paul Dourish. 1996. "Re-place-ing Space: The Roles of Place and Space in Collaborative Systems." In *Proceedings of the 1996 ACM Conference on Computer Supported Cooperative Work*, 67–76. Boston: Association for Computing Machines.

Harvey, David. 1997. "The New Urbanism and the Communitarian Trap." *Harvard Design Magazine* (winter/spring): 68–69.

Harwood, Edward. 2002. "Rhetoric, Authenticity, and Reception: The Eighteenth-Century Landscape Garden, the Modern Theme Park, and Their Audiences." In Young and Riley 2002, 49–68.

Hay, David. 2005. "Watered Down Urbanism." *Metropolis* (Oct.): 122–27.

Hayden, Dolores. 2000. *Building Suburbia: Green Fields and Urban Growth, 1820–2000.* New York: Pantheon Books.

———. 2004. *A Field Guide to Sprawl.* Photographs by Jim Wark. New York: Norton.

Hays, K. Michael. 1995. "Architecture Theory, Media, and the Question of Architecture, 1995." *Assemblage* 27 (fall): 45.

———. 1998. Introduction. *Architecture Theory since 1968.* New York: Columbia University Press.

———. 1999. "Not Architecture But Evidence That It Exists: A Note on Lauretta Vinciarelli's Watercolors." *Assemblage* 38: 48–57.

Hecht, Richard D. 1994. "The Construction and Management of Sacred Time and Space: Sabta Nurin the Church of the Holy Sepulcher." In Friedland and Boden 1994, 181–235.

Hegel, Georg Wilhelm Friedrich. 1965. "Who Thinks Abstractly?" Translated by Walter Kaufmann. In Kaufmann 1965, 114–18.

———. 1967. *Hegel's Philosophy of Right.* Translated by Thomas Malcolm Knox. New York: Oxford University Press.

———. 1969. *Hegel's Science of Logic.* Translated by Arnold Miller. New York: Humanities Press.

———. 1975. *Hegel's Aesthetics: Lectures on Fine Art.* Two volumes. Translated by Thomas Malcolm Knox. Oxford: Clarendon.

———. 1977. *Phenomenology of Spirit.* Translated by Arnold Miller. Oxford: Clarendon.

Heidegger, Martin. 1954. "Bauen Wohnen Denken." In *Vorträge und Aufsätze.* Pfullingen: Neske. Translated in Heidegger 1971, 143–61.

———. 1971. *Poetry, Language, Thought.* Translated by Albert Hofstadter. New York: Harper & Row.

———. 1977. *The Question Concerning Technology and Other Essays.* Translated by William Lovitt. New York: Harper & Row.

———. 1981. "Only a God Can Save Us." Translated by William Richardson. In Sheehan 1981, 45–72.

———. 1996. *Being and Time.* Translated by Joan Stambaugh. Albany: State University of New York Press.

Helling, Amy. 2002. "Transportation, Land Use, and the Impacts of Sprawl on Poor Children and Families." In Squires 2002a, 119–39.

Henig, Jeffrey. 2002. "Equity and the Future Politics of Growth." In Squires 2002a, 325–50.

Hernandez, Sylvia. 1997. "There Is Nowhere Like Mexico: An Interview with Sylvia Hernandez." *Hemispheres* (June): 21–26.

Hertzberger, Herman. 1991. *Lessons for Students in Architecture.* Rotterdam: Uitgeverij 010.

Hough, Michael. 1990. *Out of Place.* New Haven: Yale University Press.

Howard, Michael. 1993. Review of Eugene Rostow's *Toward Managed Peace. Times Literary Supplement,* 3 Sept., 6.

Husserl, Edmund. 1960. *Cartesian Meditations: An Introduction to Phenomenology.* Translated by Dorion Cairns. The Hague: M. Nijhoff.

Huxtable, Ada Louise. 1997. *The Unreal America: Architecture and Illusion.* New York: New Press.

Huyssen, Andreas. 2000. "After the War." *Harvard Design Magazine* (winter/ spring): 72–77.

Ingvar, Lars, ed. 1990. *Lund, One Thousand Years: A Cultural Guide.* Lund, Sweden: Wallin.

Isozaki, Arata. 1996. "The Island Nation Aesthetic." *Polemics.* London: Academy Group.

————, et al. 1991. *Osaka Follies.* London: Architectural Association.

Iyer, Pico. 1999. "Always Homeward Bound." *Architecture* (Dec.): 83–84.

————. 2000a. *The Global Soul: Jet Lag, Shopping Malls, and the Search for Home.* New York: Knopf.

————. 2000b. "A Room of My Own." *Condé Nast Traveler* (March): 150–59, 198–200.

Jackson, John Brinckerhoff. 1984. *Discovering the Vernacular Landscape.* New Haven: Yale University Press.

————. 1994. *A Sense of Place, a Sense of Time.* New Haven: Yale University Press.

Jacobs, Jane. 1961. *The Death and Life of Great American Cities.* New York: Vintage.

————. 2000a. "Jane Jacobs, Urban Agitator." *Architecture* (March): 71–72, 142–43.

————. 2000b. *The Nature of Economies.* New York: Modern Library.

Jacobs, Karrie. 1993. "The Single Box Theory." *Metropolis,* Dec.

————. 2005. "Oh Brooklyn, My Brooklyn." *Metropolis* (Aug./Sept.): 74–78.

Jaret, Charles. 2002. "Suburban Expansion in Atlanta: 'The City without Limits' Faces Some." In Squires 2002a, 165–205.

Jargowsky, Paul. 2002. "Sprawl, Concentration of Poverty, and Urban Inequality." In Squires 2002a, 39–71.

Jencks, Charles. 1995. *The Architecture of the Jumping Universe.* London: Academy Editions.

Jenkins, Henry. 2006. *Convergence Culture: Where Old and New Media Collide.* New York: New York University Press.

Joassart-Marcelli, Pascale, William Fulton, and Juliet Musso. 2004. "Can Growth Control Escape Fiscal and Economic Pressures? City Policy before and after the 1990s Recession." In Wolch, Pastor, and Dreier 2004, 255–77.

Joyce, Michael. 1995. *Of Two Minds: Hypertext Pedagogy and Poetics.* Ann Arbor: University of Michigan Press.

Kahn, Louis. 1987. "Silence and Light." In *Louis I. Kahn Complete Works 1935–1974,* ed. by Heinz Rouner and Sharad Jhavert, 447–49. Basel: Birkhäuser.

Kant, Immanuel. 1933. *Critique of Pure Reason.* Translated by Norman Kemp Smith. London: Macmillan.

————. 1987. *Critique of Judgment.* Translated by Werner Pluhar. Indianapolis: Hackett.

Kaufmann, Walter. 1966. *Hegel: Texts and Commentary.* Garden City, N.Y.: Doubleday.

Kelbaugh, Douglas S. 1997. *Common Place: Toward Neighborhood and Regional Design.* Seattle: University of Washington Press.

———. 2002a. "American Density and Sprawl: Seven Goals, Seven Policies." Ann Arbor: University of Michigan Urban and Regional Research Collaborative, Taubman College of Architecture. Available online at http://sitemaker.umich.edu/urrcworkingpapers/all_urrc_working_papers/da.data/308469/Paper/urrc_02-4.pdf, accessed April 2007.

———. 2002b. *Repairing the American Metropolis: Common Place Revisited.* Seattle: University of Washington Press.

———. 2004. "Density—The D Word." Ann Arbor: Taubman College of Architecture. Available online at http://www.architects.org/emplibrary/P4_a.pdf, accessed April 2007.

Kelly, Barbara M. 1993. *Expanding the American Dream: Building and Rebuilding Levittown.* Albany: SUNY Press.

Kierkegaard, Søren. 1987. *Either/Or.* Princeton: Princeton University Press.

Kirkwood, Judith. 1999. "Endless Summer." *USAir Attaché Magazine* (Oct.).

Kirsner, Scott. 2000. "Are You Experienced?" *Wired,* Archive 8.07, July. Available online at http://www.lo-q.com/press/Wired.htm, accessed April 2007.

Kolb, David. 1986. *The Critique of Pure Modernity: Hegel, Heidegger, and After.* Chicago: University of Chicago Press.

———. 1990. *Postmodern Sophistications: Philosophy, Architecture, and Tradition.* Chicago: University of Chicago Press.

———. 1992. "Home on the Range: Planning and Totality." *Research in Phenomenology:* 3–11. (Reprinted in *Nordisk Arkitekturforskning,* spring 1995).

———. 1998. "Tradition and Modernity in Architecture." In *Encyclopedia of Aesthetics.* New York: Oxford University Press.

———. 1999a. "Circulation and Constitution at the End of History." In Comay and McCumber 1999, 57–76.

———. 1999b. "Modernity's Self-Justification." *Owl of Minerva* 30, no. 2: 253–76.

———. 2000a. "The Age of the List." In Algreen-Ussing et al. 2000, 27–35.

———. 2000b. "Learning Places: Building Dwelling Thinking On-line." *Journal of Philosophy of Education* 34, no. 1 (winter): 121–33.

———. 2000c. "The Spirit of Gravity: Architecture and Externality in Hegel." In Maker 2000, 83–96.

———. 2001. "Hegelian Buddhist Hypertextual Media Inhabitation, or, Criticism in the Age of Electronic Immersion." In Erben 2001, 90–108.

———. 2002. "Madeline Gins and Arakawa: Architectural Body." *Continental Philosophy Review* 35, no. 4 (Dec.): 461–69.

————. 2003. "Oh Pioneers! Bodily Reformation Amid Daily Life." *Interfaces* 2, no. 21/22: 383–98.

————. 2006a. "Authenticity with Teeth: Positing Process." In Nikolas Kompridis, 2006, *Philosophical Romanticism* (New York: Routledge), 60–77.

————. 2006b. "Real Places in Virtual Spaces." *Nordisk Arkitekturforskning: Nordic Journal of Architectural Research*, no. 3: 69–77.

————. 2007. "Borders and Centers in an Age of Mobility." Special issue of the online journal *Wolkenkuckucksheim* honoring Karsten Harries, http://www.cloud-cuckoo.net.

Koolhaas, Rem. 1994. *Delirious New York*. New York: Monacelli Press.

————. 1995. *Small Medium Large Extra Large*. New York: Monacelli Press.

Koppell, Jonathan G. S. 2000. "No 'There' There: Why Cyberspace Isn't Anyplace." *Atlantic Monthly* (Aug.): 16–18.

Kostka, Stefan, and Dorothy Payne. 1989. *Tonal Harmony*. New York: Knopf.

Kramer, Jane. 1991. "Living with Berlin." *New Yorker* 40 (25 Nov.): 55ff.

Kroloff, Reed. 1998. "Suspending Disbelief." *Architecture* (Aug.): 11.

Kwinter, Sanford. 1995a. "Assembly 1." *Assemblage* 27 (fall): 33–40.

————. 1995b. "Politics and Pastoralism." *Assemblage* 27 (fall): 25–32.

Laclau, Ernesto, and Lilian Zac. 1994. "Minding the Gap: The Subject of Politics." In *The Making of Political Identities*, ed. by Ernesto Laclau, 32. New York, Verso.

Lakoff, George. 1997. "Testing the Limits of Brain Plasticity." In Gins and Arakawa 1997, 118–19.

Landis, John. 2006. Review of Robert Bruegmann's *Sprawl: A Compact History*. *The Next American City* 10, Spring Online, http://www.americancity.org/article.php?id_article=154, accessed April 2007.

Lang, Robert. 2003. *Edgeless Cities: Exploring the Elusive Metropolis*. Washington, D.C.: Brookings Institution Press.

Le Corbusier. 1986. *Towards a New Architecture*. New York: Dover.

Le Guin, Ursula K. 1985. *Always Coming Home*. New York: Harper & Row.

Leccese, Michael, and Kathleen McCormick. 2000. *Charter of the New Urbanism*. New York: McGraw Hill.

Lefebvre, Henri. 1991. *The Production of Space*. Translated by Donald Nicholson-Smith. London: Blackwell.

————. 1996. *Writings on Cities*. Translated by Eleonore Kofman and Elizabeth Lebas. London: Blackwell.

————. 2003. *The Urban Revolution*. Translated by Robert Bononno. Minneapolis: University of Minnesota Press.

Lerup, Lars. 2000. *After the City*. Cambridge: MIT Press.

Libeskind, Daniel. 1995. *Traces of the Unknown*. 1995 Raoul Wallenberg Lecture. Ann Arbor: University of Michigan Press.

Liggett, Helen. 2003. *Urban Encounters*. Minneapolis: University of Minnesota Press.

Lippard, Lucy R. 1997. *The Lure of the Local: Senses of Place in a Multicentered Society*. New York: New Press.

———. 1999. *On the Beaten Track: Tourism, Art, and Place*. New York: New Press.

Lopez, Barry. 1986. *Arctic Dreams: Imagination and Desire in a Northern Landscape*. New York: Scribners.

———. 1997. "A Literature of Place." *Portland Magazine* (summer). Portland, Ore.: University of Portland. Online at http://arts.envirolink.org/literary_arts/BarryLopez_LitofPlace.html, accessed April 2007.

Lowenthal, David. "The Past as a Theme Park." In Young and Riley 2002, 11–24.

Lyman, Rick. 2005. "Living Large, by Design, in the Middle of Nowhere." *New York Times*, 15 Aug.

Lynch, Kevin. 1960. *The Image of the City*. Cambridge: MIT Press.

———. 1981. *A Theory of Good City Form*. Cambridge: MIT Press.

MacCannell, Dean. 1989. *The Tourist: A New Theory of the Leisure Class*. New York: Schocken Books.

———. 1992. *Empty Meeting Grounds*. London: Routledge.

Maker, William. 2000. *Hegel and Aesthetics*. Albany: SUNY Press.

Marcus, Clare Cooper, and Wendy Sarkissian. 1986. *Housing As If People Mattered: Site Design Guidelines for Medium-Density Family Housing*. Berkeley: University of California Press.

Marling, Karal Ann, ed. 1997. *Designing Disney's Theme Parks: The Architecture of Reassurance*. New York: Flammarion.

Marshall, Alex. 1996. "Suburb in Disguise." *Metropolis* (July/Aug.): 71ff.

Mårtensson, Jan. 1990. "The Spirit of Lund." In Ingvar 1990, 9–13.

Massey, Doreen. 1994. *Space, Place, and Gender*. Minneapolis: University of Minnesota Press.

Mathews, Stanley. 2000. *Potteries Thinkbelt: An Architecture of Calculated Uncertainty*. Online at http://people.hws.edu/mathews/potteries_thinkbelt.htm, accessed April 2007.

McCrone, David, Angela Morris, and Richard Kiely. 1995. *Scotland—the Brand: The Making of Scottish Heritage*. Edinburgh: Edinburgh University Press.

McCullough, Malcolm. 1997. "Genetic Code." *Harvard Design Magazine* (summer): 71–72.

Mehrotra, Rahul, ed. 2005. *Everyday Urbanism: Margaret Crawford vs. Michael Speaks*. Vol. 1 of Michigan Debates on Urbanism. New York: Distributed Arts Press.

Meyer, Michael. 2000. "The Whys of Size." *Condé Nast Traveler* (March): 165, 213–15.

Meyerowitz, Joshua. 1985. *No Sense of Place: The Impact of Electronic Media on Social Behavior.* New York: Oxford University Press.

Miller, David E. 2005. *Toward a New Regionalism: Environmental Architecture in the Pacific Northwest.* Seattle: University of Washington Press.

Mitchell, William J. 1999. *e-topia.* Cambridge: MIT Press.

Moore, Charles W. 2001. *You Have to Pay for the Public Life: Selected Essays of Charles W. Moore.* Edited by Kevin Keim. Cambridge: MIT Press.

Mugerauer, Robert. 1988. "Derrida and Beyond." In Benedikt 1988a, 66–76.

Mullins, Robert. 2005. "Mall Joins 'Hy-style' Trend." *Silicon Valley / San Jose Business News,* 21 May 2004. Online at http://www.bizjournals.com /sanjose/stories/2004/05/24/story5.html, accessed April 2007.

Murray, Janet. 1997. *Hamlet on the Holodeck.* New York: Free Press.

Musso, Juliet. "Metropolitan Fiscal Structure: Coping with Growth and Fiscal Constraint." In Wolch, Pastor, and Dreier 2004b, 171–94.

Nesbitt, Kate, ed. 1996. *Theorizing: A New Agenda for Architecture: An Anthology of Architectural Theory 1965–1995.* New York: Princeton Architectural Press.

Nielsen, Jakob. 1998. "2D Is Better than 3D." Alertbox. 15 Nov. Online at http:/ /www.useit.com/alertbox/.

Nietzsche, Friedrich. 1967a. *The Birth of Tragedy.* Translated by Walter Kaufmann. New York: Random House.

———. 1967b. *The Will to Power.* Translated by Walter Kaufmann. New York: Vintage.

———. 1968. *The Twilight of the Idols.* Translated by R. J. Hollingdale. Baltimore: Penguin Books.

Nitschke, Günter. 1993. *From Shinto to Ando: Studies in Architectural Anthropology in Japan.* London: AD Academy Editions.

Nobel, Philip. 2007. "Good Malls and Bad Cities." *Metropolis* (March): 72–74.

Norberg-Schulz, Christian. 1976. "The Phenomenon of Place." *Architectural Association Quarterly* 8, no. 4: 3–10. Reprinted in Nesbitt 1996.

———. 1984. *Genius Loci.* New York: Rizzoli.

———. 1985. *The Concept of Dwelling.* New York: Electra/Rizzoli.

———. 1996. *Nightlands: Nordic Building.* Cambridge: MIT Press.

Norfolk, Andrew. 2005. "Slay Goliath, Sail the Ark." *Times Online,* 28 March, http://www.timesonline.co.uk/article438726.ece, accessed August 2007.

Ockman, Joan, ed. 1993. *Architecture Culture 1943–1968: A Documentary Anthology.* New York: Columbia School of Architecture/Rizzoli.

Orfield, Myron. 2002. "Politics and Regionalism." In Squires 2002a, 237–54.

Pallasmaa, Juhana. 1996. *The Eyes of the Skin: Architecture and the Senses.* London: Academy Group.

Patron, Eugene. 1998. "Virtual Paradise: The Cruise Industry Turns to Total Design in Its Quest for the Ultimate Destination." *Metropolis* (Feb./March): 66–68, 93–94.

Paz, Octavio. 1974. *In Praise of Hands: Contemporary Crafts of the World.* Greenwich, Conn.: New York Graphic Society.

Peterson, Iver. 1999. "Some Perched in Ivory Tower Gain Rosier View of Suburbs." *New York Times,* Sunday, 5 Dec., 1, 46.

Pinsky, Michael. 1992. "Evidence of History." *disClosure* 2 (autumn): 99–108.

Pippin, Robert. 1989. *Hegel's Idealism: The Satisfactions of Self-Consciousness.* New York: Cambridge University Press.

———. 1991. *Modernity as a Philosophical Problem.* London: Blackwell.

———. 1997. *Idealism as Modernism: Hegelian Variations.* New York: Cambridge University Press.

Poster, Mark. 1988. *Jean Baudrillard: Selected Writings.* Stanford: Stanford University Press.

Potts, Alex. 1991. "Schinkel's Architectural Theory." In *Karl Friedrich Schinkel: A Universal Man,* ed. Michael Snodin, 47–56. New Haven: Yale University Press.

Price, Cedric. 1984. *Works II.* London: Architectural Association.

Pulido, Laura. 2002. "Environmental Racism and Urban Development." In Squires 2002a, 71–98.

Quaintance, Richard. 2002. "Toward Distinguishing among Theme Park Publics: William Chambers's Landscape Theory vs. His Kew Practice." In Young and Riley 2002, 25–48.

Rakatansky, Mark. 1995. "Identity and the Discourse of Politics in Contemporary Architecture." *Assemblage* 27 (fall): 9f.

Raz, Aviad. 1999. *Riding the Black Ship: Japan and Tokyo Disneyland.* Cambridge: Harvard University Press.

Reichek, Jesse. 1961. "On the Design of Cities." *Journal of the American Institute of Planners* (May): 141.

Ricoeur, Paul. 1977. *The Rule of Metaphor.* Translated by Robert Czerny. Toronto: University of Toronto Press.

———. 1984–88. *Time and Narrative.* Translated by Kathleen McLaughlin and David Pellauer. 3 vols. Chicago: University of Chicago Press.

———. 1992. *Oneself as Another.* Translated by Kathleen Blamey. Chicago: University of Chicago Press.

Rivera, Dylan, and Bill Bishop. 2000. "High-Tech Companies Leading the Charge Downtown." *Austin American-Statesman* (3 March): A1, A10–11.

Robertson, A. F. 1994. "Time and the Modern Family: Reproduction in the Making of History." In Friedland and Boden 1994, 95–126.

Ross, Andrew, ed. 1988. *Universal Abandon: The Politics of Postmodernism.* Minneapolis: University of Minnesota Press.

Ross, Andrew. 1999. *The Celebration Chronicles: Life, Liberty, and the Pursuit of Property Value in Disney's New Town.* New York: Ballantine.

Rossney, Robert. 1996. "Metaworlds." *Wired* (June): 145–46, 210.

Rubin, Chris. 1997. "Sweet Tele-Suite." *Wired* (Aug.): 129.

Rudberg, Eva. "Building the Welfare of the Folkhemmet 1940–1960." In Caldenby, Lindvall, and Wang 1998.

Rybczynski, Witold. 1995. *City Life.* New York: Touchstone.

———. 1999. "The Virtues of Suburban Sprawl." *Wall Street Journal* (25 May): A26.

Sack, Robert David. 1992. *Place, Modernity, and the Consumer's World: A Relational Framework for Geographic Analysis.* Baltimore: Johns Hopkins University Press.

Sallis, John. 1994. *Stone.* Bloomington: Indiana University Press.

Sandin, Gunnar. 2003. *Modalities of Place: On Polarisation and Exclusion in Concepts of Place and in Site-Specific Art.* Doctoral dissertation, Lund University, Department of Architecture, see http://theses.lub.lu.se/postgrad/search .tkl?field_query1=pubid&query1=tec_721&recordformat=display, accessed April 2007.

Sartre, Jean-Paul. 1991. *Critique of Dialectical Reason.* London: Verso.

Sassen, Saskia. 1991. *The Global City: New York, London, Tokyo.* Princeton: Princeton University Press.

Savitch, H. V. 2002."Encourage, Then Cope: Washington and the Sprawl Machine." In Squires 2002a, 141–64.

Schenker, Heath. 2002. "Pleasure Gardens, Theme Parks, and the Picturesque." In Young and Riley 2002, 69–90.

Schwarzer, Michael. 1998. "Selected books by J. B. Jackson." *Harvard Design Magazine* (fall): 75.

Scully, Vincent. 2000. Article in the *Brookings Review,* summer 2000, quoted in an *Austin American Statesman* editorial, Tuesday, 18 July, A8.

Seamon, David, and Robert Mugerauer, eds. 1985. *Dwelling, Place, and Environment: Towards a Phenomenology of Person and World.* Boston: M. Nijhoff.

Sellars, Wilfrid. 1963. *Science, Perception, and Reality.* New York: Humanities Press.

Sennett, Richard. 1999. "The Spaces of Democracy." *Harvard Design Magazine* (summer): 68–72.

Sheehan, Thomas, ed. 1981. *Heidegger: The Man and His Thought.* Chicago: Precedent.

Shippey, Tom. 1996. "Burbocentrism." *London Review of Books,* 23 May, 35.

Snyder, Susan Nigra. 1999. Letter to the editor, *Chronicle of Higher Education*, 25 June, B3, B11.

Soja, Edward W. "Postmodern Geographies: Taking Los Angeles Apart." In Friedland and Boden 1994, 127–62.

Sorkin, Michael, ed. 1992. *Variations on a Theme Park: The New American City and the End of Public Space.* New York: Hill & Wang.

"Squeezed Out." 2000. *Economist*, 22 July, 33.

Squires, Gregory, ed. 2002a. *Urban Sprawl: Causes, Cosequences, and Policy Responses.* Washington, D.C.: The Urban Institute Press.

———. 2002b. "Urban Sprawl and the Uneven Development of Metropolitan America." In Squires 2002a, 1–22.

Stanley, Nick. "Chinese Theme Parks and National Identity." In Young and Riley 2002, 269–92.

Star, Alexander. 1999. "Atlantis in Reverse." *Metropolis* (Dec.): 116, 119–20.

Stephanson, Anders. "Interview with Cornell West." In Ross 1988, 69–86.

Stephenson, Neal. 1993. *Snow Crash.* New York: Bantam.

Sterling, Bruce. 1995. "Triumph of the Plastic People." *Wired* (Jan.): 158ff.

———. 1996. *Holy Fire.* New York: Bantam.

———. 1998. *Distraction.* New York: Bantam.

Stern, Robert A. M. 1986. *Pride of Place: Building the American Dream.* Boston: Houghton Mifflin.

Steuteville, Robert. 2000. "New Jersey Town Takes Public Route to New Urbanism." *New Urban News* (March).

Strawson, Peter. 1959. *Individuals.* Garden City, N.Y.: Doubleday.

———. 1966. *The Bounds of Sense.* London: Methuen.

Strickland, Roy, ed. 2005. *Post Urbanism and ReUrbanism: Peter Eisenman vs. Barbara Littenberg and Steven Peterson.* Vol. 3 of Michigan Debates on Urbanism. New York: Distributed Arts Press.

Strong, Tracy, and Marcel Henaff, eds. 2001. *Public Space and Democracy.* Minneapolis: University of Minnesota Press.

Sucher, David. 1995. *City Comforts: How to Build an Urban Village.* Seattle: City Comforts Press.

Sudjic, Dayan. 1992. *The Hundred-Mile City.* New York: Harcourt.

Svennson, Charlotte Rosen. 1996. *Culture Shock: Sweden.* Portland, Ore.: Graphic Arts Center Publishing.

Tägil, Tomas. 1990. "Lund Buildings and Lund Places." In Ingvar 1990, 49–108.

Taylor, Charles. 1989. *Sources of the Self.* Harvard University Press.

Taylor, Mark C. 2001. *The Moment of Complexity.* Chicago: University of Chicago Press.

————, and Esa Saarinen. 1994. *Imagologies*. London: Routledge.

Thompson, J. William. 1999. "Can We Retrofit Suburbia?" *Journal of Landscape Architecture* 89, no. 7 (July): 76–81, 96–97.

"Trash Overboard." 1999. *Economist*, 18 Sept., 63.

Treib, Marc. 2002. "Theme Park, Themed Living: The Case of Huis Ten Bosch [Japan]." In Young and Riley 2002, 213–34.

Tuan, Yi-Fu. 1977. *Space and Place: The Perspective of Experience*. Minneapolis: University of Minnesota Press.

————. 1998. *Escapism*. Baltimore: Johns Hopkins University Press.

Ulmer, Gregory L. 1989. *Teletheory: Grammatology in the Age of Video*. New York: Routledge.

Venturi, Robert. 1966. *Complexity and Contradiction in Architecture*. New York: Museum of Modern Art.

Venturi, Robert, Denise Scott Brown, and Steven Izenour. 1977. *Learning from Las Vegas*. Cambridge: MIT Press.

Vitello, Paul. 2005. "As Illegal Workers Hit Suburbs, Politicians Scramble to Respond." *New York Times*, 6 Oct.

Watson, James, ed. 1997. *Golden Arches East: McDonald's in East Asia*. Stanford: Stanford University Press.

Weber, Max. 1968. *Economy and Society*. Translated and edited by Guenther Roth and Claus Wittich. New York: Bedminster Press.

Wellman, Barry. 2001. "Little Boxes, Glocalization, and Networked Individualism." Powerpoint slides online at http://www.chass.utoronto.ca/~wellman/publications/, accessed April 2007.

Wellman, Barry, Anabel Quan-Haase, Jeffrey Boase, Wenhong Chen, Keith N. Hampton, Isabel Isla de Diaz, and Kakuko Miyata. 2003. "The Social Affordances of the Internet for Networked Individualism." *Journal of Computer-Mediated Communication* 8, no. 3 (April): n.p. PDF version online at http://www.chass.utoronto.ca/~wellman/publications/, accessed April 2007.

"When Life Is More Interesting Than Art." 2000. Review of *American Beauty*. *Economist* (25 March): 36.

Whitehead, Alfred North. 1958. *Modes of Thought*. New York: Capricorn.

————. 1960. *Process and Reality: An Essay in Cosmology*. New York: Harper.

Wiewel, Wim, Joseph Persky, and Kimberly Schaffer. "Less Sprawl, Greater Equity? The Potential for Revenue Sharing in the Chicago Region." In Squires 2002a, 255–91.

Wigley, Mark. 1995. "Story Time." *Assemblage* 27 (fall): 81–94.

Williams, William Carlos. 1963. *Patterson*. San Francisco: New Directions.

Wittgenstein, Ludwig. 1953. *Philosophical Investigations*. Oxford: Blackwell.

Wolch, Jennifer, Manuel Pastor Jr., and Peter Dreier. 2004a. "Introduction. Making Southern California: Public Policy, Markets, and the Dynamics of Growth." In Wolch et al. 2004b, 1–40.

———, eds. 2004b. *Up against the Sprawl: Public Policy and the Making of Southern California.* Foreword by Michael Dear. Minneapolis: University of Minnesota Press.

Wolf, Gary. 1998. "Venture Kapital." *Wired* (June): 138–51, 202–7.

———. 2000. "The Unmaterial World." *Wired* (June): 308–19.

Wood, David. 1999. "Heidegger and the Challenge of Repetition." *Proceedings of the Heidegger Conference,* DePaul University, Chicago.

Wood, Denis. 1991. "Looking for Life in the Heart of the City." *Places* 7, no. 2 (winter): 41–47.

Wright, Frank Lloyd. 1932. "Broadacre City: An Architect's Vision." *New York Times Magazine* 20 March, 8–9.

———. 1933. "Frank Lloyd Wright Tells of the Broadacre City." *City Club Bulletin* (City Club of Chicago) 25, no 7: 1–2.

———. 1935. "Broadacre City: A New Community Plan." *Architectural Record* (April): 243–52.

———. 1958. *The Living City.* New York: Horizon.

Wylie, Philip, and Edwin Balmer. 1970. *After Worlds Collide.* New York: Paperback Library.

Young, Terence. 2002a. "Grounding the Myth: Theme Park Landscapes in an Era of Commerce and Nationalism." In Young and Riley 2002, 1–10.

———. 2002b. "Virtue and Irony in a U.S. National Park." In Young and Riley 2002, 157–82.

Young, Terence, and Robert Riley, eds. 2002. *Theme Park Landscapes: Antecedents and Variations.* Washington, D.C.: Dumbarton Oaks Colloquium on the History of Landscape Architecture.

Žižek, Slavoj. 1991. *Looking Awry.* Cambridge: MIT Press.

———. 1999. "The Matrix, or Malebrance in Hollywood." *Philosophy Today* 43, supp. 1999: 11–26.

Zukin, Sharon. 1991. *Landscapes of Power: From Detroit to Disneyland.* Berkeley: University of California Press.

Index

in norms, 40; participating in,
179–80; and place making,
30; possibilities for, 57, 95, 99,
101–2, 182–83; pressure for, 170;
processes of, 201n2; resistance to,
147; sources of, 55–56, 195n14;
speed of, 9. *See also* innovation
character of places, 47, 48–52, 111,
112, 114, 201n19. *See also* unity
Chartres Cathedral, 61
Chesterton, G. K., 157
Chicago, 20–21, 119
children, 126, 133
China, 196n15, 211n10, 228n26;
theme parks in, 214n24
choices, 25, 147. *See also* disparities,
economic
Christiania (Copenhagen), 209n2
churches, 73, 77. *See also* cathedrals
circumspective concern, 65
cities: classic, 148–49; European, 191,
193n1; groups in, 15; importance
of, 150–55; modern, 10, 204n76,
228n27; role of, 221n23; suburbs
vs., 148–50
civic groups, 179
clarity, 80
classes, economic: interaction of,
158; isolation of, 224n2; and
New Urbanism, 163, 226n16;
and regional issues, 230n38;
segregation of, 142–43, 144, 145,
176; and worthiness, 220n18
classic places, 2, 30, 148–49
classism, 218n13, 218n14, 219n16,
226n16
Cline, Anne, 209n29, 211n11
cloisters, 73–74
closed places, 92, 93, 201n1, 228n27
closeness. *See* proximity

clutter, 52
Cohen, Eric, 211n12
coherence, 80
commodification: characterized, 77,
94; effects of, 59–60, 204n2; and
identities, 205n7; of places, 83–88;
resistance to, 95–102, 204n3; in
theme parks, 215n27; virtual,
205n9. *See also* consumerism;
systems
communication, 28, 157, 195n14,
223n29
community, 95, 168, 170, 220n20,
221n22
complexity: of ancient places, 69;
and architecture, 172, 202n7;
characterized, 40, 45–46, 53–54,
60–62, 74–78, 207n19; and
commodification, 85–86; cultural,
201n1; vs. density/thickness, 72,
74–78; dimensions of, 54–57; and
elsewhere, 180–83; and intensity,
57–63; in New Urbanism, 162–70;
perceiving, 63–67; revealing, 47,
78–80, 104–5, 168, 173–78; and
roles, 70; and suburbs, 148–50,
171–73; in systems theory, 201n6;
of themed places, 107, 121,
133; value of, 67–70. *See also*
elsewhere; interpretation; norms;
reproduction of norms/structures;
simplicity
concentricity, 10–11, 25–26. *See also*
nonconcentric places
concepts. *See* norms
conflicts, 157–58; in awareness,
207n19; in contested places,
14–15; and diversity, 174, 227n22;
handling, 69; kinds of, 90, 203n12;
of norms, 43; political, 38